APPROPRIATELY INDIAN

APPROPRIATELY INDIAN

GENDER AND CULTURE IN A NEW TRANSNATIONAL CLASS

Smitha Radhakrishnan

Duke University Press

Durham and London   2011

Printed in the United States of America on
acid-free paper ∞

Designed by Heather Hensley

Typeset in Chapparel Pro by Keystone
Typesetting, Inc.

Library of Congress Cataloging-in-
Publication Data appear on the last printed
page of this book.

For Avva, who first inspired me to write

about the everyday life that surrounds me.

CONTENTS

Acknowledgments   ix

INTRODUCTION On Background   1

1. PRIVILEGE Situating India's Transnational Class   25

2. GLOBAL/INDIAN Cultural Politics in the IT Workplace   53

3. MERIT Ideologies of Achievement in the Knowledge Economy   87

4. INDIVIDUALS Narratives of Embedded Selves   115

5. FAMILY Gendered "Balance" and the Everyday Production of the Nation   145

6. RELIGION When the Private Is Transnational   173

CONCLUSION Apolitical Politics   199

Notes   207

Bibliography   215

Index   227

ACKNOWLEDGMENTS

As with all long-term projects, this book has stacked up a series of intellectual and monetary debts along its way. The fact that this book draws from research conducted on three continents in five different cities expands the network of indebtedness even further.

At the outset, I thank my father, B. D. Radhakrishnan, whose rich stories of the young women and men of India's burgeoning technology industry piqued my interest in this topic as early as the mid-1990s. Thanks to his long experience in the global IT industry, I began this project with an "insider" view. Aside from that, my father provided me with encouragement, initial contacts for my pilot studies in Bangalore and Mumbai, and constant support, even when it became clear that my approach to the topic was clearly at odds with his own numbers-driven technical approach to problem solving and analysis.

At the Sociology Department at the University of California, Berkeley, I was blessed with a dream dissertation committee. Raka Ray, my fearless chair, personal advisor, and friend provided every kind of intellectual and mental support possible, and I continue to be indebted to her for her generosity as my primary mentor in my academic career. Peter Evans encouraged me to pursue the ambitious task of ethnography on three continents and persisted in getting me to ask tough questions of my data. Gillian Hart, without whose support I never would have ventured toward South Africa, also exerted a profound intellectual influence upon me, and I am grateful for her constant support, starting from my days as an uncertain undergraduate.

I have been fortunate to have always had strong funding for this project. The American Institute of Indian Studies provided support for the bulk of the research in India conducted in 2004–5. The graduate division of the University of California, Berkeley, funded the fieldwork in South Africa and Silicon Valley, as well as my writing period in 2005–6. After leaving Berkeley, I had the luxury of being a part of the Global

Fellows Postdoctoral program at UCLA's International Institute, which provided me with funding for the final stretch of research in 2007 as well as the time and intellectual environment for the work of beginning to turn my dissertation into a book. Since my move to the East Coast, Wellesley College has provided the funding, administrative support, and autonomy for me to complete my project in good time.

In all of the locations I conducted research, I am most of all grateful to my 137 interviewees, who generously offered me their time and entrusted me with their stories and perspectives. This work would obviously be impossible without their insights, beliefs, and struggles, which lie at the heart of this book.

In India, a network of friends old and new kept me sane, focused, and connected. During my stay in Mumbai, I was grateful for the counsel, friendship, and connections of Komal Dubey, Jyothi Bhat, and Mukta Raut. My friends Vallari and Rajesh Shah connected me to housing in Andheri, and Shashi Suryanarayanan kept me laughing during the bleak and trying days of my first Mumbai monsoon. Nirmala Balasubramaniam and her parents provided me with a loving, open home to turn to always. In Bangalore, Bharathi Chainy, Sun Kumbakonam, Rajavel Manoharan, and S. Mohan helped me with contacts and made me feel comfortable immediately. Meeta Gangrade and Champaka Rajagopal have become wonderful friends.

Although South Africa makes up only a chapter of this book, my ability to include it stems from a previous year of fieldwork and research in Durban in 2001–2. Many of those I met at that time continued to provide the amazing support I needed to make the research for this project possible. I am very grateful for the connections, friendship, and camaraderie of Suria Govender, Kanagie Pillay, Devan Royan, Nalini Naidoo, Beena Jugjivan, and Clive Pillay. In Johannesburg, I found a warm and welcoming home with Kogie and Rodney Subramoney.

Over the years, this project has enjoyed the input of wonderful intellectual interlocutors. I would like to especially acknowledge Cinzia Solari, my closest partner in crime from graduate school and the best sounding board for my work ever, and Meredith McGuire, who provided great feedback on an early draft of this manuscript. In Boston, a reading group with Caitrin Lynch and Sarah Lamb played a key role in helping me to transform this project into a book. Their advice, encouragement, and always constructive feedback are visible in almost all of the chapters included in this book. So many others have helped me realize this project along the way, including Rachel Behler, Eric Hayot, Peggy Levitt, William Mazzarella, Casey Miller, Nina Sylvanus, Bagya Thyagarajan, Steph Tung, and Jaye Cee Whitehead. Ken Wissoker at Duke University Press has patiently nurtured this project along with great faith in my abilities, and the anonymous reviewers for this manuscript have been amazingly careful, detailed, and perceptive in their feedback over our long exchange. I am deeply grateful for their time, energy, and critical input.

A much earlier version of chapter 5 appeared in *Qualitative Sociology*'s June 2009 issue under the title "Professional Women, Good Families: Respectable Femininity and the Cultural Politics of a 'New' India." Some sections of chapters 1 and 3 appear in *Theory and Society*'s January 2007 issue under the title "Rethinking Knowledge for Development: Transnational Knowledge Professionals and the New India." Many of the framing concepts of the book presented in chapter 1 and peppered throughout the book were originally developed in the context of a conference in Delhi organized by Raka Ray and Amita Baviskar on the Indian middle class, which took place in March 2007. The paper I produced for that conference appears in the edited volume, *Both Elite and Everyman: The Cultural Politics of the Indian Middle Classes* (2010) from Routledge.

My family in many ways sets the context for this book, as our story of migration, change, and gendered "balance" helped to set up what eventually became the framing intellectual questions of this book. I am grateful to my mother, Sharada, for her ability to restore my faith in myself when the going got rocky, my grandparents, M. K. and Vatsala Karunanithy, for opening the door for future generations, and my brother, Prasant, for laughter, wit, and unbelievably reliable compassion. Finally, I thank my partner in life and love, Ganesh Ramachandran, who has been my tireless supporter from the earliest stages of this project, and whose quiet admiration and critical eye have kept me strong, clear, and focused.

The cover of the popular Silicon Valley magazine *Wired* of February 2004 features a headshot of a beautiful copper-skinned woman bedecked in jewels. With her palm concealing the lower half of her face, she gazes out at the reader from heavily lined eyes. The palm is covered in the traditional Indian decoration known as *mehndi*, usually seen in the abstract designs and floral patterns that adorn the hands of Indian brides and Bollywood starlets. "The New Face of the Silicon Age," declares the headline. At a closer look, the viewer sees that the *mehndi* designs are not what he might expect—the *mehndi* is software code. The caption reads, "Kiss your cubicle good-bye. Tech jobs are fleeing to India faster than ever. You got a problem with that?" (figure 1). The corresponding story inside the magazine introduces the "real" woman the glamorous model on the cover was meant to refer to: Aparna Jairam, a thirty-three-year-old project manager in Mumbai described in the following passage by the journalist Daniel H. Pink: "Her long black hair is clasped with a barrette. Her dark eyes are deep-set and unusually calm. She has the air of the smartest girl in class—not the one always raising her hand and shouting out answers, but the one who sits in back, taking it all in and responding only when called upon, yet delivering answers that make the whole class turn around and listen." Pink goes on to cite Jairam's practical, yet authentic reading of the ancient Hindu text, the Gita,[1] and Jairam's sharp, composed responses to American counterparts accusing her of stealing their jobs. A photograph of Jairam shows her just as Pink describes her, with simple jewelry and a small black *bindi* (figure 2).

This issue of *Wired* came out just as I was beginning the research for this project. As I was already interested in the particular role of female information technology (IT) professionals in the

FIGURES 3A AND 3B
A feminized "global" India.

ference—a generic, transferable set of "Indian" cultural norms that are palatable to Western cosmopolitan culture. Cultural streamlining and the production of appropriate difference allow Indian IT professionals at the frontlines of the global economy to assert their symbolic position at the helm of a "new" India. The principles that sustain and drive cultural streamlining and the boundaries of appropriate difference are embedded in the everyday experience of the IT industry and the knowledge economy. From the workplace, these principles move into the private sphere of the home through individual IT professionals who are themselves already embedded in gendered, religious, national, and class histories. In the sphere of the home and the family, conceptions of "Indian culture" are reworked, upheld, and rendered authentic and appealing to national and international audiences, including others who identify as "Indian" living in India and abroad. This book traces these specific cultural processes as they move from the realm of the public to that of the private.

The economic and social transformations of the 1990s and beyond have fueled new kinds of job opportunities for an educated, English-speaking group of mostly urban Indians. In the 1960s and 1970s, the sons of such urban educated families fueled the skilled migration of engineers to the United States. While many of the new jobs initially created in India were at the absolute bottom of the international IT value chain, this position has shifted as IT talent and skills in India have become more sophisticated. Talented urban Indians with the appropriate technical training can today enter the IT industry and realistically hope to advance far enough in their firms to travel far and wide. Regardless of whether or not these technologists actually travel the world or migrate abroad, the ethos of mobility and achievement in India's IT industry forms the basis of a class culture that reshapes meanings of Indianness to fit the conditions of globalization.

Background as Keyword

On a humid monsoon afternoon in July, I am interviewing Shubha in a crowded, suburban Mumbai coffee shop. Shubha,[2] a twenty-four-year-old IT professional who has been working for a large Indian multinational corporation for the past three years, is one among the tens of thousands of Indian women who have entered the lucrative field of Indian IT in recent years. She has lived in the United States for work, has broken conventions of caste and community to marry a man of her choosing, and is moving up the corporate ladder at a steady clip. I ask her if she finds herself to be very different from women who work at the State Bank of India. Government bank jobs have conventionally been considered good jobs for women in urban India, yet few women in the IT industry would ever consider a career in the nationalized banking sector. Her response highlights the importance of "background," a multifaceted term that gets to the heart of cultural continuity and change in India's transnational class of professionals:

SHUBHA: Well, it's difference in education definitely. They [the bank workers] probably don't have any major qualifications backing them. We [IT workers] go to school, college, play sports, that makes a lot of difference. Many of them probably can't make a straight sentence in English. So, it's education to some extent and to some extent background also.

SR: What do you mean, background?

SHUBHA: The kind of family that they come from. Meaning, they come from lower middle-class families, probably. So, the entire outlook—not outlook, but—well, the way they talk and the way they interact is different. I mean, the background that I come from is also so different from most of the other people in [my firm] . . . Many of them are from families where their fathers are also in similar kinds of jobs. Like, I have a friend, her father's working in the Middle East somewhere. So probably, her income helps the family in some way. She'll buy a washing machine for her parents. Maybe it's not a responsibility but definitely . . . if she buys something for the family, it probably helps. For me, that's just not the case.

Shubha comes from a wealthy family, a family that never intended for her to work at all. Her income makes no difference to her parents whatsoever. From Shubha's elite position, she is acutely aware of "background," a term that characterizes class, caste, education, family ties, and even the responsibility and behavior of daughters. Bank workers and IT professionals might all consider themselves to be "middle class," but for Shubha the distinctions between them seem to be obvious. Through the idea of "background," Shubha is able to distinguish easily why she is different from the women she perceives to be working at the bank (although she does not know such women personally and might be mischaracterizing them) and, more importantly, between herself and her peers at her own workplace. In its deceiving neutrality, "background" demarcates a place for everyone in society—not only does it tell Shubha where people come from, but where they might be going. Because Shubha pursued a career in engineering rather than the more luxurious life her parents envisioned for her, Shubha's own background did not dictate her future. Yet, the mismatch between her adult life and the life she was raised to live makes her all the more aware of the importance of background.

In the parlance of middle-class India, the term "background" comes up in conversation almost daily. In professional contexts, a question about one's background can be a question about educational achievement. In a family conversation about a prospective bride, a question about background refers to a combination of class and caste position. Especially in the latter context, the designations, specifications, and nuances that distinguish one position from another are myriad and are never easily addressed by a simple set of categories. Perhaps the most ambiguous and ill defined of these categories is the claim to be of a "middle-class" background. For example, a "middle-class" background in Bangalore, a large metropolis, might viably include hairdressers, IT professionals, and rickshaw drivers, depending on whom you might ask. In a rural area, a landowner with large land holdings may consider himself to be middle class as well. Moreover, in both of these settings, being a middle-class Brahmin (the highest caste) contains different meanings than being a middle-class Gowda (a lower caste, categorized in the state category Other Backward Classes, or OBCs), differences that the identification "middle class" alone fails to capture. As a result, many analysts of India's middle class refer to them as a plural group—India's middle *classes* (Fernandes and Heller 2006; Rajagopal 2001b; Ray and Baviskar 2010).

To stay with the example of choosing a potential bride, finding out about her "background" not only means coming to know all of these nuances, but also coming to understand what her family is like. Did her mother stay at home or did she work? How committed is the bride's mother to her family? Did the bride's parents educate her? If so, in a private or government school? What kind of a house did the bride grow up in? In what part of town? What sorts of appliances does she have at home? What religion do they practice at home and to which gods do they pray? How do they celebrate festivals?

FIGURE 4 *Wired* magazine offers more faces of Indian IT.

is unique in this wish. Most of the women I spoke to were proud of the particular version of Indian femininity portrayed in the magazine, as it seemed to adjudicate between the "Indian" and the "global" in a way that resonated with them. This resonance suggests that professional women play an important symbolic role in defining exactly what those boundaries are and how they may be appropriately transcended, bringing Indian middle-class femininity to the center of the cultural innovations of IT professionals. More specifically, the unique symbolic position of professional IT women allows them to legitimize the success of the elite class of knowledge professionals through their navigations of "global" and authentically "Indian" culture. This power enables them to help set the terms for cultural streamlining and the production of appropriate difference. As professional Indian women enact, reinforce, and reinvent a new, respectable femininity, they also legitimate a vision of India and Indian culture that reflects the successes of the transnational professional class.

"Background" refers not only to overt class markers, but also to the gendered character of the domestic sphere, which is implicitly linked to class standing. Good family backgrounds are composed of heterosexual families in which middle-class women make appropriate decisions for their husbands and children—decisions that were enacted self-consciously and enthusiastically by most of the women I interviewed in all three countries. Indeed, good families lie at the heart of a reinvented transnational Indian culture, and it is the repeated naming of this value, which my informants always contrasted with the deterioration of Western families, that comprises one of the key methods through which tensions between the "global" and the "Indian" are reconciled with one another. It is invariably middle-class Indian women who feel responsible for this reconciliation. The navigations that professional IT women in particular make in "balancing" values of the "global" as well as resonant notions of "Indianness" and family help to imagine, stabilize, and consolidate a new kind of Indian culture for a broad transnational audience.

So, who exactly are the women who become IT professionals? In which social norms are they complicit, and which social norms do they violate, transform, or create? Unlike women in the United States, young Indian women from urban families, especially upper-caste ones, encourage their daughters to study science and math.[5] Although these subjects remain dominated by men at the college level, the availability of IT jobs, combined with the widely accepted perception that these jobs are some of the only "good" professional jobs for women, has attracted more and more women to engineering and computer science degrees (Parikh and Sukhatme 2004). Most of the women I interviewed had job offers by the time they had graduated from college. Indeed, incoming cohorts of new recruits to large IT firms have an almost one to one ratio of women to men, although over time that ratio deteriorates rapidly, leveling off at about one to two in the industry overall (Suriya 2003). In contrast to a previous generation of middle-class women, the young women who enter IT today have a sense that they wish to achieve financial independence prior to getting married. Yet, the issue of marriage continues to loom large for IT women. As I will show in subsequent chapters, many women opt to marry men of their choosing rather than adhering to the conventional arranged-marriage system that most of their parents went through. Sometimes, women decide not to marry at all, although this is still rare. A large proportion of women, however, work for a few years, get married through the conventional arranged-marriage system, and then leave their IT jobs altogether. The status they have acquired in working in the IT sector makes them more desirable in marriage markets, where urban men express interest in having educated, working wives, even if the wives are required to give up or cut back on that work when they marry.[6]

Thus, although IT work does open up a wide range of options for women, it does not completely eliminate conventional expectations that their families might have of them.[7] Still, their earning power, as well as the high status of their work, seems to give them a significant say in their own life trajectories. This decision-making power is reflected in later ages of marriage and childbearing among these women compared to the previous generation, and the increased frequency of "love marriages" (as opposed to "arranged marriages"). The expectation to work or not to work also varies greatly according to exactly those specificities and nuances of background I have outlined above. For some families, a daughter, daughter-in-law, or wife working in the IT industry for life would be a source of great pride, while for others a woman working outside the house at all would be unacceptable. These differences arise from caste, class, and gender conventions specific to each family. Even within the narrow group I am studying, there is great diversity in these practices. In this sense, the particular form of femininity that women enact in the home and at work is shaped precisely by the constraints of the "background" from which they come, even as they create and reshape the contours of a broad notion of "Indian culture" for a new generation.

An "Indian" Background

At the heart of the cultural terrain that Indian IT professionals navigate is the idea of belonging to India—"Indianness"—and, by association, the idea of India and "Indian culture" more generally. What is at stake to say that this privileged group is remaking Indianness? And how is this particular effort to remake and streamline what it means to belong to India significant in relation to other attempts to fix ideas of Indianness that have been widespread since the early nationalist period of the late nineteenth century? Can it possibly mean similar things to make a claim to "being Indian" or "having an Indian background" in cultural milieus as different as India, the United States, and South Africa?

The questions of defining the idea of what India is as a cultural entity, and what it means to belong to this entity, have been salient since the colonial period, first to outsiders interested in the region, and later to the elite nationalists who rallied together in the anti-colonial nationalist movement. While there exist numerous accounts of the origins and development of Indian nationalism and the difficulties of defining a unified India, scholars agree that the issue has never been resolved with any degree of certainty or finality (Chatterjee 1986; Khilnani 2004). Indeed, the persistence of a multiplicity of ideas of India and Indianness, paired with the shifting role of the Indian state as an arbiter of those meanings, has left open the possibility of renegotiating those meanings even further in the contemporary context.

Since India's independence from British rule in 1947, perhaps the most important tension in defining the culture of India has persisted between ideas of India that place the values of secularism, modernity, and equality at the forefront on the one hand, and those that emphasize religion (specifically, Hinduism) on the other. The dominant voices of Western-educated elites sought to create a secular state that included all religions, and it was these elites who forged the new state. Alongside this dominant movement, however, were also the voices of Hindu nationalists who opposed Gandhi's teachings of non-violence in favor of a militant, masculinist model of the new nation. Hindu nationalists defined themselves exclusively by what they determined to be "Hindu values" and culture, a distinct take on Gandhi's more inclusive interpretation of Hinduism and Indianness. Although Hindu nationalist voices had become organized in the nineteenth century in the context of the larger nationalist movement, they were marginalized as the European-influenced ideas of the anti-colonial Indian National Congress, led by Jawaharlal Nehru, took center stage. Their marginalization, however, did not erase their continued presence on the Indian political landscape (Corbridge and Hariss 2000; Malik and Singh 1990).

The economic and political philosophies of Nehru, the nation's first prime minister, emphasized a secular state and an economy driven by state-sponsored investment—a set of preoccupations that dominated Indian politics for decades. Still, the hegemony of Nehru's idea of India was always shaky. A moment of economic and political crisis, building up through the 1970s and culminating with the assassination of Prime Minister Indira Gandhi in 1984, laid bare longstanding communal tensions. Economic stagnation and political instability signaled a failure of Nehru's ideals and provided a political opening for the revitalization of Hindu nationalism, which sought to create an idea of a singular nation, united under a singular religion, making India by definition a Hindu country rather than a secular one. In 1989, a Hindu nationalist movement, fueled by allied organizations around the world comprising the Hindu Sangh Parivar or Hindu family, entered the national mainstream. The movement's attempt to "reclaim" the iconic city of Ayodhya, the alleged geographic location of the birth of Ram, an important Hindu deity, gained speed by drawing on existing feelings of a division between Hindus and Muslims that had continued from the partition of India on religious grounds in 1947, and which had been simmering just beneath the surface of institutionalized political debate. Building upon the groundswell of popular support driving the march to Ayodhya, which culminated in the destruction of the sixteenth-century Babri Masjid mosque, the Bhartiya Janata Party (BJP), a Hindu nationalist party, came to political power by a narrow margin in 1998.

The continuing tension between a secular idea of India on the one hand, a religious idea on the other, and the shifting legitimacy of the state in enforcing those ideas and ideals is precisely the tension at the heart of which the educated, metropolitan elite of Indian IT workers comes to be important and meaningful. The advent of global modernity[8] in the 1990s was made distinctly Indian through the revitalization of ideas of devotion to God, familial piety, and domestic consumption. A particular type of rebranding and reinvention of Hindu religious practice, filtered through the collective of the family, was central to these cultural processes. As Sunil Khilnani vividly explains,

> Rising consumerism and the extension of the market during the 1980s did not fuel an individualistic hedonism nor breed liberal individuals. Rather, it was experienced as an opportunity to sample the pleasures of modernity within collective units like the family . . . [and] through the conservative filter of religious piety, moralism, and domestic virtue. This has spawned a novel Hinduism, where holographic gods dangle on well-used keychains and cassettes of devotional *ragas* are played in traffic jams (2004, 186).

In this description, Khilnani offers a sense of what a new, capitalist version of Indianness might look like for middle-class Indians in India and suggests that this new version might be importantly constituted through the domestic sphere of the family. While not a direct challenge to the more secular notion of India forged by India's founders, this version certainly also embraces Hinduism as a constitutive part of the cultural sphere that is experienced primarily in the realm of the private, even as it overflows to the world outside it. This idea—that critical cultural shifts and innovations among India's educated urban classes have taken place in the private realm—is one that resonates throughout this book.

Parallel with these shifts occurring in India, notions of Indianness were being navigated in the diaspora, oftentimes in ways that were in direct conversation with emerging notions of Indianness within India. In the United States, Indianness not only defined a set of cultural and religious values and a sense of connection and heritage to a land far away but also provided an ethnic identification in an increasingly multicultural terrain. As cultural difference became more celebrated in the mainstream of American cultural production, Indianness in the diaspora acquired a new "cool," allowing Indian racial minorities to draw upon cultural artifacts to underscore their exotic difference from the white mainstream (Maira 2000; Mani 2003). Indianness in the diaspora was importantly defined through gendered performances, practices, and moralities as well, maintaining a resonance with Indian nationalist discursive practices that placed the essence of Indianness in the private sphere (Bhattacharjee 1999; Das Gupta 1997). In South Africa, ideas of Indianness were always produced and sustained within the context of a racist state regime. The end of apartheid opened up space for renegotiations of Indianness as a primarily cultural, rather than racial, identity, where gendered performance and practice also remained key (Radhakrishnan 2005). As I show in this book, however, shifting ways of being Hindu in India are ultimately what has drawn some South African Indians into transnationally shared meanings of Indianness. Within the global IT industry, Indian cultural identity became the subject of managerial interest—an essential aspect of the changing global business that had to be identified, catalogued, and then effectively managed (Upadhya 2007b).

All of these spheres of cultural navigation have been interacting with one another, feeding off the shifting hegemonies of competing ideas of

Indianness in India while also incorporating the diverse desires and experiences of that strand of the diaspora that cared to participate in these cultural processes. And while the official politics of the state in some ways reflected the heightened visibility of Hinduism as a constitutive part of Indian identification, in other ways the public sphere set the pace and tone for the new articulations of Indianness that were surfacing, while the state followed far behind. Unlike Aihwa Ong's account of state-driven notions of Chineseness that navigate flows of culture and capital among Chinese transnationals, in India, the state seems to come later, while an ever diversifying transnational middle class negotiates new ways of embodying what it means to be Indian (Ong 1999).

For my respondents, some notion of "Indian culture" was always informing their ideas of why globalization was good or bad for India, what changes were acceptable and unacceptable, and, indeed, what constituted a good or bad background. While there was little explicitly shared agreement on the content of this elusive "Indian culture," the historical context in which these discourses came to be suggests first that Hinduism plays a central, constitutive role in this culture, and second that this culture is inextricably linked to ideas of the family. Moreover, the persistent concern with "Indian culture" among my respondents suggests that what is at stake here in the new, emerging notion of Indianness they are making is the beginning of a *new* hegemonic consensus to replace the seemingly unviable secular socialist democracy envisioned by the founders of an independent India—a new (trans)national elite, a globalization-friendly version of Indian culture, and a new vision with which to take the nation forward.

Transnational as Location and Concept

What does it mean to call Indian IT professionals a "transnational professional class?" In the context of this study, I use the term "transnational" to signify three specific meanings. First and foremost, I use the term "transnational" to describe the scope of the class I am examining. In sociology, the social formation of class has been studied almost exclusively as a social structure contained by the nation-state. Theorists of class ranging from Weber to Bourdieu have examined class stratifications and divisions in the context of national economies and societies (Bourdieu 1984, 1995; Weber 1978). In these discussions, class stratifications are meaningful relative to others living in the same nation-state. Moreover, these nation-states were often implicitly placed within a global political economy that made nation-states unitary actors. Prior to the emergence of studies that grappled directly with cultures of globalization, development literatures emerging from a Marxist tradition tended to dichotomize the world into the binary terms of first or third world, developed or underdeveloped, or core or periphery (Frank 1967; Wallerstein 1974). In this approach, class divisions within a nation-state remained crucial, but the binary categorization *between* countries obscured the possibility of analyzing class divisions *across* nation-states. More recently, discussions of a transnational capitalist class have examined the practices of the businesspeople who control capital in multiple national settings (Ong 1999; Sklair 2001). These studies examined people occupying a very elite class segment for whom national boundaries are unimportant. Yet, even in these cases, the motivations and practices of the state shape class privilege and national ties.

The IT professionals I write about here are not, for the most part, included among the elite transnational capitalist class examined in other studies; rather, they are *professionals* for whom the traversing of borders (or the possibility of doing so) is critical to their socialization, belief system, and expression of cultural belonging to India.[9] The notion of Indianness that India's transnational professional class creates and projects, I argue, profoundly shapes the meaning of India and Indian culture for audiences at home and abroad. The production and navigation of these cultural discourses occur across multiple national settings and through specific practices in the realms of work, family, consumption, religion, and travel, among others. In all of these spheres, the actions and beliefs of these professionals are shaped by the knowledge that they could be employed in any number of countries, and that their careers are likely to take them to many places around the globe. Because of my focus on a transnational professional class, my analysis is restricted to professionals working in the software and hardware sectors, which employ primarily engineers or others with specialized, usually technical training. I do not include workers employed in the business processing outsourcing industry, which includes call center or transcription workers who are unlikely to work in the same industry abroad.[10]

Second, I invoke the term "transnational" to denote my use of a method that examines the connections and relationships between different places, rather than a comparative approach that seeks to describe and analyze commonalities and differences. A transnational method acknowledges that the bounded nation-state may not be the most appropriate scale for examining social phenomena, and that many such phenomena may be constituted through interactions between multiple locales (Levitt and Khagram 2008; Mitchell 2002; Yeoh, Willis, and Fakhri 2003). Although centered in the rapid changes occurring in urban India, my multi-sited qualitative method grows out of the premise that a revitalized notion of "Indianness" is created and mobilized by a class of professionals in multiple locations, though not all of these locations are equally privileged in their ability to create these meanings for other Indians. As I will show, upwardly mobile Indian professionals in the United States and India are the most privileged in creating cultural meanings; those who travel back and forth between these locales occupy an especially powerful position from which to define and articulate meanings of Indianness. Meanwhile South African Indians, operating on the sidelines of these cultural processes, are aware of a new and exciting notion of Indianness that makes belonging to a "new" India desirable. For South African Indians, globalized Hinduism becomes a vehicle through which they can connect with the transnational professional circuit of Indians and the meanings of Indianness that are produced in that circuit. These differential positionings and privileges offer us insights into the unevenness of cultural interactions across multiple boundaries.

This differentiation leads to my final intention in utilizing the term "transnational"; I assert the continued importance of the "national" even as it might be transcended. I choose "transnational" for analytic purposes, then, as a conscious choice over the word "global." Although "global" is often used in popular media and corporate contexts to signal some kind of taken-for-granted cosmopolitanism, in the context of scholarship, the meanings assigned to ideas of the global are divergent and ultimately vague, offering little in the way of analytic traction (Moore 2004). In some of the most important scholarly treatments of globalization, the "global" refers to multiple things, most often a realm of interaction that is counterposed with the "local (Castells 1997; Friedman, Randeria, and Toda Institute for Global Peace and Policy Research 2004; King and State University of New York, Binghamton, Department of Art and Art History 1991). When the notion of the "global" is mapped onto empirical contexts, however, it becomes difficult to designate in a rigorous way which practices are produced in the realm of the "local" and which are produced in the "global," as most studies examining these have shown repeatedly that the workings of the "global" always take shape and become concrete in the "local" (Burawoy et al. 2000; Hart 2002). Given that the influence of global capital is pervasive and becomes concrete in an infinitude of lived practices and experiences the world over, the term fails to bring to bear a useful set of theoretical tools or concepts for understanding empirical realities.

In scholarly treatments of the term, "global" is often meant not just to transcend national borders, but also to presume such borders to be relatively unimportant (Appadurai 1996, 158–77). It is in fact this transcendent conception of the "global" that my informants most readily embrace and identify with. Although I will devote considerable space in this book to understanding the significance of the "global" in the culture of Indian IT professionals, I treat the term strictly as a folk category and not as an analytical one.[11] In choosing the term "transnational," I underscore my interest in the borders of the national, even when new definitions of the nation travel across territorial borders. For the transnational class I examine here, the geographic territory of India remains the privileged site of Indian culture, even as this culture is actively navigated and mediated in other locations. Indian professionals in all of the locations I examined acknowledge this privilege, which is reinforced through ideas of authenticity associated with generational proximity to India. That is, Indian emigrants or children of emigrants feel more entitled to assert and participate in discourses of Indian culture than those who are many generations removed from India, such as those in South Africa. For the latter group, travel to India, made possible through enhanced financial means, consumption of Indian cultural products, and religious practice all serve to fill in a perceived gap in authenticity. These patterns, then, support the need for an approach that acknowledges the varied discursive, material, and geographic bounds within which a shared sense of cultural belonging is constructed. The nation, as a territorial and cultural discourse, remains critical. The term "transnational" denotes this centrality.

My "Background"

In 1972, my father, a bright engineering student from Bangalore, India, packed a suitcase for his one-way journey to North America. He had a full scholarship for a master's program at the State University of New York,

Buffalo, where he would pursue his second graduate degree. When his passage to the United States was confirmed, his photo appeared in the local newspaper, the *Deccan Herald*, along with the handful of other outstanding students from Bangalore who had earned their tickets out of India. On the day of the flight, all of his siblings and relatives traveled to Madras to see him off at the international airport. He was the first in the family to take such a trip, but because he was the youngest in a large family it was not surprising that he should be breaking new ground. He knew, as did his family, that the course of his life to follow would be fundamentally different from theirs.

After finishing his degree and securing a job, my father returned to India in 1975, but it was not a return in the true sense. He came back to Bangalore for his wedding, after which he and my mother proceeded to a new life in Canada. They settled in the United States, eventually, where they raised my brother and I as American citizens. India was always "home," but at a distance. In their time, my parents had "succeeded," having beaten the odds. They emigrated from India during a time of economic stagnation and chronic unemployment, and they established a comfortable life for themselves and their children in a land far away.

It is this migration story that helps to set the stage for the powerful transnational class of Indian technologists who would come of age a generation later. It is also, at least in part, the story of my own "background." As the daughter of immigrants with this particular story, my own position as a scholar emerges from the peculiarity of the "push" factors that led my father to leave India and the "pull" factors that led my parents to stay in the United States. This story is a typical one, centered on a talented male engineering student arriving in the United States from afar, one in the wave of educated migrants from Asia who started to arrive in American universities in the late 1960s and 1970s. The United States needed the technical talent, and top Indian universities were among the few in the world providing world-class technical educations. But more importantly, for middle-class Indians of my parents' generation, India held few opportunities for engineers like my father. The decision to emigrate, then, was a straightforward one at a personal level. For India, however, the decisions of people like my parents seemed detrimental—labeled as "brain drain," the trend seemed to ensure that India's brightest minds would never serve India's own national development goals.

But immigrants like my parents continued to maintain ties to India, even though they no longer lived there. They made trips home to visit families, provided remittances to family members, donated to charities, and made regular phone calls. Travels to India introduced new consumer goods and new stories of life abroad to their families in India. In the United States, they raised their children as Indian Hindus and cultivated relationships with other similarly educated Indian immigrant families. In most of these families, it was the mothers who were most invested in the task of cultural preservation. Although college-educated, often these women did not work outside the home. They were seen as the bearers of Indian culture, and they spent time cultivating community and religious networks meant to uphold their connections to their home country and culture. As a daughter of this subculture, then, I have been a participant in the forms of respectable femininity that Indians living in the United States have helped to produce. In conducting the interviews and field-work that comprise the empirical basis of this book, I engaged these aspects of my own positionality vis-à-vis my informants, who viewed me as someone sharing something fundamental with them—as someone participating in the production of a new kind of Indian culture that was nonetheless grounded in the authentic.

A New Indianness?

The symbolic power of India's transnational class comes in part from their formidable economic power, but more importantly it comes from their ability to navigate between the realms of the "global" and the "Indian" to produce a new discourse of belonging to India. *Cultural streamlining* is the process of simplifying a dizzying diversity of cultural practices into a stable, transferable, modular set of norms and beliefs that can move quickly and easily through space. In India's transnational class, this streamlining process transforms interpretations of "Indian culture" that emerge from the specificity of this transnational professional class's position in the global economy into something generically "Indian" that can be adopted as national culture anywhere. It is this process of cultural streamlining—of reconfiguring specific class practices such that they appear to be generically "Indian" ones—that the subsequent chapters of the book describe and analyze. I show that the IT industry in itself, driven by the logics of a global knowledge economy, helps to foster this cultural process, and that the influence of the knowledge economy on the one hand and the norms of the "certain background" that IT professionals reproduce on the other hand provide the inputs for cultural streamlining. Individuals then shape how Indian culture becomes streamlined on an everyday basis, in a give-and-take relationship with their own subjectivities. One of the most compelling effects of cultural streamlining is the production of *appropriate difference*. The new form of Indianness realized by Indian IT professionals strengthens a bond to India as an eternal, unchanging source of cultural belonging and forges a sense of unity with Indians around the world. Yet this kind of belonging is necessarily divorced from the divisive messiness of everyday life in India. The appropriately different version of Indianness that emerges, then, is self-consciously distinct from the cultural behemoth of "the Western" while at the same time compatible with a Western, cosmopolitan lifestyle.

The chapters of this book detail specific sites and discourses through which cultural streamlining takes place, and outline the contours of appropriate difference that appear in each of these contexts, moving from the public sphere of the workplace to the intimate sphere of family and religion. The first chapter explains in depth the various facets of material and symbolic privilege that India's transnational class enjoys. Explaining and theorizing their position of privilege provides a starting point from which to understand the conditions that enable the narratives of culture making that follow. The next two chapters examine the notions of culture and value that circulate in the workplace. Chapter 2 examines managerial and cross-cultural discourses of the "global" as they are actively reconciled with the "Indian" and shows how these competing discourses are enacted by IT professionals in the workplace, setting up a framework for cultural streamlining while providing specific models for appropriate difference. Chapter 3 elaborates on the ideologies that underpin achievement and success in the Indian IT industry and in the knowledge economy more generally, considering the importance of individual achievement in a world presumed to be an even playing field. Here, we see how ideologies of middle-class India converge with those of the knowledge economy, allowing the views of Indian IT professionals to resonate in multiple transnational settings. Subsequent chapters turn to the private lives of Indian IT professionals, exploring how the processes of cultural streamlining set in motion at work are absorbed into everyday lives, producing personalized, resonant notions of appropriate difference. Chapter 4 examines narratives of individuality, using the life stories of IT professionals to understand the ways in which the logics cultivated in the knowledge economy enter into private lives, even as individual "backgrounds" influence the specific ways in which those accommodations take place. Chapter 5 examines the production of the "good" Indian family and the gendered balances that comprise it, demonstrating how the cultural streamlining that begins in the workplace finds its ultimate realization in the private sphere. Chapter 6 then turns to the role of Hindu religious belief and practice, focusing primarily on the example of South African Indians, to understand the specific ways in which Hinduism is made into a mobile discourse of belonging meant to unite Indians, thus highlighting the constitutive role of Hindu identification in the culture of India's new transnational class. Finally, in a brief conclusion, I consider the implications of the peculiar culture of transnational Indianness having become dominant in India. On the one hand, the individualistic yet family-oriented version of Indian culture produced within this class offers an empowering, flexible cultural blueprint around which to create and stabilize national unity in a moment of rapid social and economic change. On the other hand, the peculiar version of Indianness promoted in this class conceals the failures of economic liberalization while also obscuring the diverse, local, non-dominant cultures within India and its diaspora.

SITUATING INDIA'S TRANSNATIONAL CLASS

Indian IT professionals are privileged through their ability to imagine and live out personal and professional lives in multiple places. This privilege stems from their dominant position in the global economy as well as their material and symbolic privilege within India. The privilege of India's new transnational class is embedded in national/domestic hierarchies, global capitalism, and India's class structure. In this chapter, I examine the multiple layers of IT professionals' privilege and power, paying attention to symbolic, material, and economic privileges, while always remaining attentive to the role of geographic mobility in establishing and reinforcing those privileges. The logics of individuality and respectability produced within this matrix of privilege enable the project of culture making analyzed throughout this book.

Locating India's Transnational Class
Bangalore, 2005

Thirty-three years after my father packed his bag in Bangalore, I am seated in a comfortable home in a new suburb of Bangalore, eating a meal with a young family in surroundings not unlike those of my childhood in the United States. Around the perimeter of the large dining table are seated Ram, Shreya, their two children, and Shreya's mother. We eat lentils, vegetables, and rice from Corningware plates as Ram's and Shreya's son angles for his parents' attention as they speak to me. Ram had left India for the United States in 1992, with a degree from a top Indian university in hand and a lucrative job offer from a company in Virginia. He worked for two years, came back to India to marry Shreya in 1994, and returned to the United States, where his career eventually took both of them to Silicon Valley. Like my parents, Ram and Shreya maintained ties to India through their families and their friends. They raised their children to have a strong sense of Indianness and Hindu values but never had any intention of moving back to India. On a trip home in 2003, however, Ram sensed that things in India had changed. Indeed, he began to sense that the better opportunities in terms of career, economic mobility, and lifestyle were not to be found in the United States at all, but, surprisingly, in the very place he had left. More importantly, it seemed to him that he could offer his children a more secure cultural identity in India, rather than the delicate balancing act between "Indian" and "American" he felt they were forced into in the United States.

Bangalore is the beating heart of India's IT industry, the most visible city in a short but growing list of Indian IT cities that includes Mumbai, Hyderabad, Chennai, Pune, and Gurgaon. Most large multinational technology firms have operations in Bangalore, and the success of multinational capital has dramatically transformed the landscape of the city. In Bangalore, more than practically any other Indian city, the positive effects of the IT industry seem pervasive, whether in the crowded mall or the mushrooming tech parks, in the innumerable engineering colleges or the new high-end international airport (see figures 5–7). All of these trends have also made Bangalore the prime location for non-resident Indians (NRIs) to relocate after several years in the United States.

Ram's and Shreya's decision to relocate to Bangalore stemmed from recognition not only of a changing India, but also of a transformed Bangalore in particular. Once they arrived in Bangalore, they went about making their American-turned-Indian dreams a reality. At the time I spoke with them, they had almost finished constructing their brand-new five-thousand-square-foot home in a residential enclave outside of Bangalore (see figure 8). Their new home is luxurious—far beyond anything they might have afforded in Silicon Valley. Indeed, the move back to India was not, as it might have been in a previous generation, a sacrifice or a step down; rather, it was a step up in every way. In his Bangalore-based job, Ram earns in dollars but spends in rupees, thus converting what would be an upper-middle-class salary in the United States into an even more elite lifestyle in India. Shreya, who had been working a lucrative biotech job in the United States, could afford not to work in India. She took time off to spend with her children before starting a part-time teaching job.[1] Both felt that life in Bangalore took them out of the U.S. "rat race," allowing them more time with their children and extended family. For them, the move back to India underscored

FIGURE 5
A busy mall
interior in
Bangalore.
Photo by Ganesh
Ramachandran.

their family and cultural values, even as it afforded them a larger house with a more luxurious lifestyle.

Ram's and Shreya's story has become exemplary of India's transnational professional class and unfolds during a distinct moment in the history of India and in the history of the global economic system. My parents were their predecessors—converting a technical education acquired in India into social and geographic mobility that allowed them to live comfortably in the United States while maintaining ties to India from afar. Unlike my parents, however, Ram and Shreya have helped to transform concerns of "brain drain" during my parents' generation into hopeful narratives of "brain circulation," allowing them to participate directly in India's new development trajectory (Saxenian 2005). Indeed, Ram is one among an estimated sixty-thousand transnational Indian professionals who have returned to India since 2000 (Ray 2007). In the Bangalore office

FIGURE 6 Heightened consumerism in a commercial district.
Photo by Ganesh Ramachandran.

FIGURE 7 Cisco's Bangalore office. Photo by Ganesh Ramachandran.

FIGURE 8   New gated residential enclaves outside Bangalore. Photo by Ganesh Ramachandran.

or his California-based multinational, he is joined by other transnational colleagues—experienced IT professionals like him who have chosen to move back to India after a long stint abroad, or younger folk, who aspire for the opportunity to leave India, even if only to return.

Whatever improvements in lifestyle they might be experiencing, however, Ram and others like him do not choose to be in India solely for economic reasons; rather it is their identification with India as a cultural and spiritual "home" that motivates the decision to return. Ram explained that he wished for his children to experience what he had experienced as a child, growing up in a small semi-rural town in South India. Ram explained that there is something unchanging about India that persists despite all the changes he sees: "The beauty of India, what I have seen with my own eyes, is that it does not change. It does not . . . You may allow certain changes to happen. Top one or two layers of people keep changing newer cars due to IT . . . [But] it is given that not everybody can achieve the same goal . . . Being contented with what comes is one of the greatest things here. People's expectations are not high; nobody is on a fast track. In India, the fast track is not on."

Ram's beliefs about Indian society are rooted in his own class history. Born into an "ordinary middle-class" family, Ram became a knowledge worker whose savvy and skills led his family from the American dream in

California to another kind of dream in the land of his birth. The privilege of his transnational status allows him to view India and Indian culture from a distance, even as he lives within it, producing an Orientalizing view of life in India that allows him to romanticize India from a position of power and privilege. In this way, Ram and his family influence and participate in a "new" idea of what it means to belong to India, but they also reinforce resonant notions of India as a space of cultural stability.

Santa Clara, California, 2005

A warm, smiling woman of thirty welcomed me into her comfortable suburban home in the heart of Silicon Valley one sunny day in August. Her new baby daughter, just three weeks old, was sleeping in a cradle in the family room. Aarti invited me to be seated at the dining table, overlooking a spacious kitchen flooded with light. Indian immigrants like Aarti and her husband have played a critical role in the production and sustenance of the American IT industry, and this influence has been most pronounced in Silicon Valley. Most graduates of the prestigious Indian Institutes of Technology (IITs) who left India for the United States in the 1960s and 1970s played an active role in bringing the American IT industry to maturity, particularly in California's Silicon Valley. Graduates of these schools helped to found nearly every major Silicon Valley firm, including Microsoft, Intel, and Sun (Saxenian 2005). Since then, talented educated immigrants from Asia, like Aarti and her husband, and before them, Ram and Shreya, have found Silicon Valley to be something of a promised land, offering high salaries, good weather, and a generation-old Indian community with its own temples, community centers, and shops. At the same time, this affluent minority group has also become more and more mainstreamed in American politics and society. This history, as well as Silicon Valley's continued dominance in the global IT industry, continues to attract large numbers of the best Indian talent to northern California, but increasingly, these migrations seem to be short-term, as more and more Indian immigrant couples decide to return "home" after a long stint in the United States.

Aarti met her husband while working in a particular kind of environment in India—a sphere of life in which going abroad to the United States was a logical, presumed option: "My husband and I used to commute together. The profile of people from that area was all kinds of young graduates—mostly engineers—who used to travel together. There were computer science people too. We all had a lot in common, and that's how we met. Half those people went to the U.S. [My husband] was trying to go to the U.S. to do MBA. He got admission to a good school in Bombay, but he wanted to come here. I got the visa [first]." Unlike most of the women in Silicon Valley I interviewed who came to the United States on a spousal visa, Aarti traveled to the United States for her master's degree on her own, even though her mother would have much preferred that she get married first. Because her chosen mate had not yet secured admission in the U.S. school of his choice, marriage prior to migration was not possible, but Aarti stuck to her decision. Soon, her intended husband joined her in the United States; they courted briefly and were engaged. After finishing their respective degrees, they headed west to California, where they had been living for several years at the time that I met her. Having achieved upward mobility and the American dream of homeownership in one of the most expensive real estate markets in the United States, Aarti and her husband appear to be quite settled, especially with the new daughter asleep in the cradle.

As soon as we began talking, Aarti explained to me that she had taken maternity leave from her job but planned to return to work within a few months. Before long, however, it became clear that the pause in her career was about more than just the sleeping infant. Within this "break," Aarti was assessing her career and her future, and perhaps most importantly, whether that future would continue in California or back in India. The birth of her daughter created a moment of professional confusion for her, in which she was reevaluating for herself what she really wished to do in her career, and, more importantly, it created an opening that could potentially propel her and her family back to India. Like Ram and Shreya, Aarti and her husband have become aware of the winds of change in India and want to be a part of those changes:

> We were in India in January for a wedding. I kind of got the idea that India is booming. Got the feeling that "oh, my country is changing!" [And here,] I have lately been thinking—why am I consciously talking so much of money when I wanted to do other things? I am moving away from my roots. So it is definitely an option. A very serious option. But my husband wants to make sure. After living here for a long time, personally, professionally, and socially, it has to work out in India. He wants U.S. citizenship. If we are not happy in India, we need

to get back. We need a plan B. Lots of people say, "Once you decide, throw your green card in the ocean." I do not think of it that way. We are too open to the whole world.

Like other Indian couples in Silicon Valley who are thinking through this decision, she is cautious about letting go of a hard-won life in the United States, even as she is excited about participating in the vibrancy of her home country. She wishes to make the decision in the most secure manner possible—U.S. citizenship for her daughter, her husband, and herself, and, thus, the perpetual possibility of returning to a life in California that they might be choosing to leave behind.

Aarti's ambivalence is a common sentiment among professional Indian couples in their thirties in the United States. With her concerns and hopes she sounds just as Ram and Shreya might have sounded a few years earlier. Like Ram and Shreya, Aarti says that she finds social life in California to be too formal, without the spontaneity of being able to drop in on friends without notice, a practice she believes to be common in India. She also is wary of raising her daughter in the United States. In India, her daughter would be raised to respect her school and teachers more. Also, because Aarti would be able to hire domestic help in India, she would be able to spend more time with her family when she returns from work, rather than having the responsibility of cooking and cleaning, as she would in California. Aarti's ability to effectively compare and contrast the possibilities of very privileged lives in two different locales stems directly from a position in the global economy that allows her to realistically imagine job prospects for herself and her husband in both India and the United States. At the same time, economic considerations seem to be only part of the story; her sense of "home" allows her to imagine a better, more meaningful life in a new and improved India—a life that she feels might bring her closer to "her roots" in the long haul. In contemplating how to bring together the lifestyle she enjoys in the United States with the sense of "home" and cultural stability she feels in India, Aarti is already putting into motion notions of a "new" India that resist binary categorizations.

Durban, South Africa, 2005

I first met Raneshni at her office, nestled in a large office park in central Durban. As she invited me inside, I noticed she wore a *bindi* on her forehead despite her otherwise Westernized attire of slacks and a blouse.[2]

Raneshni was extremely forthcoming about her love for and identification with India, even when I did not specifically ask questions about it. Over my many visits with Raneshni—at her home, over lunch, and on religious occasions, I came to understand her deep and abiding feeling of connection not only to India as a privileged site of "her" culture, but also to Indians elsewhere. Perhaps to an even greater extent than her counterparts in India and the United States, "being Indian" fundamentally constituted who Raneshni perceived herself to be as a person.

South African Indians have remained relatively isolated from a changing India, having emigrated over a century ago, first as indentured laborers and later as merchants. Since the end of apartheid, however, South African Indians, whose ties to an Indian identity were maintained through the isolation and insulation of colonialism and then apartheid, have invested significant energy in connecting with a larger transnational circuit of Indian meanings. Upward mobility for some South African Indians in recent years has made it possible for them to visit India in increasing numbers, a dream that was almost inconceivable for most of their parents. Although most South African Indians remain working class, the symbolic power of an upwardly mobile, mostly Hindu group has helped them to reimagine Indians as being at the cutting edge of the new South Africa.

Raneshni works in the IT world, but not in a technical capacity, as did most of those I interviewed in India and the United States. She deals in sales and marketing, but is also required to have a good working knowledge of technology. Her connection to a major multinational firm allows her to travel widely for conferences and workshops, networking with the IT elite of South Africa and the world. As I sit down and begin speaking with Raneshni, I realize that her position in IT within South Africa has made her acutely aware of India's dominant role in the IT world internationally, a status not widely acknowledged among South Africans. Even though Raneshni is a fifth-generation South African Indian with no experiences of India as "home," this distance does not keep her from imagining a parallel life in India, where she can participate in India's IT boom even as she more authentically and joyously partakes in what she sees as her own special cultural heritage, which she has witnessed during her recent trips to India: "There [in India], everyone is so calm and humble. I mean, I could do with that pace of living. I just love it. If I had to locate anywhere, well, in my business, Joburg [Johannesburg] is the height. I could get a job there tomorrow. I've had offers. But it's not for me. I don't want to take my family to Joburg and lead that kind of life. It's terrible! If I had a choice and I could go, I'd go to India. Nowhere else . . . And anyway, India is the fastest growing IT country in the world!"

In 2008, three years after our initial meetings, I met Raneshni at her office again and we went out for lunch. She had just traveled to India, and this recent trip seemed to underscore further the views she had shared with me before. She had friends in Whitefield, the enclave of NRIs outside of Bangalore, and had witnessed firsthand their high-powered jobs and privileged lifestyles. Still, she was amazed by what she called "the humility and simplicity" of these extremely affluent Indians. Although she has accepted that her own life will mostly likely be lived out in South Africa, she continues to imagine an alternative life in India. For Raneshni, India is more than a place of origin; it is a place where she would be able to adhere to her cultural and spiritual values more closely and interact with other Indians who share her philosophy and moral values. In contrast to Ram, Shreya, or Aarti, Raneshni has never lived in India herself. But as an IT professional for whom India looms large in her professional life, she has access to a contemporary set of imaginings about India shared by other Indian IT workers with more direct connections to India.

In spite of the very divergent lenses through which Ram, Shreya, Aarti, and Raneshni imagine a life in India, for all of them India remains the authentic space in which to "be" Indian, whether that means upholding the family, participating in the vibrancy of a transforming Indian social and economic landscape, or feeling closer to one's spiritual and religious home. In their stories, belonging to India is not simply a consideration of heritage; it is also something that comes with a specific kind of virtuous morality that seems to abide amid all of the rapid economic changes they witness.

The Material and Symbolic Privilege of a Transnational Class

What are the various layers that comprise the privilege of India's transnational professional class? What does it mean to call them an elite? As in all situations of privilege, that of IT professionals is relative and does not extend to every circumstance. Still, their position of privilege is derived not only from their dominant position in the worldwide story of globalization and the "success" of India, but also in their ability to represent "everyman" in India, thereby disguising their eliteness.[3] It is the multiple layers of privilege of Indian IT professionals, and the naturalization of these privileges, that allow the cultural streamlining processes taking place within this class to produce influential, resonant notions of a new and improved "Indian culture"—an appropriate difference compatible with cosmopolitan sensibilities.

The Upper End of the Global Economy

The language of software code and participation in global networks place Indian IT workers in a hegemonic upper tier of the global economy. Robert Reich's now classic formulation of work in the global economy characterizes symbolic analysts as the most privileged workers in the global economy (Reich 1991). Symbolic analytic work includes "problem-solving, problem-identifying, and strategic-brokering activities" that must compete in a global market and encompasses work ranging from software engineering to public relations. But unlike routine production work, which involves repetition, symbolic analytic work is not standardized and must compete on the basis of its specific creative contribution to a larger production process, usually stretched across space (Reich 1991, 177). Many accounts of India's software sector characterize IT work in India as being more like routine production jobs that require routine coding and maintenance and that do not call for specialized problem-solving skills (Khadria 2001; Konana and Balasubramanium 2002). More recent accounts argue, however, that India is moving up the value chain and is no longer simply a low-wage destination (de Jonquières 2005; Kaul 2005; Richter and Banerjee 2003). Aneesh Aneesh's recent ethnography on Indian IT workplaces suggests, however, that it is the symbolic language of code in itself that structures the interactions between India and the rest of the globe. If the symbolic language of code serves as a vehicle of access and belonging to global networks, as Aneesh's account argues, then Indian IT professionals occupy a specialized, privileged segment of the global economy. Whether or not Indian IT professionals earn wages comparable to those earned in the United States or Europe, they are included in a symbolic system that allows them to "virtually" migrate, thus placing them in a privileged position in relation to other workers (Aneesh 2006).

The standard working arrangement for most Indian IT firms in which I conducted interviews and fieldwork is based upon an "offshore" outsourcing model that presumes the "virtual migration" that Aneesh describes. This model has been remarkably successful in India and has fueled the software industry boom. In this model, companies located (usually) in the United States or Europe relocate specific projects to a team abroad, which completes the work either on a contract basis, or as a subsidiary, branch, or partner of the client firm. An "offshore" model, at least in theory, offers the advantage of lower economic costs as well as the opportunity to work around the clock.[4] In the case of Indian/U.S. partnerships, for example, because of a favorable exchange rate, highly qualified software engineers in India cost roughly one-third of what similar talent would cost in the United States.[5] Because of the time difference, software engineers in India work while the "onsite" team in the United States sleeps, expanding the productive hours of the firm. This model has allowed Indian IT firms to establish partnerships with leading global multinationals, and these ties have grown stronger as the industry has matured and talent in India has become more sophisticated. As a result of these arrangements, IT professionals in India are likely to interface frequently with management in the United States or Europe through phone and e-mail. They speak in English and must overcome any communication barriers that may arise. In addition, more and more engineers go "onsite" for short periods to work for a client firm, expanding dramatically the opportunities for thousands of young Indian IT professionals to have the experience of living and working in the United States or Europe. Most of those I interviewed in India had spent at least some time working abroad in an industrialized country. In the context of this virtual production process that works in synchrony across oceans and borders, various definitions and meanings of "the global" emerge and become significant.

Knowledge Professionals on the Frontlines of India's "Success"

Within India, the success of IT professionals is embedded in the rhetoric of "knowledge" as a powerful new development discourse that replaces the conventional modernization paradigm. "Knowledge" is linked to broad social and economic goals, included in the notions of "knowledge for development," the "knowledge economy," or the "knowledge society." Knowledge is meant to signal attention to broad-based development goals, but in practice it tends to foster and enhance the development of an educated professional class. The term "knowledge economy" had been coined in the context of New Zealand's success in developing a high-tech economy in the 1990s, but it was the publication of the World

Bank's *World Development Report 1998/99: Knowledge for Development* that turned the word "knowledge" into a mantra in the arena of international development policy. Since its release, countries from every region of the developing world claim commitment to fostering and encouraging a knowledge economy at home as a path toward broad-based development (World Bank 1998).

On June 13, 2005, Prime Minister Manmohan Singh appointed the elite National Knowledge Commission. Consisting of eight highly influential individuals from academic, business, and policy settings, the commission's mandate is to devise reforms that will "transform India into a strong and vibrant knowledge economy in coming years." The commission is premised on the idea that a focus on knowledge will allow India to "leapfrog in the race for social and economic development," and that a society with equal access to knowledge will be one that will develop most successfully and dramatically (*Hindu* 2005).

The rhetoric of knowledge for development (K4D) relies upon a discourse of "leapfrogging," meant to signal the ability to skip ahead along the implicitly linear model of industrial development that has dominated development thinking since the end of World War II. In the conventional modernization and development paradigm, agricultural nations must progress to modernity through the vehicle of industrialization. By this conventional logic, agricultural economies like India should be most centrally concerned with the task of transformation to an industrial economy. It was this idea of industrial modernity that influenced the policies set forth by India's leaders well into the 1980s. Only after industrial modernity had been achieved, it was believed, could national economies like India's aspire to become service-oriented informational economies, typical of advanced industrial nations today. The K4D thinking provided an alternative to this view by suggesting that the "step" of industrial modernity could be skipped altogether, and that poor agricultural nations could "leapfrog" ahead to engage in an information economy without a well-developed industrial manufacturing sector. "Knowledge," then, defined as technical skills, expertise, and entrepreneurship, was posed as a kind of magic bullet, a "revolution" even, that could promise broad-based development to savvy countries with the technical know-how, skills, and proper policy commitments (Utz and Dahlmann 2005). Unlike industrial manufacturing, knowledge does not require concentrated capital investments, but rather human capital, and thus seemed to promise a way to channel the energies of countries with large, youthful populations into a viable development strategy.

Since the turn of the millennium especially, India has become the darling of such discussions, especially those taking place in the institutional context of the World Bank. India's booming IT sector, along with impressive levels of economic growth in recent years and a rising per capita GDP, seemed to provide clear evidence that "leapfrogging" was not only desirable, but also attainable. The World Bank's policy recommendations have focused on how India could further harness the power of the knowledge economy for its development, even as it used the evidence of India's success in developing a vibrant IT sector as a model for other countries to follow. These policy recommendations suggest the continuation of dramatic economic reforms, particularly those friendly to global capital and foreign investment, and assert that such practices will transform India into a "knowledge society." Implicitly, becoming a "knowledge society" would allow India to join the league of advanced industrialized nations.

But K4D policy recommendations reflect fundamentally divergent notions of knowledge. While knowledge is believed to be light, mobile, and open to all, policies meant to foster knowledge for development tend to focus on technological skills and expertise that require an education available to relatively few. This very specific "knowledge" has emerged as the dominant way to operationalize the term, taking over competing conceptualizations of knowledge in the development literature. Since the 1990s, radical critiques of development have focused on "local knowledge" as a rich source of environmental and ecological knowledge that counters dominant development paradigms (Agrawal 1996; Escobar 1995; Ferguson 1994). In these accounts, the everyday practices and beliefs of "authentic" place-bound communities are seen as the only alternative to the disasters of institutionalized development efforts, which have conventionally devalued place-bound knowledge as irrational and prescientific (Mohanty 2003; Nygren 1999; Shiva 1988). Although these arguments gained traction in academic and activist settings, radical critiques of development never completely translated into World Bank policy packages focused on "knowledge," although they did succeed in channeling new energy into such themes as "community empowerment" and "social protection."

As industrialized nations began focusing on expertise and high-tech as the basis of a new global economy, however, K4D became a narrowly defined strategy aimed at bringing technology, expertise, and infrastructure to the developing world. "Knowledge for development" discourses emphasize the development of "expertise" and "expert knowledge," and, implicitly, focus upon those individuals who either already possess them or are about to. This focus obscures the relative class position of the skilled, global experts engaged in the knowledge economy and helps to make an elite project appear broad-based and democratic.

It is no coincidence that India should provide such striking support for the K4D paradigm. Indeed, Jawaharlal Nehru, India's first prime minister, made an early commitment to science and technology as the path toward development for the nation. Science and technology were not viewed as Western, but rather as "practical," and thus were seen as available resources for India's development (Abraham 1998, 46–47). This set of convictions was embodied in the institutions that it created; elite engineering colleges, such as the famed Indian Institutes of Technology (IITs), fostered the development of globally competitive technologists rooted in a "modern" Indian value system (Nair 1997). Ironically, Nehru's efforts, meant to spur India toward industrial modernity, had the effect of fueling the "brain drain" of the 1960s and 1970s, creating technical talent with few outlets for creativity and mobility in India's previously closed economy. Yet those efforts toward technical education did create a pool of technical talent unlike any in the developing world, making India a particularly receptive setting for K4D discourses.

India's transnational class of knowledge professionals, then, is importantly located at the intersection of national and international development discourses, the boundaries of which are necessarily unclear. Technologists who today comprise the pool of Indian IT talent have been produced in part through India's early efforts to achieve industrial modernity, but they have come to the fore in a historical moment that views them as mobile purveyors of "knowledge" who are meant to participate in India's development by spurring economic growth. As I will explore in depth in later chapters, participation in the knowledge economy also encourages specific beliefs and practices that come to define the ethos of this new class of Indians. Central to this belief system is the importance of individual merit, which appears to be available for anyone to achieve. It is this belief that creates knowledge professionals who are at the frontlines of the global and national economy while at the same time creating a class that sees its position as attainable for everyone, thus obscuring its own privilege.

The India That Was "Shining"

Indian IT professionals have become prominent in the national imagination at the confluence of two seemingly conflicting trends: unprecedented economic reforms on the one hand, which have opened up the economy to foreign investment and privatized most major industries, and the rise of Hindu nationalism into the political mainstream on the other hand (Corbridge and Hariss 2000). The confluence of these two trends perhaps became most evident in 2004, when, as a part of the bid for the election of 2004, the Hindu nationalist Bhartiya Janata Party (BJP) spent tens of millions of taxpayers' money to launch a massive, high-end publicity campaign, "India Shining." In this glossy campaign, made highly visible through banners, TV ads, and an extensive website, the government projected India as a country that had finally arrived on the global scene. Emphasizing economic growth largely resulting from IT, access to car and home loans, and the desirability of India as an international tourist destination, the India Shining campaign produced a "feel-good factory" through rosy images portrayed through world-class marketing techniques.[6]

India Shining portrayed the success of those class groups that had benefited from globalization and economic reform, and, in so doing, was able to portray India as a nation reborn. The image of India offered in the campaign highlighted the new financial opportunities offered by global capital, while stressing a patriotic message of nationalist renewal and hope for all. At its core, the campaign was meant to emphasize the ostensible success of the liberalization policies that the BJP actively pursued, following in the footsteps of those before them who had laid the groundwork for economic reform. But, just as importantly, the campaign helped to create a new kind of nationalism that distanced the BJP from the Hindu nationalist rhetoric and communal violence that had helped bring the party to power. India Shining presented a "soft" nationalism to the nation and the world, a nationalism that viewed economic prosperity and global presence as achievements that redefined India (Chakravartty 2006b; G. Das 2004; Sirohi 2004). This type of nationalism bears a striking resemblance to Indian organizations in the United States that were similarly enthusiastic about the exciting economic developments occurring in India (van der Veer 2004). In contrast to the violent and xenophobic model of nationalism characteristic of Hindu fundamentalism, the kind of nationalism portrayed in India Shining looked to the professional and upwardly mobile classes for validation and fulfillment, and acknowledged India's strength in the global economy.

The fate of the India Shining campaign also served as a metaphor, perhaps, for the blind spots in this new kind of nationalism and the class it meant to target. The backlash against the campaign was swift and direct. As the competing Congress Party mounted an oppositional election campaign focusing on the rural areas, where a spate of farmer suicides had sparked national attention, it denounced the BJP for neglecting the majority of the country and spending taxpayer money to do it. The exorbitant cost of the campaign, as well as its bias toward the successes of the upwardly mobile classes in India, may have been the key factor that cost the BJP the election (Ahluwalia, Kochhar, Lal, Oldenberg, Karmali 2004; Tully 2004). Contrary to the prediction of most political pundits, and amid a skyrocketing stock market, the BJP was soundly defeated in the election of 2004.

Yet, even the newly elected Congress Party government did not stray far from the economic policies that had been implemented by the BJP. Led by Manmohan Singh, the architect of India's economic liberalization policies prior to the BJP's election, the new Congress Party government continued to support and promote the development of the IT industry, leaving the status of the professional class lauded in the India Shining campaign relatively unshaken. For all the criticisms leveled at the government for the inappropriateness of running the campaign in an election and its lack of inclusiveness, the image of a new shining nation was one that did have the effect of elevating a small elite to the level of national symbols, representing a "new" India for the nation and the world. During a time of rapid social and political change, then, when India as a nation was navigating weighty questions of economic growth, national culture, and broad-based development, Indian technologists became (and remained) the nation's heroes.

The power of the upwardly mobile to represent India in nationalist portrayals such as India Shining was not new, however. India's middle class has long played an important role in representing and imagining the nation. Scholars of the Indian middle class have long argued that the middle class holds special ideological weight in imagining the Indian nation (Chatterjee 1990; Deshpande 1993, 2003; Fernandes 2000c; Varma 1998). Moreover, it appears that the composition of this group has remained more stable over time than dramatic accounts of post-liberalization India may suggest. In the earlier Nehruvian model of Indian nation building, the "old" middle class was made up of government workers who served the nation by working for it. In a globalized model of the Indian nation, the middle class engages in a global economy of work and consumption, serving the nation by, ironically enough, directing itself away from it. This latter middle class, entering the limelight of globalization, has been dubbed a "new" middle class and is generally characterized by conservative cultural or nationalist values, a hunger for global consumer goods, and a conscientious integration into the global political economy (Deshpande 2003; Fernandes 2000b; Mazzarella 2005; Rajagopal 2001b). This "new" middle class is most often described as comprising those who are employed in high-end service sector jobs. What appears to be "new" about this class, however, is *not* its composition. Most of those who make up what has been dubbed India's "new" middle class had parents who were a part of the "old" one. New industries brought to India by globalization have brought new wealth but have not fundamentally shaken up India's class structure. The symbolic privilege of the old middle-class formation in representing the nation is reproduced in a new sociopolitical climate, thus constituting a "new" middle class.

The dominance of India's middle class in the political and cultural imagination of the nation is a product of powerful class segregation practices that have persisted over time. These practices have allowed older forms of social, economic, and cultural capital to be transformed constantly to suit shifting sociopolitical climates while keeping class divisions intact. For example, as middle-class status seems to be derived from the possession of specific kinds of professional skills, education appears to be a mode through which economic and social mobility can be realized. Yet, as Leela Fernandes and Patrick Heller (2006) have noted, in the Indian context, education serves as a central field through which class segregation is perpetuated. Advantages of urban location, education, caste, and language compound themselves, making the combination of these advantages more powerful than each of the individual components. In short, those who are acquiring the skills and professional education to become upwardly mobile already possess a significant amount of economic and symbolic capital. Educational credentials and the subsequent professionalization of personal identifications serve to mask the continuity of class dominance; such credentials come to be viewed as evidence of personal "merit." "Merit" then becomes a powerful, benevolent-sounding feature of upwardly mobile work culture, but its allure masks the continued inequalities that it justifies. What is "new" about this segment of India's new middle class, then, is not necessarily *who* they are, but *how* they perform their position in the nation.

Transnational Indian IT professionals transform a previously existing middle-class category by associating it with particular kinds of work and lifestyle patterns. This transformed category is more exclusive and yet also appears more accessible. In practice, however, clear limitations on mobility remain, and despite the exuberance of this class, few readily accept that *anyone* in India can gain access to it, as the divisions between this class and the marginalized majority remain striking. Yet, this special segment of the "new" middle class draws upon the continuities built into middle-class status in India to maintain its cultural dominance.

Internal Hierarchies of the Indian Middle Class

So, who *are* India's knowledge professionals? Who are those on the margins of that category? And how are those distinctions managed? Among the jobs created by India's new focus on high-tech service professions there exists a hierarchy of at least two tiers: the tier occupied by those in the transnational knowledge economy, which includes engineers, graphic designers, and technical writers, and the tier occupied by those in the business processing outsourcing (BPO) industry, which includes call center workers, medical transcriptionists, and simple data entry positions. This book focuses on the culture of the former. Information technology professionals working in the knowledge economy (from now on, "IT professionals," in contrast to BPO or call center workers, as appropriate) tend to be well versed in technical and managerial languages that are translatable across national boundaries, while BPO workers acquire skills that allow for a more limited kind of mobility, both economic and geographic. Reena Patel's ethnographic work with call center workers, for example, shows that entry-level positions are not given much credibility in India's middle class. Although the position requires a proficiency with English that very few youth outside India's dominant middle class possess, most middle-class kids consider BPO jobs to be "beneath" them (Patel 2008). Entry-level positions in both fields may offer similar salaries, but there is a symbolic hierarchy between the two that not only tends to feminize BPO work, but also feeds the perception that call center workers are associated with moral decay (Patel 2008, 74–75). This hierarchy was underscored in the narratives of IT women I interviewed in India when they reflected upon the rise of the BPO industry in India. Sunita, a twenty-eight-year-old engineer in Mumbai, described it thus: "I don't think people really respect those [BPO] jobs. I feel respect in this job . . . Because of education. Because people in this field have done graduation, and after that, a few courses and they achieve something . . . Now people are getting into these call centers. Getting more salary and more exposure, night shifts. They make good money. But I don't think it is a respectable job. It's because of education, qualification, again. When I started working, I was making 5,500 per month. And now, people starting in call centers start at 17,000."

While there is little evidence to suggest that BPO workers are indeed less educated than their counterparts in IT, and since most industry reports on IT in India tend to lump both of these groups together,[7] Sunita's remark is puzzling, although by no means unique. The software services industry is itself older and more established in India in comparison to the BPO industry, and it has an older average age among its employees. The profusion of research and media attention on call center workers, who work at night in order to service clients in Europe and the United States, suggests that they are a well-educated group, usually holding college degrees (Clark 2008; Shome 2006).

There are, however, some differences that seem to be especially salient to IT professionals. For example, while BPO jobs are open to most college graduates with fluency in English, IT jobs require a specialized, technical education, such as an engineering degree. Also, unlike IT workers, call center workers undergo intensive cultural training that teaches them to interact comfortably with clients living in the United States or the United Kingdom, including training in sports, popular media, and weather (Poster 2007). The adoption of American names and personas has been a standard practice in these firms for many years. In the IT industry, by contrast, there was never any overt push to change any aspect of employees' identities, even though, as I show in chapter 2, IT companies do manage the cultural identities of their employees in more subtle ways. The distinctions that IT professionals perceive between themselves and their counterparts working in call centers do not, however, seem to stem from any of these differences alone. Instead, questionable "backgrounds," a term that tends to stand in for inappropriate sexuality, bad families, and/or a "lack of culture" among call center workers, stand at the center of their relative lack of symbolic legitimacy.[8] The ability of IT professionals to question the backgrounds of call center workers speaks in large part to the symbolic privilege of the ethos of the transnational, and all the special distinctions that come with it.

These distinctions come out particularly clearly in various discussions of the "downside" of globalization in India; Indian IT workers often project the anxieties of rapid cultural change (as well as perhaps status anxiety) onto call center workers. Information technology professionals with extensive experience abroad especially tended to mark the difference between the culture of IT and the culture of the call centers as a difference in background, which was always linked both to notions of appropriate Indianness and to the possibility of global mobility. Ashok, a thirty-three-year-old technical consultant, explained his decision to remain in India in terms of a commitment to a non-materialistic ethos, yet he immediately explained that call center workers were changing that ethos: "People here have become more materialistic and so permissive, but I will limit that to the call center industry . . . Call center companies have actually started neglecting things . . . If you move away from your culture, you lose . . . People in IT are less susceptible to this. I think there is a different culture here."

Similar sentiments were echoed in the narratives of several interviewees. Ram felt discouraged by the cultural changes he saw among call center workers:

Take the kids working for BPOs. No background, their parents have never seen money—some get into drugs. It's very, very negative. The culture is opening up for a whole lot of wrong kinds of things. The reason why the Indian culture has been able to keep a tab on these things has been economics. [When you were young,] you were economically dependent. Now a BPO guy comes back at 2 a.m.; on his way back he is going with two [or] three girls, dropping them off, doing whatever—his father or mom cannot even ask because he is making enough money . . . They share offices with my firm and I can see it is bad. IT culture is very different. Basic background of education which becomes very different. In those industries, someone with B.A. who would have made 5,000 is now making 20,000 and is becoming a status symbol . . . it is corrupting the framework here.

In Ram's narrative, it becomes clearer that BPO and call center workers are losing and corrupting the Indian "framework" because of their lack of "background." In contrast, what Ram perceives as the longer educational and earnings trajectory of IT workers combines a more desirable "background" with a more moderate and well-paced path to economic independence.

In both Ashok's and Ram's narratives, they assert a knowledgeable elite position vis-à-vis BPO workers, not only in terms of their work, but also in terms of their culture. There was a general understanding among my interviewees and the mainstream media in India that BPO workers are more susceptible to the dangers of losing themselves or "forgetting" their culture in comparison to IT workers. While the scope of these observations goes far beyond the workplace itself, it speaks importantly to the conviction with which IT professionals assert their status in part through a reaffirmation of not just any Indian culture, but a particular kind of Indianness, defined by class and "background." This becomes especially clear in the narratives of individuals like Ashok and Ram, who have lived abroad for long periods of time.

Not all technologists agree with this interpretation, however. Malini, a thirty-year-old project leader in Bangalore, viewed call center and BPO workers as the main drivers of globalization and positive cultural change in urban India. For Malini, the challenges that call center workers brought to her understanding of Indian culture and convention were a welcome development:

Forget IT. IT support and call centers is really becoming big. You have ordinary graduates earning 10,000 or 11,000 rupees per month, which is a big deal. And they have to spend this kind of money. I think there is a movement in place. I think if you see the roads, if you see the shops, if you see the kids, I think there is a movement in place. My perception is that when there's money, there's time, and when there's time, things will start changing, people will start questioning. You will have an impact . . . We as Indians have never thought beyond our own family or our own community or our own caste and that has to change. I can see that is changing with globalization.

Malini is well aware of the fact that most Indian technologists look down upon call center and BPO workers for the reasons that Ram and Ashok articulated very clearly. But for Malini, globalization and attaining the global have to do with financial prosperity, which she believes will force India to shed a parochialism she despises. Call center workers are part of the change she sees and wishes to see more of.

Evidence from Patel's ethnographic work as well as anecdotal evidence in the field seems to suggest that call center workers and other BPO workers may come from a broader range of caste and class backgrounds in comparison to IT professionals. If this is the case, it is possible that the real stories of rapid mobility in India's post-liberalization landscape do indeed lie in the BPO industry, as Malini suggests, wherein young women and men acquire incomes that radically transform the social and economic standing of their families.[9] A savvy youth from a rural or lower middle-class family can more easily acquire the nontechnical skills needed to participate in the BPO industry when compared to the more rigorous standards of technical training required in software and software services. In this sense, "education," as Sunita and many other informants name it, indicates not only the degree but also a much more subtle quality of background: the social and cultural location that makes an advanced technical education possible. This means coming from a family that never needs its children to produce income for the family, a family that can afford private school fees in a country where the public school system cannot provide basic skills, a family that can create an environment that allows its children to gain the skills to compete and obtain valuable seats in college, where they will do well enough to succeed in a highly competitive applicant pool. The BPO industry, in being more flexible about the types of acceptable educational requirements, provides opportunities for a broader range of people. It is this subtle distinction that accounts in large part for Sunita's feeling of superiority over call center workers. This feeling of superiority does not translate outside of India; those Indians living in Silicon Valley do not view call center workers as somehow less successful or respectable than other IT professionals in India, suggesting that these distinctions are actively being produced within Indian cities. Whatever the explanation, however, the culture of call center workers in particular, and BPO workers more generally, seldom figures into transnationally resonant ideas of Indian culture, even as it does seem to stand in for a kind of Western modernity (with all the promises and threats that come along with that) within urban India (Nadeem 2009).[10]

Within India's borders, then, hierarchies of "background" translate to some degree into the relative prestige of different segments of the IT industry, thus defining one type of boundary of India's transnational class. Government workers, bank workers, and shopkeepers remain the staple jobs of Indian middle-class life, but they are, for the most part, outside the realm of India's transnational class. Certainly, this perceived "old" middle class is outside the sphere of social and professional interactions of most of those I interviewed, even though most come from families supported by such jobs.

A Feminist Take on Privilege as an Analytical Tool

In her book *Feminism without Borders*, Chandra Mohanty outlines a one-third world/two-thirds world framework for understanding global inequality. She moves away from the conventional first world/third world model, subordinating geography and colonial histories to her interest in "draw[ing] attention to the continuities as well as the discontinuities between the haves and the have-nots *within* the boundaries of nations and *between* nations and indigenous communities" (Mohanty 2003, 227). Her approach allows us to acknowledge the existence of a privileged One-Third world located geographically in both the global north and the south, as well as a Two-Thirds world majority. Mohanty's conceptualization allows her to theorize political and economic positions that defy easy categorization. For example, Mohanty identifies herself as socially, economically, and geographically located in the One-Third world, even as she wishes to explain and assert her alliance with the Two-Thirds world. Indian IT professionals are similarly geographically located partly in what we might associate with the Two-Thirds world (India) and partly in what we might associate with the One-Third world (United States), but this transnational class is economically, socially, and often even politically firmly within the privileged One-Third world. This privilege is the result of IT professionals' dominant position in several intersecting realms: material and symbolic hierarchies of "background" within India, the contingencies of international development discourses that view knowledge professionals as primary agents of economic and social change in the global south, and, more broadly, a global economy that privileges "symbolic analysts" over "repetitive workers." In India especially, as I have mentioned, these skills are only made available to individuals with certain backgrounds. Once attained, however, the acquired skills of the symbolic analyst unlock the door to the One-Third world.

Professional IT women occupy a peculiar positionality within these hierarchies. Understanding IT women as powerful symbolic agents offers a critical lens for understanding cultural contradiction and change. Patricia Hill Collins (1991) famously argued that middle- and upper-class black women, in occupying a simultaneously dominated and dominating position, illuminated precisely the intersections of class and gender that cannot be examined separately. Transnational feminist scholarship includes a critique of capitalism and colonialism in its effort to situate patriarchal nationalisms in all their particularity (Grewal and Kaplan 1994). Here, I build upon these theoretical traditions, examining the symbolic power of elite women in a patriarchal, postcolonial setting during a moment of economic reform and religious nationalism.

Middle-class women have long acted as idealized markers of Indian national culture, and they have been a key mode through which "modernity" gets reconciled with a perceived "authentic" culture. In early Indian nationalist discourse, middle-class Bengali women stood in for the spiritual essence of Indian culture, located in the home, while men were located outside the home, engaged in the realm of the material. Thus, men, whose identity was linked to the public sphere, could and should modernize to support the nation. Women, in contrast, could be educated and refined, but they were not to be "essentially" modernized. Rather, as the protectors of the nation's superior essence, located in the private sphere, they had to remain Indian in essence (Chatterjee 1990). Over time, representations of idealized Indian womanhood have shifted, reflecting sociopolitical and economic changes, though the domestic role of women has remained central to this imagination (Bhattacharjee 1999; Puri 1999; Rajan 1993; Sarkar 1995; Sen 2002).

Since the 1990s, a "new" Indian woman has come into focus in the public realm. Her newness is marked simultaneously through her potential for professionalism in the workplace *and* through her adherence to an essentialized notion of Indianness that hearkens back to earlier nationalist ideologies. As such, the "new" Indian woman, epitomized in the success of India's beauty queens in global pageants since the 1990s, is thought to signal advancement for women in a country long thought to be burdened by the shackles of oppressive traditions (Ahmed-Ghosh

2003; Parameswaran 2004). The "new" woman has become a subject of capitalist desire as a consumer, as well as the subject of a middle-class panic about changing sexual norms (Bhaskaran 2004; Oza 2006). Upwardly mobile professional women, then, as *exemplary* "new" women, must simultaneously reinforce the values of the nation while legitimating the integration of the new cultural and economic influences of global capital.

The ways in which a particular appropriate, middle-class femininity is upheld within the private sphere of the family are critical for understanding cultural streamlining and appropriate difference—the process through which a new, rationalized version of "Indianness" that is compatible with globalization is produced. Scholars of gender and nationalism have noted that in times of dramatic social change the clear demarcation of the boundaries between the private domestic sphere and the public sphere, always a gendered division, serves to provide the guidelines for the cultural future of the nation (Chatterjee 1990; McClintock 1995; Yuval-Davis 1997). In the context of India, contemporary constructions of the domestic hinge upon a notion of the Indian (implicitly Hindu) family (Mankekar 1999; van der Veer 2004). The Indian family and its values become part of a core cultural discourse through which the superiority of national culture is affirmed and reinforced. Respectable femininity, expressed importantly through the preservation of "good families" among professional Indian women, offers a point of entry for understanding how gender, articulated through class privilege, produces the logics and beliefs of a reinvented culture whose authenticity and sense of cultural continuity hinges on the family. As a concept, respectable femininity can help us examine the interplay between nationalist constructions of womanhood, contemporary urban enactments of femininity, and the integral role that respectable femininity plays in constituting the ideal Indian family.

Pierre Bourdieu's notion of symbolic capital, when approached through his conception of gender, provides a set of concepts through which we can examine practices of respectable femininity as they are embedded in patterns of class dominance and national culture. In Bourdieu's treatment of symbolic capital, its bearers exert power from a dominant position, but this dominance is "misrecognized" as natural and permanent, thus making it appear as if the dominant group is not exerting power at all (Bourdieu 1990, 1991, 1995). The strength of Bourdieu's emphasis on symbolic capital as cultural authorization also opens up space for grappling with the embeddedness of gender in these processes, offering a conceptualization of respectable femininity as a constitutive element of *symbolically authorized middle-classness*. In this framework, it is not only education or taste that constitutes symbolic capital; respectable femininity and its association with the family constitute equally critical forms of symbolic capital.[11]

By conceiving of the broad range of practices associated with respectable femininity as symbolic capital, we can be attentive to the embeddedness of gender within class meanings. Specifically, we can understand how class privilege enables the production of gendered class practices that uphold nationalistic meanings of the domestic sphere. As respectable femininity is enacted in everyday practice, we can analyze historically rooted patterns of middle-class dominance and the continued resonance of gendered symbols of the nation, but more importantly, we can see the creative navigations of individual women that modify and reshape these patterns. This framework, then, offers a lens through which to understand how professional women working in software set the terms for cultural streamlining processes that shape the culture of a "new" India built largely around the aspirations and achievements of the new middle class, producing an appropriate difference that showcases Indian culture to the world.

Cultural streamlining as a process can only be put into motion by individuals who are authorized by the nation, through their symbolic power, to engage in such a cultural innovation. The product of these innovations—the specific meanings of Indianness that resonate *as* Indian, while still being palatable to a Western, cosmopolitan sensibility—is governed by the values and meanings of this matrix of class privileges. Thus, the multiple layers of symbolic and material privilege in India's transnational class are closely intertwined, such that each of these layers reinforces the others. A history of a particular "background" of class privilege enables entry into a position of dominance in the global economy and participation in India's knowledge economy—the story of Indian success that has refigured what India means to the world. That same background also offers IT professionals a symbolic privilege that is profoundly gendered in its character: shaped by shifting expectations of women in the public realm, its power is realized in the realm of the private and domestic.

The IT workplace comprises an important starting point for understanding the stakes and benefits of cultural streamlining, while also providing an initial model for appropriate difference that individuals then imbibe, adapt, and modify as they channel the lessons learned at work into their personal lives. Given the complexity of the backgrounds of Indian IT professionals, how does the workplace draw together, reshape, and create new models for Indian culture on an everyday basis?

CULTURAL POLITICS IN THE IT WORKPLACE

I really stress the word global. And not American. Because even if their co-workers are predominantly American . . . that's changing. So they may work with someone from Poland or China. So the skills that we talk about are going to be useful globally. And that's about being transparent and clear. Because you need that. In virtual teams, you need this kind of communication . . . And it's a very appealing term. I mean, who doesn't want to work globally? And they [the Indian engineers] love it!—LUELLEN SCHAFER, THE FOUNDER AND DIRECTOR OF GLOBAL SAVVY, A CROSS-CULTURAL TRAINING FIRM IN SILICON VALLEY

Because I'm global, I tend to be more interested in reading something about the U.S. or whatever. I think a lot of that has got to do with global-ization. And even with my television, my news, my movies. My restau-rants. When I go out, I eat Italian food, and that makes me curious. So, in that way, I think globalization has really helped me. And, you know, when I was growing up, all this was just "modern" or "Western." I think a lot of that is really going away. I think it's getting to be a part of Indian life . . . So everything is not just Western and modern, and hence, not so good. Things are changing. Because we have always been aware of the global world, but we have always shut it out. Now, we're letting it in. Always, there's a challenge, right? You have your own way of life and there's another way of life coming in. While it's coming in, while you're creating a new identity for itself, there will be casualties, a bit of confusion. It's okay.—MALINI, A THIRTY-YEAR-OLD PROJECT LEADER IN BANGALORE

Malini, a longtime employee at a major Indian multinational in Bangalore, has traveled the world and has very specific ideas about what it means to be global. She defends globalization, praises its virtues in India, and does not mind it if the more parochial fea-tures of India's society and culture fade away. A few casualties and some confusion, inevitable in the cultural shakeup, are fine with her. For LuEllen Schafer, in contrast, "global" is a keyword meant to describe a particular set of skills that she helps to foster in the IT workplace—an appealing, pragmatic set of skills that is transferable and applicable anywhere. It is Schafer's job to transmit these skills to Indian engineers in a way that does not threaten their sense of Indianness, but rather allows them to maintain what she understands to be their culture. When does the acquired skill of effective global communication become something that defines a person more fundamentally? What are the mechanisms through which this happens? How might Indians working in the IT industry acquire not just the skills to "work globally," but also the personality traits and attitudes that make them feel "global" on a much deeper and more personal level? And finally, what might be the implications of these skills and shifts on the class culture as a whole?

This chapter traces the production of "the global" in the IT workplace and beyond, and the shifting place of "the Indian" that is always alongside it. Taking a step back from the seemingly self-evident truths about the "global" character of the IT industry, I focus upon the competing, overlapping meanings of the folk term as it circulates among Indian technologists who travel from workplaces in India to workplaces abroad, and back again. I argue that the private beliefs and lifestyles of IT professionals that I will explore in subsequent chapters are powerfully shaped by discourses of "the global" that circulate in IT firms. Information technology workplaces actively seek to create new kinds of people, with a new orientation to themselves and the world. And IT professionals themselves take an active role in shaping the ideas of "global" and "Indian" as these ideas flow from the workplace into their personal lives.

Navigating Cultural Terrain at Work: Corporate Perspectives

Indian IT companies do not just produce software products or sell their technical skills to clients abroad; they also produce a new breed of workers. The culture of the IT workplace, and, consequently, the transnational class of Indian IT professionals, is importantly derived from what informants repeatedly called a "global work culture." This culture is defined in myriad ways, the most prominent of which I describe and analyze here. "The global" can indicate a kind of new corporate culture that is separate from either Indian culture or Western culture, although this culture can be very thinly defined, leaving it open to interpretation. A cultivated sense of placelessness and insulation in office interiors, paired with a new awareness of corporate branding, offers little that is distinctive from which to build a new corporate culture. "The global" also refers to certain types of processes, communication styles, and skills, all of which are low context (in that they rely more on words and language than situational or relational cues), standardized, and transferable anywhere in the world. Finally, "the global" refers to a particular kind of organizational and managerial style, indicating flat hierarchies and innovative, empowered employees that emerge from new-age management and globalization discourses. Discourses of personal empowerment have particular resonance for professional women, although in their navigations, the gaps and shortcomings of corporate discourses of empowerment become apparent.

All of these competing meanings of "the global" set the stage for cultural streamlining. In corporate hallways and cross-cultural training sessions, culture becomes something that can be apprehended and absorbed, something transferable and strategically deployable. Corporations are invested in fostering a "global work culture" because it offers the promise of better efficiency and productivity, which improves their bottom line. Individuals, in contrast, are invested in being "global" because it promises a cosmopolitan sensibility that connotes status and refinement outside the workplace, as well as added bonuses within it. Such a strategic approach to culture that begins in the IT workplace, stemming from the capitalist imperative to streamline differences for the sake of efficiency, becomes a way of understanding culture more generally, as corresponding notions of "Indian" take shape alongside competing notions of the "global."

Sometimes, notions of what is "Indian" stand in contradiction to the global, while at other times, they are in concert. The dominant relativist rhetoric of "the global" encourages Indian technologists to maintain an "Indian" core and to adopt a global professional persona purely for the purposes of their own productivity and advancement. In this setting, India is ostensibly being preserved, but it is also being redefined as definitions of "the global" proliferate. This sense of India—at once new and abiding, both informed by discourses transmitted to technologists in the workplace and created by the engineers themselves— reveals itself most clearly in the narratives of professional IT women, whose behaviors within the workplace reflect their commitment to being simultaneously "Indian" and "global," a reconciliation that forms the basis for the cultural navigations that streamline Indian culture into mobile, globalization-friendly appropriate difference.

Early industrial workplaces sought to create particular kinds of people to make up a new class culture, sometimes in very dramatic, paternalistic ways. Henry Ford's implementation of the five-dollar-a-day wage after the dawn of the twentieth century was meant to create an American middle class of consumers who would buy the cars being produced. But Ford was not interested only in putting money into the hands of the men in his factory; he also wished to supervise their transition into what he saw as an appropriate lifestyle for the burgeoning American middle class. The Ford Sociological Department oversaw the living conditions and habits of its employees, offering grants for better housing and encouraging workers not to live in immigrant-style crowded quarters. Those who could not be "improved" by the company within six months were let go. Such efforts were part of a larger Americanization program designed by the Ford Sociological Department that aimed at assimilating a diverse immigrant workforce into a homogenous American middle class. The graduation ceremony, the highlight of the program, consisted of each graduated employee first appearing in his national garb, then climbing into a large pot that was then "stirred" by the teachers in the program, and finally emerging as an American worker with an American flag. The program did not succeed in making workers give up their national culture and was eventually cut due to funding constraints (Hooker 1997; Hull 2001). Although the enculturation of employees in Indian IT workplaces can hardly be compared to this extreme paternalism, the Ford example does offer an important historic precedent for thinking through how corporations self-consciously promote a homogenous culture, not only for purposes of efficiency and productivity, but also as part of a larger agenda of social betterment that appears benevolent and even progressive to those in power at the time.

India's IT heroes certainly endow the IT industry with a sense of transformative purpose that is a distant echo of Ford's attempts to improve America. Narayana Murthy, the co-founder of the Indian tech giant Infosys, might arguably be the Indian IT parallel to America's Henry Ford. As a symbol of India's new middle class, Murthy is a powerful figure, having lived out his own Indian version of the Horatio Alger story. Infosys was the first Indian company to be traded on the NASDAQ and it has played a key role in branding India's tech industry as a global one. In 2005, Infosys opened the doors of its Global Education Centre in Mysore, the largest corporate training center in the world. In an interview with the premiere Indian news website, rediff.com, Murthy explains, "We have realised that our challenge is to take the reactive mindset of Indian youngsters and change them into proactive problem solving ones. By and large, because of our culture, family background, etc., we are reactive. To change that, we have to understand problem solving as a science and an art. We have to understand algorithmic thinking. . . . We have to understand interacting with people from other cultures, the ability to get into a new unstructured situation and use our generic learning to ask questions in a systemic way" (Roy 2005). In Murthy's explanation, becoming global requires a move away from a particularly "Indian" mind-set, again, determined by culture and background, toward a more abstract and broadly applicable mode of thinking that can allow Indians to compete with other technologists around the world. His words contain not only an idea of what an Indian mentality looks like, but also a plan and a vision for transforming that mentality, and, by association, the nation itself. At the same time, Murthy's vision does not threaten or undermine what it means to be Indian; it only enhances it.

Cultural trainers who work with IT firms have a clear idea of such differences in "mind-set" as well and reproduce those ideas in training sessions designed to make workers aware of their own cultural proclivities, often using psychological language and principles to help workers understand "who they are." These cultural proclivities are also dynamic, and cultural trainers change their own models of culture to reflect their notions of a changing India. For example, Dr. Zareen Araoz, a cultural trainer who has worked with both Indian and U.S. companies for more than two decades, explained in a phone interview, "Everything has changed. [Compared to] things that I used to teach them then [in the 1980s] about India, you teach them almost the opposite in many ways . . . Like in the 1980s we taught that Indians cling to tradition and are closed to change, their difficulty in accepting new things and change. Today, the Indians are hungry for change and newness and nice ideas and creativity and all of that." Still, Araoz agrees that there are underlying, persisting differences that continue to shape the ways she deals with both Indian and American workers: "Maybe a few major differences are the much more individualistic or independent approach in the U.S., as opposed to a much more collective and, shall we say, directed, hierarchical approach in a traditional Indian company. And I think the much more direct, assertive approach here [in the United States] as opposed to a more indirect and maybe the desire-for-harmony-approach that comes from India."

Aroaz's assertion of this fundamental difference, at odds with her assertion of the dynamism of attitudes she has witnessed and produced during her career, is well supported by Carol Upadhya's observations of such cross-cultural training in Bangalore firms. Upadhya finds that cultural trainers work from outdated anthropological models that specify traits for national cultures, especially Hofstede's model of culture, which has become the gold standard for understanding cultural diversity in the business management literature.[1] As much as the relativistic language of the training emphasizes the need to break from stereotypes, Upadhya finds that these trainings end up reinforcing and reproducing those same stereotypes, pitting "collectivist" cultures against "individualistic" ones and encouraging Indian IT professionals to adopt particular behaviors purely for the sake of their professional development (Upadhya 2007b).

In the concept of transforming a particular kind of "mind-set," the abstract strategic innovations of corporations get translated into the culture of IT workplaces in India, even when the content of that "mind-set" is underspecified, presumed, and perhaps even reproduced in the midst of efforts to transform it. Cultural streamlining as a corporate goal begins to take on a broader meaning as shifting a "mind-set" becomes a way of discussing how Indian technologists can become "global," both among cultural trainers and among IT professionals themselves. These professionals do not view this kind of a mind-set shift as either a kind of Westernization or even necessarily a strengthening of Indian identification, but rather as an adaptation to discourses that dominate the upper crust of India's IT industry. This strategic adaptation lies at the core of the "appropriate difference" produced in the Indian IT workplace—a difference that improves upon "being Indian" without violating it. Ram, who returned to India from Silicon Valley as described in the previous chapter, explained that a significant part of the satisfaction he derives from his job comes from acting as a kind of transformative cultural bridge in his capacity as a mentor to produce exactly this kind of strategic adaptation. As a senior-level manager, he mentors and guides younger hires, some of whom have gone on to become managers themselves. He explained to me, "I am able to transform the Indian way of thinking, the Indian way of looking at foreigners, of looking at people from abroad, and [helping them in] finding out what is missing in the way they look at things, bringing in the pragmatism and practical functioning of [the] U.S. culture of working."

In his account, Ram's capacity as a mentor emerges from his experience working in the United States. Yet, in bringing in U.S. work practices, he does not see himself as diluting Indian culture in any way, but rather as helping to cultivate an improved corporate ethos in his workplace. Experts in cross-cultural issues in IT indicate that individuals "originally from India, but with higher education and long-term residence in North America" can be extremely useful for managing cultural differences for complex projects, as they are able to communicate effectively with employees on both the Indian and North American sides of a project (Krishna, Sahay, and Walsham 2004). Thus, for individuals like Ram, a focus on bringing together or bridging two different mind-sets fulfills not only a personal goal, but also a goal of the company.

To what extent, then, is the culture of Indian technologists controlled by the agendas of corporations striving for the upper echelons of the global economy? Is cultural streamlining and the production of appropriate difference anything more than a form of corporate-led homogenization? A burgeoning literature on India's IT industry suggests that top-down processes are indeed at work here, and that it is these processes that might play the most important role in determining how and why employees embrace "the global." Carol Upadhya argues convincingly that discourses of "global" and "Indian" have been used not only to empower Indian IT professionals, but also to control them and make them a more pliant workforce (Upadhya 2007b). Other sociological and anthropological studies of the Indian IT industry have tended to focus more upon the subordinate status of these professionals vis-à-vis their foreign clients, as well as their job insecurity, though they do not directly examine questions of workplace culture (Chakravartty 2006a; Khadria 2001; Upadhya and Vasavi 2006). Yet, my interactions with IT professionals suggest that it is difficult to claim that sheer top-down cultural hegemony drives the production of the new cultural forms that are apparent here. Indeed, the culture of IT work, and the very specific arrangements and procedures of the workplace, inform and help to constitute the subjectivities of the workers themselves, but in a more back-and-forth, participatory manner than it might initially appear.

Indian IT professionals make meanings that importantly shape their own subjectivities, even though the IT industry, management, and cultural training sessions are all important influences in these processes. While I do not wish to underplay the importance of claims that these professionals have little power relative to foreign clients in a large, segmented, and diverse industry in which many workers find themselves in subordinate positions, the vast majority of the professionals I spoke to saw themselves as agents in charge of their own meanings and destinies, viewing those same issues of relative power and job security in a very different light. High turnover at Indian IT firms in Mumbai and Bangalore, due in large part to the growing demand for IT talent, allows young technologists to hop from company to company for better pay. This phenomenon in itself lends credence to the idea that whatever the particular managerial constraints they may face, individuals actively shape the corporate culture of the IT industry at the broadest levels. The process of cultural streamlining and the production of appropriate difference in the workplace, then, emerge not only from corporate imperatives, but also from IT professionals themselves. The "global" character of the IT industry's corporate culture is produced at multiple sites—in the setting of the workplace, in the vocabulary and practices of management, and in the symbolic hierarchies that IT workers produce about other workers of other backgrounds who are not considered "global."

A "Global" Setting

On a hot and dusty afternoon in 2005, I find myself in an auto rickshaw bouncing along the badly rutted road to Whitefield, once a satellite industrial town, on the outskirts of Bangalore. I clutch the directions to the office of a multinational technology firm, i-gate, where I have scheduled an interview with a software professional. Along the main road are signs of a dying industrial backwater: deserted, dingy factory buildings, large lots full of broken-down trucks, and the occasional tire store, the latter perhaps the only establishments that show signs of vitality. Without notice, the rickshaw veers off the main road onto an unmarked dirt lane, which is, to my eyes, empty. Gaping open lots stretch before us, punctuated now and again by huge construction sites with busy laborers. When I feel convinced we are going the wrong way, the driver pulls over to ask a laborer how to get to i-gate. The laborer tells us in Kannada to continue on the road we are on, turn right at Dell, and then a left at IBM; i-gate, he tells us, will be on the left, opposite SAP Labs.

As the man promised, Whitefield's expanses of empty lots slowly give way to the futuristic office buildings of multinational tech firms. Stretches of the road are paved, while most are not. Finally, we arrive at i-gate, a brand-new building of several stories, glass and steel glittering in the harsh sunshine. There is barely a dirt road leading up to the door of the office, but as soon as I cross into the driveway, a security guard snaps my picture on a digital camera and prints a visitor badge for me from his computer station. The guard remotely pages the woman I have come to see, and I am suddenly standing in the middle of a chilly, air-conditioned lobby done up in muted tones and minimalist styling. Once inside, I realize that the building is only one part of a huge, self-contained campus that consists of immaculate and contemporary common areas surrounded by carefully landscaped outdoor areas that had been invisible in the haze of dust at the main gate. Outside the lobby, IT professionals stroll along manicured lawns down granite pathways, oblivious to the dirt road they took to come to work that morning.

The interior office environments of most large IT firms in India are designed to look like their Silicon Valley counterparts, or more accurately, to look placeless, as if they could be "anywhere."[2] In their interiors, the offices of major multinationals I visited in California and even in South Africa were similar to those in India in scale, materials, and security arrangements, although there was considerable variation in the external settings. Offices in Silicon Valley and South Africa are often surrounded by a moat of parking spaces, such that employees arrive in private cars and walk as little as possible to arrive at their cubicles. Cisco's enormous campus in Silicon Valley is an excellent example of this setup. In India, there is great diversity in the external settings of IT offices, ranging from new gleaming buildings on the outskirts of town, such as i-gate, to older office buildings in the midst of dense urban settings (figures 9–12). Regardless of this variation, however, the entrance into the air-conditioned serenity of an IT office with a swipe of a magnetized security badge is fundamentally similar. Technologists in India feel assured that the work they do each day is done under conditions that, in their cultivated placelessness, feel comparable to conditions for technologists anywhere in the world. Those who travel abroad

FIGURE 9 Infosys, Bangalore: Software Development Block.

FIGURE 10 Climate-controlled cubicles: the same as anywhere.

for work on the client's side shore up that belief; in each new location they travel to they find the same cubicles and computers in a similarly contained, climate-controlled environment.

It is the ostensible neutrality of the interiors of IT environments, which form a sometimes shocking contrast to the exteriors of offices in urban India, that in part contributes to a feeling of "being global" experienced by employees. American multinationals in India, such as IBM, BroadCom, Honeywell, Accenture, and others, try as far as possible to reproduce the physical structures of their American offices in India, making adjustments where necessary to accommodate local situations. For example, because of the existing high density in urban India, American

FIGURE 11 A retreat from India's urban landscape.

FIGURE 12 Embedded in the urban landscape. Photo by Champaka Rajagopal.

corporations cannot quite accommodate the large surface parking model of Silicon Valley and tend to build tall parking structures instead that are meant to accommodate only some of the employees, while most take private buses chartered by the corporation. But even Indian multinationals, such as Wipro, Tata Consultancy Systems (TCS), and Infosys, many of whose founders got their start in Silicon Valley, have interiors that are similar to their American counterparts. The arguments to be made for this appear immanently practical and common-sensical: computers require air-conditioning, engineers require cubicles, high-tech firms need security. When there is already a prototypical interior model that accommodates all of these requirements, why reinvent the wheel? I would argue, however, that there is a cultural payoff to maintaining the status quo of IT interiors in all of these firms: the employees feel that they are a part of something "global."

The cultural payoff of the interiors of IT workplaces is not just their similarity to other IT workplaces elsewhere in the world, but also their palpable insulation from their surroundings. Interviewees most clearly expressed the importance of this insulation with regard to the appropriateness of IT work for women. Indian middle-class women who have worked outside the home have often worked in banks and in government service positions, but have faced an uphill battle in corporate fields that required extensive travel within the city or interactions with clients. Neethy, a twenty-eight-year-old project leader working for an American multinational in Mumbai, explained that she switched into IT primarily due to the working environment, which her family saw as a safer place for women by virtue of its insulation from the outside world. She was trained for a career in marketing but was forced out of the job by her parents, who did not want her in a job that required so much face time with clients. Neethy understood that IT would be a more respectable job for her, one that would be more appropriate for her because she is a woman. Mital, a twenty-four-year-old woman working as a project leader in Mumbai, explained, at least in part, why Neethy's story is not an uncommon one:

> IT has really given an opportunity for women to work. If you see computer work, you're sitting in front of a computer, but there's no, like, physical exertion. And you don't have to run around the whole town, selling something. And there's something very comfortable about sitting quietly in an air-conditioned office in front of a computer. And you're earning money at the same time. So, I think this will pretty much be the work that women will take. And it's like a job that you can really get into. It's not like getting an MBA where it's very selective and only very few can get into it.

Many interviewees, both women and men, echoed Mital's assessment of IT as a safe and appropriate job for women. While there are many reasons why this is the case (see chapters 4 and 5), one of the key elements of this perceived safety is the insulated settings of the IT workplace. By eliminating the need for mobility or interaction with those outside the office, the IT workplace creates a seemingly placeless environment rendered safe for middle-class women to enter.

A Third Culture?

Are Indian corporations just trying to emulate American ones, then? Is the reproduction of American corporate settings reflective of deeper kinds of emulation? How do corporations define what is "global" and how do those definitions become meaningful to their employees?

Both Indian and American multinationals have integrated the rhetoric of "the global" into the everyday vocabulary of corporate management. In practice, however, Indian corporations often struggle with how to achieve global status and credibility. Corporations from all over the globe recognize the need for special cross-cultural training in order to perform competently and competitively in a business model that requires a spatially stretched production process. These concerns have led to a flourishing industry of cross-cultural trainers, especially in the United States, who train teams around the world to function in multicultural settings. The websites and materials of several cross-cultural training firms suggest that firms in every part of the world must move away from a nationally defined corporate ethos to a global one that is distinctive and new. This means that it is not only firms in India and China that must make this transition, but firms in the United States and United Kingdom as well must recognize cultural practices that are different from their own. LuEllen Schafer of Global Savvy, a veteran trainer in Silicon Valley, emphasized in her interview that the shifts toward the development of a global work culture must be a two-way street; Indians must adjust to be global, but American firms and American employees must also make cultural adjustments and managerial changes. These descriptions suggest that a global work culture is a third culture, related to (but not determined by) the (usually) two cultures of the firms that might be involved in one process. Yet, the meaning and significance of this third, supposedly culturally neutral culture is contested and surprisingly open-ended. Even among cultural trainers themselves, the definition of what constitutes the "global" and the objective of "global" training are constantly shifting discursive grounds. Dr. Araoz, for example, explained,

I don't define a global employee as having x, y, z traits only. I think it depends on where they're coming from and where they're going. And of course, there are a few general traits, like flexibility, the ability to observe and adapt, a good sense of humor, a desire to communicate, to understand and be understood. But how you do that in different environments is different. So, if I'm preparing an Indian IT person to go to Japan, I would teach him to be a little more low key and more moderate than if he were coming to the U.S., in which case I would teach him to be more outspoken and assertive.

Dr. Araoz seems to call for a degree of cultural specificity as part and parcel of what is "global," and there were other cultural trainers who seemed to concur with her. Other cultural trainers, however, avoided such relativism, opting instead for more universal definitions tied to the physical production process. A cultural trainer based in the United States who wished to remain anonymous, for example, is more accustomed to working in groups of mixed cultural backgrounds, rather than specifically mediating the India-abroad interface. In his interview, he emphasized the virtual setup of global teamwork and the development of a culture suited to that particular model of work as being global rather than emphasizing how to overcome perceived fundamental cultural differences. This trainer explained, "[Global work] is about teamwork, it's about time and space, it's about how to maintain your stakeholders, because in virtual teams the people are not co-located; everybody's boss is a stakeholder in what happens. And there are cultural differences in how technology is used in communication." For this trainer, learning to manage the peculiarities of the logistics of working virtually is fundamental to producing global workers, while cultural differences are more marginal.

Despite the apparent vagueness of "global" either as a cultural descriptor or as an objective for training, Indian IT firms often go to great lengths to underscore their "global" character. Large Indian firms in part prove their global scope by promoting their American connections. At the same time, however, there seems also to be an effort to establish a "global" work culture that is Indian in character. The website of a major Indian multinational, which I will call Inditech, includes a list of quotes from satisfied clients, all of which are large, established, American and British multinationals, including Motorola, Chrysler, and British Airways (accessed July 2008). The banners of quotes from satisfied corporations abroad remind potential clients that recognizable corporations have vetted the firm. Yet, Inditech is also interested in the cultivation of a distinctly Indian corporate ethos, similar to the corporate culture of Japan. This interest has arisen in large part from a newfound awareness on the part of Indian corporations that the branding and marketing of a corporate image are critical to a firm's success.

Sneha, who was a new hire at Inditech when I interviewed her in 2004, explained these shifts most clearly. A graduate from a top business school, Sneha was hired specifically to cultivate the "global look and feel" of the firm. Sneha described Inditech's desired ethos as more concerned with cultivating cultural distinction. Even as it emulated certain practices clearly developed in the context of corporate America, Sneha's narrative suggests that there has been a kind of growing self-awareness about how India's culture can be maintained and even asserted in a global corporate environment, which validates India as "part of the bigger picture":

> Earlier, when we were entertaining guests, we would have given them French wine. Where now, instead of that, we are telling them, "Let's take you on a visit to the Taj, let's get you an authentic Indian thing to have." You know? So, I think we're recognizing that we're good, and that we can wow people with traditional India. And I think that sense is coming not only from interacting with the West, but also others. Like, when you look at Japan, and see how proud they are of their culture, how they cling to their culture . . . if you go to Japan, they will give you sake, not French wine.

Sneha's insistence on the fact that Inditech aims to cultivate a distinctly Indian corporate culture seems to be based only on a narrowly defined set of practices that represent an essentialized India to foreign visitors. A key part of defining what it means to be simultaneously "global" and "Indian" in the workplace, then, must re-package India and Indian culture for the easy comprehension of foreign clients, thus producing a corporate brand of appropriate difference that still makes sense to employees like Sneha.

A new moment in Inditech's corporate development has prompted a burgeoning desire to develop a new brand of distinctly Indian corporate culture. Inditech's decision to hire a business school graduate like Sneha reflected a fundamentally new consciousness on the part of the firm that it needed to do more than just provide low-cost services. This change speaks to a shifting strategy of management that is more focused on the culture of the company than it has been in the past. The newfound global status of Inditech seemed to demand that shift, as Sneha explained: "[Inditech is] global by virtue of its presence, by virtue of its business, its turnover. It's present in any city in India, we're there in 116 countries. We've got offices all over. We are doing business for all the Fortune 500, Fortune 1000 companies, . . . so I think they [the corporate leaders] just got up one day and said, 'Hey, you know what? We're as global as any other multinational, so why don't we have the same look and the same feel?'" The recognition of this global status and the pursuant expectations to "be global," however, are not well defined. Indeed, for employees like Sneha, hired specifically to make this transformation, the task of going global is surprisingly open-ended. Sneha explained how exciting the job sounded to her when she got the offer:

> Inditech has worked on the low-cost model, but they've had to shift to a global model because they are a huge global company. And they were very set in their Indian ways of doing things, so it was exciting. When they hired me, they said they didn't know what I'd be doing—you can do what you like. Point is, they wanted to bring about a change of perspective because they'd never hired MBAs before, only engineers. [Previously] they didn't believe in branding, marketing, a whole lot of things. There's been resistance to those things. So [for me] the whole thing sounded so good. Intimidating in the beginning. There's a lot of the old perspective still [among employees in the company], but it's changing. We [the global business team] get to do whatever we want, move into wherever we feel there should be change.

Sneha's narrative suggests a clear shift in priorities, away from the nuts-and-bolts work of software development and toward the development of an internally cultivated ethos, even at a time when the company is not exactly sure what that ethos will look like. Sneha's work is directed more at the internal staff than at the external marketing of the firm. In a way, she must market the global status of the firm to the employees themselves, working on projects such as universal wireless networks within Inditech buildings and employee incentive programs to encourage and reward extraordinary individual performance. These markers of the company's global status are derived from American multinationals, yet Inditech as a firm seems to want to cultivate these markers while rejecting anything that might suggest emulation of the United States.

Not everyone at Inditech buys the argument that the firm is already global and just needs to cultivate a matching global ethos. Mital in Mumbai felt that global location did not inherently make her firm a truly global company. Mital has had extensive travel experience through her participation in an international student exchange while in college. Because of this experience, she felt she understood the challenges and promises of being global but saw Inditech as not having achieved that yet:

> Indians only network within the Indian community. They hang onto Inditech people only. . . . They almost resist making friends with Americans. In that sense, I don't think Inditech is global. . . . [Our American client] said that if you want to be global, you should be able to recruit a Chinese person in China and have the same culture. The way [the client] has a culture. Anywhere, an individual in [that firm] feels the same. They may be part of something else, but they are also part of the [firm's] culture, which is global. . . . If Inditech can have offices in different places, and we just send our people over there, then, sure, you're doing work across the globe, but you're still not global.

Mital differentiates between work done in different parts of the globe and what she thinks of as global, which she sees as developing a common corporate culture that will produce a common sense of identity among employees of varied cultural and ethnic backgrounds. In Mital's view, then, "being global" is a new cultural innovation that companies like Inditech have to undertake in tandem with working in multiple countries. Mital's account also emphasizes the extent to which Indian multinationals like Inditech might rely upon linkages with other Indians to work, which Mital does not find to be a convincing indicator of global status.[3] Although Mital and Sneha seem to define "global" differently, both speak about it as a culture yet to be realized, a third culture that is neither Indian nor Euro-American, and one in which corporations play a role in defining.

Almost all of the IT professionals I interviewed who worked for large Indian multinationals attested to the self-conscious cultivation of a distinctly "Indian" ethos, but in none of those cases were individuals able to name expressly what "core values" distinguished an Indian global firm from other firms. Although there appears to be a wish on the part of the largest Indian IT firms to cultivate a distinctive corporate culture, this vision is still vague and ill defined. Yet, a very specific kind of Indian culture—a pared down, neutralized, simplified kind of difference—is shored up in the effort to cultivate a global, ostensibly neutral one.

Vocabularies of "the Global"
Communication

The virtual working arrangement that acts as the baseline for most of India's software development must necessarily standardize certain practices in order to make the production cycle more efficient and ensure that all professionals are operating with similar standards and understandings of the work to be completed. This enforced standardization contributes significantly to the cultivation of a working environment that feels global. The ability to understand, interpret, and respond effectively to standardized business practices serves on the one hand to effectively homogenize a workforce of Indians from a diversity of linguistic and regional backgrounds and on the other hand to highlight the importance of very specific skills that are transferable to multiple environments. These skills are grouped broadly around the rhetoric of "good communication." Individuals who have good communication are validated by an elite education or transnational work experience.

Standardized work practices across locations make all individuals working for a faraway client able to begin work with similar technical and cultural knowledge bases, and to work in the firm on equal footing whether employed by the client firm itself, a subsidiary, or a contracted firm. Oftentimes, the conviction that the work is "global" in this sense even leads employees to tell others that they work for the client firm, rather than for the Indian firm or subsidiary that pays them. Workers have important reasons for their apparent allegiance to their foreign client rather than to their own firm. Mital explained that her firm is organized into "client-based verticals" such that employees are "inducted" into the culture of the particular client whose account they will be working on. In this case, Mital was inducted into the corporate culture of Inditech's largest client, which provides work for all of the six thousand employees working in two high-rise office buildings in the northern suburbs of Mumbai. After being hired, Mital and her colleagues first went through a two-month orientation to help them make the transition from college to the industry. They were then required to undergo a certification program that would train them to operate under six sigma, a quality certification process specified by the large American client. Many Indian companies train their employees in six sigma, which ensures that the work of Indian engineers meets a global standard. In the case of Mital's firm, the six sigma process structures the various interactions between the Mumbai offices and the client. Mital described this as "speaking in the client's language."

Mital's reference to language is more than a metaphor for specific business processes. The standardization of linguistic skills, including the cultivation of "good English," and, more broadly, "good communication skills," is an important marker of global status. Cross-cultural training firms place a heavy and sometimes exclusive emphasis on cross-cultural communication in their training sessions. Communication is broadly defined, but often it is the quirks and nuances of individual words and linguistic habits that comprise a large part of cross-cultural training sessions. For example, trainers focusing on Indian/American interactions point out that when Indians ask Americans for their "good name" they want to know their given name. They also point out that American business idioms like "slam-dunk the project" will not be understood by most Indians, just as Americans are unlikely to understand that when Indians say they feel "fagged out" they mean that they are tired. The focus on language habits allows for a global work culture to be a culturally relativistic one, in which the "core" of a national culture is sacred and should remain untouched, while the external communication habits and patterns can be trained to be compatible with a global work environment. "Good communication" thus becomes a key strategic cultural adaptation for both firms and IT professionals.

LuEllen Schafer of Global Savvy calls the practice of adopting a standardized, streamlined method of professional communication a "global dance." In an interview, she explained that her workshops with Indian engineers are geared toward closing a "gap" in communication styles and habits. When new habits are adopted for the purposes of work, employees can be better at their work and produce a better product. But, like a dance, these new habits are just a set of acquired skills that are not meant to transform a person fundamentally. The practices that Schafer fosters in her workshops are based upon a "gap analysis" method of cross-cultural training, in which she studies teams of engineers in multiple settings and hones in on the differences she finds. Primarily, she draws upon the linguistic tools of Edward T. Hall, an anthropologist who has defined the field of cross-cultural communication with his distinction between "low-context communication" and "high-context communication." Hall differentiates between "high-context" cultures that rely heavily on contextual clues and body language and "low-context" cultures that focus more on the specifics of words and language without reference to situational or relational cues. Since global collaboration often takes place without the benefit of face-to-face contact or preexisting relationships, "low-context" communication, associated with Western cultural norms, is the encouraged standard (Hall 1976).

In her trainings, Schafer emphasizes speech practices that can help improve communication. For example, one exercise she says she does with Indian engineers is to have them practice giving compliments to their co-workers abroad. She finds that they are not used to praising co-workers and feel uncomfortable when asked to do so. Schafer trains her students to say perfunctory phrases such as "I just want to take a moment to thank Bob for all his hard work. This really wouldn't have happened without him." She finds that these small practices greatly enhance the professional experience of her students, who report back to her with very positive results.

Cross-cultural training has become not just another vehicle through which Western corporations train their Indian teams; it has also matured into an enterprise in India as well. Global Adjustments, a cross-cultural training firm based in Chennai, India, and run by an Indian team, offers cultural training both for non-Indians coming to India for work as well as for locals. The firm's website, www.globalindian.net.in, urges the viewer to "become a global Indian" and provides a series of online courses in cross-cultural knowledge and communication (accessed December 15, 2008). The website also carries a large archive of articles on various culture clashes that are bound to occur without appropriate training, including conflicts over deadlines and even conflicts over how to have conflicts. Such situations mimic those that Schafer named as well, suggesting that all these actors draw from the same understanding of cross-cultural interactions in corporate settings. Global Adjustments names four broad areas of cross-cultural education: "understanding cross-culture [a term that seems to mean 'cultural differences between cultures'] and the need for cross-cultural education, knowing India and yourself as an Indian, knowing other cultures, and international etiquette." The importance of knowing India is highlighted here, but this knowledge is detailed and trivial. Indians who take the course learn about such details as India's political system, India's first lady, and the basic beliefs and attitudes of Indians, who are presumed to be Hindu. In Global Adjustments' materials, India is represented as a Hindu country, and "global Indians" are trained to be adept in interpreting and explaining religious symbols associated with popular deities, such as Ganesha, alongside the symbolism of the national flag. According to the company, this knowledge will "allow you to have interesting conversations" with people around the world. In this way, generic and translatable knowledge about India, palatable to interested westerners, becomes a way for students of the course to better understand themselves and their "own" culture, as defined by the cross-cultural trainers. Such knowledge renders Indianness as a simple, appropriately different culture that can fit nicely into frameworks of cultural relativism that are attractive both to corporations as well as to IT professionals themselves. As in Sneha's narrative of delivering the Taj Mahal or Indian food to foreign visitors, cross-cultural training involves the development of a body of knowledge that repackages India and Indianness as appropriate difference, which allows Indians to represent themselves to clients abroad. This knowledge must then be asserted by Indian workers as knowledge of their *own* culture, differentiated clearly from the cultures these workers will encounter and easily adapt. Improvements in communication, then, ostensibly the core aim of sites like globalindian.net.in, in fact produce and legitimate new forms of knowledge about India and new ways of being legitimately Indian in a "global" business environment.

Within the everyday lives of IT professionals, the ability to communicate through standardized methods such as conference calls and e-mails sets apart the "technical guys" from those with management capability in a definitive hierarchy that privileges English skills. In this kind of communication, employees with exceptional educational backgrounds or with extensive experience abroad saw themselves as better than their colleagues. Malini spoke at length about her dissatisfaction with the poor communication that she says is endemic to the Indian IT industry. She seems to locate the problem in Indian culture itself, yet the solution, as she understands it, leads back to the question of background:

MALINI: Generally, in IT the communication skills are very poor. People are extremely poor in communicating, whether it is to the client, or to people in their teams. I don't know—Indians have a very big problem in completing their sentences. They would just say a few words and expect you to understand the whole thing. I think communication as such is a problem, but it's also a challenge that's being thrown at everyone's face. It's one of the feedbacks that goes back to everyone—that we're not communicating well. That communication is one of the challenges we face.

If you're a good communicator, you have a distinct advantage in this country. And people tend to put you in front of customers. A lot of kids are very good in math and science, but have very poor language education. So, the same guys speaking in a local language speak very poorly, so it's not English. It's just general communication that's flawed. Their absolute inability to express themselves is so pathetic. It's very frustrating. Even when they're unhappy, they can't express themselves. Even if they're frustrated, they can't express themselves . . .

SR: What would help it?

MALINI: In my case, it was just education. I had a good education, I had a good grounding in reading and all that, and I had a good friend circle. So, that just made a difference for me. [That would be harder] if someone came from a rural background. Yes, see, in this industry, your English is not really important, your communication is important. And you work with people who cannot speak good English if they are from China or something . . . For a hundred people, there will be two or three good communicators. It just so happens that people place those two or three people in front of everyone and the remaining ninety-seven are hidden. The ninety-seven have a problem.

Malini clearly defines the limitations that most Indian IT professionals face as a communication problem that needs to be remedied. However, she is also acutely aware of which kinds of difference are appropriate and which are not. As a concept, "communication" captures and adjudicates which is which: "We need to become culturally more educated. In the sense that, well, there are issues. You have your South Indian engineer going to a client meeting and eating curd rice with his hand. Those kinds of things. But that's a stereotype. It doesn't really happen. But then, there are problems around that. Not being well read. Not knowing what's happening in the movies. Not having an opinion on too many things. Not being able to really express an opinion. That kind of cloistered kind of living and going through life."

Malini's account sets up a clear hierarchy between skilled technicians and skilled communicators. She believes IT should be more about communication than technical skill, but she recognizes that it is her education that sets her apart, offering her not only the communication skills but also the cultural education that makes her effective at work.

Chaitali, a thirty-two-year-old manager based in Bangalore who had returned to India after nearly a decade in Silicon Valley, explained that her experience in the United States made her more global in large part because she could understand the accents of those on the American end and could help her colleagues in Bangalore understand where their American counterparts were coming from. In explaining to me that she felt "global" because she could work with "anyone," she elaborated:

> When I sit here [in Bangalore], and people tell me "I do not understand the language, the accent," I can say, "Yes, it is common. I know it's English, but if it is a Chinese, you cannot understand, and you need to say speak slowly." . . . In every other country they have a problem—other people will not understand them [because there is] not much of interaction with others. I have that experience [of interacting with others]; I can tell the people here, "Do not be so restricted because of that [communication barrier], we can still work." . . . In that way I do not think only as an Indian, [but as] much more. Today I can sit and support anyone in the United States—I say, "No, no you cannot say this." I can sit and explain to the people [that] there is the other side, because I really like people over there [in the United States], so I will go out of the way to do it; other people do not know.

Chaitali links her ability to work globally with her ability to understand both the American and Indian perspectives, derived from her transnational experience. She sees herself as privileged in her ability to speak English clearly and be understood, but also to demand clarity when it is not forthcoming (as in the case of the Chinese colleague whom she feels justified in not understanding). Her work experience in the United States has given her the confidence to say that she is a "global" professional who can support anyone in her field, regardless of national background. This conviction is supported not only by her English abilities, but also by her ability to think like her American colleagues, to understand their perspective, and to foster mutual understanding between the U.S. team and the Indian team.

Flatness

Thomas Friedman's bestselling book of 2005, *The World Is Flat*, got its title from a conversation with Nandan Nilekani, the CEO of Infosys, during a cab ride in Bangalore. In describing the changing landscape of the global economy and explaining how it is that a country like India can compete with the wealthiest of nations in IT, Nilekani said that the world "is a level playing field now." From this, Friedman extrapolated the title of the book. The provocative title has become a metaphor for being global, though critics have regarded this extrapolation as inappropriate, farfetched, and facile, especially in India, where disparities in wealth are marked and access to the supposedly "flat" world is highly circumscribed (Prashad 2005; Tharoor 2005; Varadarajan 2005). The idea of flatness, already popularized in the international management literature and associated with efficiency, empowerment, and lack of hierarchy, has become an even more catchy way in which Indian corporations can market themselves as "global." Not surprisingly, Infosys has embraced the "flat world" concept most heartily, promoting itself as a "flat world company" and associating itself with Friedman's conclusions throughout its website. Rather than using derivative prestige from other Western corporations to brand itself as a global company, Infosys deploys keywords like "flat management," "innovation," and "collaboration." But these do not seem to be just buzzwords meant for marketing. Indeed, Infosys has been deeply involved in research and education around "flat world" issues, examining the impact of the "flat world" on various business practices. A major study it released in early 2008, called "Mind the Gaps," surveyed five hundred executives from around the world to push Friedman's thesis of a flat world. The founding premise of the study was described in the preface as the following: "To successfully compete in the Flat World, companies need to shift operational priorities, change business mindsets, and leverage the trends that define and drive the changing global economy" (Srivastava and Sampath 2008).

In the discourse of the flat world, "being global" has very specific strategic implications for the corporation as a whole. Infosys not only embodies these flat world strategies in its own practices but also helps to produce new discourses of the global economy that highlight the role of emerging economies like India and China and emphasize the potential for horizontal competition in high-tech fields especially.

The flat world philosophy contains within it a theory of the individual, focused on individual empowerment and drive. While "empowerment" has been a buzzword in corporate management training for decades, the term has taken on new meanings in the Indian IT industry. Cross-cultural training emphasizes the need for Indian technologists not only to be better communicators, but also to be more empowered problem solvers and to take personal responsibility for the work they do. Most American multinationals in India also train their Indian employees to be empowered professionals working in a flat managerial system that is focused on individual development and performance for fueling the success of the company. These broad imperatives often translate into specific initiatives and efforts both in individual firms and on the part of the industry as a whole. In these initiatives, gender comes to the fore as an inequality to be eliminated through empowerment, while abiding issues of class and caste remain under the radar screen of diversity.

Indian technologists often explained to me that their work not only made them able to communicate better, but also fundamentally changed the way they looked at social hierarchies. In these narratives, the flat world discourses promoted in companies like Infosys make employees who have come of age in the IT industry see the world very differently. Some of the most striking comments in this regard had to do with interactions with domestic workers, or servants, as they are called in the Indian context. Dhiraj, a twenty-seven-year-old technologist working in Bangalore for a large American multinational consulting firm, explained that working in the IT industry for the past five years has taught him not only to manage workloads, time, and customer calls, but also how to relate to senior management as well as those working for him. According to Dhiraj, "All this learning replicates in your behavior when you go home. Let me think of an example; maybe when you talk to your servant. Five years before I never used to think on these lines. I now replicate his working with my working. This is how my lead approaches me; this is how I get work from fellow colleagues. To get it done by my servant I do not have to treat him like a servant. I have learned that you need to talk to a different way; [you have to] think you are talking to your junior [colleagues, to whom you do not condescend]."Dhiraj feels that his experience in companies that emphasize flat hierarchies and empowering management strategies has made him treat his servant as an individual with a job to do, in the same way that he sees himself, his senior management, and his junior team members as all just individuals with jobs to do. He finds himself identifying less with hierarchical relationships of all types.

Empowerment

Gender equity and gendered empowerment have become key goals of the IT industry. In these discourses, women must be empowered not just for reasons of social or political correctness, but also as an important input for the firm and for the industry as a whole. The National Association of Software and Service Companies (NASSCOM) has taken up its Gender Inclusivity Initiative as one of only a handful of initiatives, citing the need to diversify the workplace for the benefit of the industry. This attention to gender conveniently sidesteps caste biases endemic in the industry. Attention to caste diversity, however, has been resisted in IT due to the thorny issue of reservations and their association with a lack of merit, to be discussed in depth in the next chapter.

The Gender Inclusivity Initiative has carried out studies on the levels of women's employment in the industry and the challenges women face with regard to balancing home and work. The Initiative encourages and organizes women in leadership positions and identifies areas in which more work can be done to include women in the industry. While NASSCOM's language on its website supports the inclusion of women as a gesture toward diversity, better business, and an effort to bridge the labor crunch, individual firms and professional women link the involvement of women in the IT industry to the question of empowerment. Most of the women I spoke to provided some account of feeling empowered by work in the IT industry. So, how do workers respond to their firms' explicit attempts to achieve empowerment and gender equity?

Mital explained that ideas of gender equity in terms of hiring and management came not from within her firm, but from its large American client. When the client firm began making efforts to even out the gender ratios in its own organization, it presented those same requirements to its vendors. This effort resulted in an influx of women into the particular account with those requirements, but not into the firm as a whole. Slowly, however, as more and more women go to engineering college, Mital has seen the number of "fresher girls" rise. When she began working, she was the only woman on the team, but at the time of the interview, she had had at least one boss who was a woman and several female co-workers. Mital felt that this was progress, and that this progress came out of both the impetus from the client and change happening at home in colleges around the country. Especially in South India, science-related careers seemed to her to be the only desirable professional option for middle-class women.

Most of the women and men I spoke to expressed satisfaction at these trends and consistently indicated to me that they viewed these burgeoning opportunities for women as signs that India was leaving its parochial past behind in favor of something more progressive, even if not explicitly "global." Discourses of women's empowerment, however, always tended to place this kind of empowerment in a gendered binary. Well-paid work for women, like a "global" third culture, could optimize Indian culture by imbibing the positive aspects of globalization. At the same time, this empowerment could go too far, just as becoming "global" becomes undesirable when it mimics the West or threatens existing notions of a good woman and a good family. To examine these issues, I first focus on a firm known for its very successful strategies for including women in its everyday operations—an IT support firm in Mumbai that I will call Infoworld.

Unlike other firms I visited, the majority of Infoworld's employees do not work at the office, which dramatically alters how their employees experience the IT industry. Still, Infoworld provides a striking example of the kind of transformation that skilled information work is thought to bring to women, as well as the limitations of such transformation. Infoworld employs an original and highly successful business plan that draws simultaneously on middle-class gender norms in India and the empowering potential of well-paid technical work for women. As the only example of an IT support firm in my sample, Infoworld neither works on the actual software coding nor does it provide customer call support. Rather, Infoworld handles outsourced data work, ranging from data entry to data analysis, financial services, and a growing range of related BPO services. The largest company of its kind in India, Infoworld became profitable due to a unique recruitment strategy—the majority of its employees work at home. Infoworld targets housewives with master's degrees in a technical field and employs them on a piece-rate basis. These "home professionals" or "knowledge associates," as they are called, are given a variable amount of work each week, depending on their schedules. Infoworld responds to the amount of time they invest and how quickly they pick up the required skills by giving them appropriate amounts of work, with increasing levels of volume and difficulty for fast learners. For a handful of these home professionals, this kind of home-based work serves as a transition to a desire to work outside the home, and some of these women eventually join the small internal staff at the firm's rapidly growing office.

The main office itself is set up with keen attention to the deeply gendered character of the firm, though its website and other materials do not reveal this key dimension. The reception area surrounds a circular center, in which the exclusively female support staff members are seated. These women provide personal and technical support to the home professionals, mostly over the phone. On the community boards information is posted about support groups for women seeking to improve their work and to find support from others struggling to balance home and work responsibilities. Also posted are employee awards with photos and a personal tidbit about each recognized employee. The ways in which this communal space has been personalized and gendered are unique, emphasizing this firm's attention to women's empowerment as one of its key aims. However, this strong image of women-driven economic empowerment is more likely to be a side effect of its profitability. By relying predominantly on a workforce that does not require office space or materials, and for whom this work is only secondary to the income of their husbands, Infoworld significantly reduces its costs in a classic, well-documented move to "feminize" low-end work (Freeman 2000; Mies 1982; Pearson 1998; Scott 1988; Ward and Pyle 1995). Still, part-time work can be highly empowering for women who are restricted from working outside the home.

Nandini, a thirty-five-year-old entrepreneur, provides a classic example of the transformatory possibilities of information work. Before she joined Infoworld as a knowledge associate, she had a master's degree in chemistry that she had never put to use. After she was married, she lived in a joint family with her in-laws, who forbade her from working outside the home. When she heard about Infoworld, she saw it as an opportunity to make some extra money without leaving the house on a regular basis. She began with just a few hours of work per week. Her first paycheck, of just a couple thousand rupees, thrilled her. Previously, although she was entitled to buy whatever she wanted, she had to ask her husband or in-laws for money. Her control over her new earnings was something of a revelation—one that other women in the firm agree is a common experience among home professionals. She quickly began training for more specialized kinds of work and increased the number of hours she was working. Eventually, not only did she join the internal staff of the company, which was still in its beginning stages, but she also managed to save enough money to convince her husband that it was financially feasible for them to live in a separate house while continuing to support his parents.

Since then, Nandini has become a dedicated career woman, a role that has transformed her outlook and lifestyle. She and her husband have made the decision not to have children, and she has since left Infoworld to start up her own small business in the tech sector. Her success as a career woman transformed her marriage and her role in the family as well. She experienced new autonomy in relation to her husband and started to be called upon to make important decisions in the family. During her interview, she emphasized how much she has come to value her own space, even to the extent of building a separate bathroom for herself in the limited space of her flat in suburban Mumbai so that she would not have to interact with her husband in the morning. She realizes how far away from the norm she has traveled, but she is proud of her accomplishments and not concerned about the criticism she receives for her choices, especially from her extended family.

The ways in which Infoworld's business plan directly affected Nandini's life trajectory highlight the potential of IT work to transform the lives of educated middle-class women, but this potential is filled with limitations and contradictions that Nandini's story alone does not reveal. In Nandini's narrative, the mental stimulation of work as well as the newfound capacity to be an independent consumer had a transformative effect, not only with regard to her sense of self, but also on her position within her family. Work has taken over all other priorities in her life, and for Nandini this has been an unquestionably positive development. Nandini believes such empowerment to be imminent for women who step into professional workplaces like Infoworld.

Asha, a thirty-five-year-old manager for Infoworld who works both with the internal staff as well as on the mentoring of home professionals, provided a more nuanced view. Like Nandini, Asha believes that the absolute economic dependence of housewives lies at the root of their subordinate status. Asha argued, "The greatest indignity a housewife suffers from is having to extend her palm for even a ten-rupee note." This indignity, Asha explained, can be diminished substantially even with a small monthly income. But Asha was quick to recognize that the kind of empowerment that Infoworld offers is only available to a small slice of the educated middle class and is taken up by an even smaller slice of those eligible. Most home-based knowledge associates do not go on to become career women at all; rates of turnover are high, and it is not uncommon for a woman to quit because her child has an exam coming up. While Asha cited this trend as evidence for the immutability of Indian middle-class conventions, the trend reveals something deeper: that Infoworld's profitability ultimately relies upon precisely the kinds of financial dependence among educated women that its own rhetoric of gendered empowerment aims to alleviate. Although Infoworld appears to empower women through the provision of a small income, its home-based, piece-rate approach ultimately serves to reinforce, rather than erode, a certain model of domestic seclusion for middle-class women. In this manner, the example of Infoworld illuminates the important ways in which new forms of professional knowledge work can capitalize upon the restrictions that many middle-class women face while furthering the apparently benevolent goal of female empowerment.

Despite the many contradictions that a company like Infoworld presents, such companies contribute to a discourse of gendered empowerment in which technical work for women is equated with progress, empowerment, and independence, while a lack of such work is equated with patriarchal constraint. This binary takes on equally dichotomous cultural connotations, where empowering work for women is associated with the "global" while staying at home is associated with the "traditional." Indeed, IT workplaces, in helping to create these binaries, also help to create gendered constructions of "global" and "traditional" work. In IT offices where men and women work full-time, although the gender dynamics operate very differently, the association between global professional work and empowerment persists, producing unexpected tensions.

Questioning Empowerment

Bharathi of Mumbai, a technical writer in her mid-twenties with a keenly critical eye of her own social world, was one of just a few interviewees to voice concerns with the model of gendered empowerment implicitly promoted through the IT industry. She argued that this kind of empowerment is limited and perhaps even misplaced. Her critique of women's lives in the workplace was intertwined with her critique of the kind of middle-class value system she feels is being promoted in the workplace, whose growing power she finds disconcerting:

> The new middle class, I don't know from when, has started to believe that working eighteen hours a day is okay. This is the fundamental thing I want to understand. What makes it okay? What makes being overworked and underpaid okay? Since when? And girls are doing it. And that was one category that was oppressed or whatever, but for the middle class it was still a category that was supposed to be sheltered and protected. And today, they are out . . . You start working to be financially independent so you don't have to be under your husband or your brother or your son anymore. But now, there's a boss who can call you anytime and you're there. What makes that okay? Just because you're getting money for it? Because before housework was like free? What has made that equation all right?

Bharathi went on to explain that most women in the industry have not had a chance to prioritize their lives. In the effort to makes themselves more independent, she argued, women of her generation had actually limited their own possibilities. The management and organization of the global workplace produce pressure to demonstrate a gender equality, construed as "global," which often leads women to lose the ability to place limits on their own working schedules. According to Bharathi, who frequently works anywhere from seventy to eighty hours a week, the lifestyle promoted within the IT setting is one that is absolutely incompatible with a real personal life.

Women must navigate between the pressure to work—the promise of independence—and the pressure to work less or not at all, equated with the norm of staying home. The complexity of these navigations indicates the tensions and contradictions built into the production of professionalism in the Indian IT workplace. To adhere to the ethics of gender equality promoted in the rhetoric of the industry, women must work as hard as men to prove that they are not like women. Bharathi explained, "I have not been able to stand up for myself enough and say no when I know I won't be able to handle it, just because I can say, 'No, I'm good enough, as good as the next guy.' And the next guy is a guy. You know? It shouldn't make me less of a worker to say, 'Beyond ten hours, I'm out.' Just because a guy is doing it, doesn't mean that I have to . . . he has his own compulsions. He doesn't want to be thought of as a girl, or whatever."

The potential for work to produce independence among women, then, is constrained; any effort on the part of the female employee to curb her working hours cannot be viewed as an issue of employee rights, but only as a choice between prioritizing work, understood as "global" and "independent," or home, understood as "Indian" and "traditional." Such tensions suggest that professional work is creating a "global" system of values, while also recreating a set of "Indian" values to oppose it, and thus defining the boundaries of "the global" more clearly, a theme I return to in examining gendered balances between home and work in chapter 5. The production of an ultimately conflicted discourse surrounding gendered empowerment reveals the tenuousness of this binary. The division appears to draw upon common-sensical, preexisting notions of old and new values but is instead produced in the context of everyday meanings of gender and work within the IT workplace. As such, the meanings of "global" and "traditional" values are constantly being crafted and negotiated.

The apparent success of professional IT women who continue to enter the workforce in increasing numbers attests to the idea that progressive global culture is being promoted in the IT workplace. A discourse of empowerment and gender equality becomes a language for women to express their independence from traditional roles and their commitment to a global work culture. As this happens, however, professional women become unable to articulate their commitment to the workplace in any language that avoids cultural binaries. To ask for a reduction in hours becomes an indicator of "traditional" values or the inability of women to work hard. Conversely, by accepting and internalizing the demands of equality and empowerment, professional women mark their own participation in a work culture defined as "global." These women experience a newfound sense of equal opportunity in the workplace and take pride in the ethics of equal opportunity, even though they are aware that the pressure of equal work in the workplace is borne differently by men and women. Such awareness does not seem to contradict their perceptions of IT as an empowering industry for women.

The empowering potential of IT work for women comes to epitomize the transformative properties of IT work on a personal level. Although men and women alike almost always agree that the IT industry has changed them, the manner in which the industry is thought to transform women's lives in particular is a critical dimension of what makes the industry representative of progress. There are clear signs, however, as we see in Bharathi's account, that the generalized conviction that IT work signals a new era for women in India is constrained by the pressing realities of everyday work pressures. The need to perform in a system that rewards empowered individuals places extra strains on women who are not recognized as such. Alongside Nandini's dramatic story of personal transformation lie the stories of women who question the ways in which women's choices remain coded in strict binaries (work equals global and independent; home equals traditional and constrained).

Cross-cultural trainers stay far away from thorny questions of gender in their workshops. The neutral third culture that they help to produce in Indian corporate workplaces explicitly avoids responsibility for the kinds of dilemmas that women like Bharathi face. The twin cultural logics of global/Indian are set up in the IT workplace as a kind of shell that technologists fill with their own beliefs, practices, and concerns. Because of this continuous back-and-forth transfer between the world of the IT industry and the world outside it, global/Indian rhetoric becomes a powerful language through which IT professionals can assert seemingly neutral ("middle-class") identifications that disguise their relative class positions. In this way, the cultural logics of global/Indian come to set up the language in which new ideas of "Indian culture" are made real in the everyday lives of Indian technologists.

The key buzzwords of "global" vocabulary—communication, flatness, and empowerment—rely heavily upon the individual IT professional to rise to the challenge of embodying appropriate difference in the workplace. Cultural training programs encourage the individual worker to strive to embody these values, but it is the everyday interactions between IT professionals within the workplace, and the hierarchies that form among them, that most significantly affect the ways in which workers assert these values. In their abstractness, vocabularies of the global place up front the importance of strategic cultural adaptations that individuals must take on, while glossing over differences in background that may privilege some workers over others.

The ways in which corporations streamline culture and produce corporate versions of appropriate difference offer a language and framework for individuals to assert in their own personal lives outside the workplace. The cultural processes of global/Indian are inextricably intertwined with the logics of merit that underpin advancement within the industry and in the knowledge economy at large. The production of appropriate difference that begins in the workplace and is supported by the logic of merit gives rise to powerful narratives of the individual self that come to constitute personal subjectivities.

IDEOLOGIES OF ACHIEVEMENT IN THE KNOWLEDGE ECONOMY

Meritocracy: A word coined by Michael Young (*The Rise of Meritocracy*, 1958) for government by those regarded as possessing merit; merit is equated with intelligence-plus-effort, its possessors are identified at an early age and selected for an appropriate intensive education, and there is an obsession with quantification, test-scoring, and qualifications. Egalitarians often apply the word to any elitist system of education or government, without necessarily attributing to it the particularly grisly features or ultimately self-destroying character of Young's apocalyptic vision.—*FONTANA DICTIONARY OF MODERN THOUGHT*

There are people who are coming from very conservative backgrounds and through sheer merit, they're globetrotting . . . They get that kind of exposure. There's this guy. And if you met him, you'd see he had like a very strong South Indian accent. I couldn't make out if it was Andhra or Tamil. But you can tell he comes from a very small town in South India and he's talking about [the season] fall. And I'm wondering—we don't have fall here! And he says he doesn't spend enough time here to remember. I asked him which office in Mumbai he works out of and he says he only comes to Mumbai to renew his passport.—SNEHA, A TWENTY-FOUR-YEAR-OLD GLOBAL CORPORATE IT STRATEGIST IN MUMBAI

In India's new middle class, the IT industry serves as space for personal transformation. Opportunities to travel, to experience new ways of being, and to expand one's own idea of being Indian are some of the many diverse benefits that an IT professional like Sneha's colleague could experience. But the ticket into this transformative club is not something that can be won; it is something that, at least ostensibly, must be *earned*. Sneha speaks of the transformations the IT industry brings, but the vehicle for this metamorphosis is merit, or, as Sneha puts it, *sheer* merit—talent and hard work unaided by external advantages. Like Sneha, most in the

IT industry view others in the industry as endowed with merit by virtue of having broken into an extremely competitive industry. Merit, in Sneha's explanation, becomes a way to *overcome* the limitations of background. Ironically, though, as Fontana's definition reminds us, the achievement of "merit" is already reliant upon access to an elite education, presupposing the very class (and in this case, caste) background it seeks to overcome. Indeed, by juxtaposing her colleague's small-town South Indian background with his globetrotting habits and knowledge of the seasons of western climes, she papers over the elite educational opportunities that her colleague had to have received to be living the life he does now. Having come from a wealthy Delhi family that Sneha sees as inherently advantaged over her South Indian colleague owing to class, caste, and cultural privilege, Sneha perceives a distance between herself and her colleague, and it is his ability to bridge this distance through the magic of sheer merit that she finds to be an exciting vindication of the industry in which she is working.

What is the nature of this sheer merit and what are the implications of merit, the magic ticket to a transformative industry? Who are the individuals who have merit, and how do they distinguish themselves from those who do not have that merit? And more importantly, what are the implications of the powerful ideology of merit, so dominant within the IT industry, in a country of deep inequalities?

Most of the IT professionals I spoke to in Silicon Valley and Bangalore did not speak of their work in IT as just another job, but as an actualizing job, one that recognized and rewarded their merits as professionals while encouraging them to grow as individuals. The majority of IT professionals I spoke to view their participation in the industry as virtuous and even inspiring because of the challenge of constant growth, achieved through perpetual education, constant travel and interaction with people abroad, and even long hours and tight deadlines. Such ideas of empowerment, individual accountability, and personal striving do emerge importantly from globally circulating managerial discourses, some of which are described in the previous chapter. But perhaps more importantly they emerge from the logic of merit—a logic that is folded powerfully into knowledge economy discourses and the rhetoric of a "new" India that has left behind the quasi-socialist bureaucratic government jobs of the past.

Merit is not just a concept associated with the new India and a new economy, but is a multi-layered, contentious term, especially in the Indian context. For decades, the language of merit has been used to oppose affirmative action policies that aim to correct historic caste inequalities. As Zoya Hasan has said of merit in the Indian context, "The obsession with 'merit' is unique in India. . . . In India merit has taken on an almost mystical significance as a quality inherent in some chosen people, not something that can be acquired through training and effort" (Bidwai 2006). The founders of the Indian constitution were committed to eradicating the atrocities of caste-based exclusion and inequality, and had thus written into the constitution policies of quotas and reservations for people of the most excluded caste groups in government jobs. Reservations policies earmarked a large percentage of government jobs for lower-caste groups. These earmarking policies have meant that, in practice, individuals belonging to lower castes do not have to meet the same criteria for placement in government jobs as those from higher castes. While a select group of castes was targeted in earlier policies, reservations policies were expanded to include a broader range of caste groups in the Mandal Commission Report (1979), which created a new umbrella term for excluded castes, the Other Backward Classes (OBC), and increased the percentage of reservations to 49.5 in government jobs. When the recommendations of the report were implemented in 1989, the move sparked massive, almost unprecedented protests from especially lower-middle-class, upper-caste youth, famously including the self-immolation of several students (Corbridge and Hariss 2000; Malik and Singh 1990; Mankekar 1999; Singh, Santosh, Avasthi, and Kulhara 1997). The protests produced a renewed language of equality and merit in opposition to the principle of reservations, which has been seen as benefiting only the "creamy layer" of lower-caste groups—the rich—rather than those who are both poor and low caste (and hence perhaps more deserving of special quotas). As such, those who oppose the expansion of the reservations system, who tend to be elite themselves, view it as a primarily self-interested tactic pursued by politicians to gain votes.[1]

The notion of merit as inherent personal worth and talent thus contains within it the historic complaints of India's elite. The evocative ideology of merit-based advancement presents an alternative to the contentious, politicized domain of caste politics that has played a defining role in India's public life. Merit-based advancement appears to affirm individual personal worth in a way that transcends petty caste politics, thus validating the nation as a whole. The ideology of a meritocracy provides the language with which to connect the development of personal expertise, central to discourses of the knowledge economy, to the improvement of the nation, and it manifests itself in a set of discourses that set up the following dichotomies (table 1), in which the left column presents a set of closely associated benevolent practices and objects, while the right column presents their opposite.

In a society historically rooted in caste, class, and regional divisions, the ostensible meritocracy of the IT workplace provides a set of ideas about how India ought to be run by creating a dichotomous, oppositional language that views the practices and beliefs listed in the right column as of a single kind—the kind to overcome. Belief in the morality, efficiency, and practicality of a meritocracy pervades not only the institutionalized practices of the IT workplace, but also, as I will show, the actions of IT professionals and the industry at large.

This discourse of merit takes a particular form in IT workplaces, one that is rooted in the free-market-oriented, individualized language of the knowledge economy, which offers the opportunity to rekindle and reinvent a language of merit historically associated with India's elite. Knowledge workers use the seemingly neutral language of merit, further legitimated by its coincidence with the principles of the knowledge economy, both as a way to understand their own mobility or lack thereof and to imagine a future India free of parochial sensibilities and corruption. In this way, IT workers not only live out the rationality of knowledge economy discourses, but also offer a powerful embodiment of a new India in which each advances according to his or her individual merit rather than according to parochial categories. By glossing over the inequalities of the elite educational system in India and understanding their own status as a result of their own hard work, talent, and effort, IT professionals thus provide a compelling alternative to a caste-ridden political history and are able to project convincingly a vision of "Indian culture" that renders such divisions invisible.

The rationality of merit is so deeply embedded within the logics of the IT industry that it especially convinces professional IT women that they work in a gender equitable industry in which each woman advances according to her own merit. While the low percentages of women in management should provide evidence to women that the industry is not as equitable as it appears (Suriya 2003), women consistently explain away

TABLE 1 Dichotomies of IT Ideology

Merit	Reservation
Private sector job	Government job
Economy/Free market	State
Professionalism	Politics/Corruption
Global	Parochial
Efficiency	Bureaucracy
Virtue/Hard work	Laziness/stagnation
Individual growth	Suppression of individual
Flat management	Hierarchy

those trends through the language of personal choice. The effectiveness of the rhetoric of choice attests to the centrality of individualized drive and desire within the industry. The ways in which professional women connect the ideology of merit to their own personal decisions—a set of linkages that become clear in the following chapter—also provide insight into how a new Indianness is produced at home and in families. As women especially shore up the ideology of merit-based advancement through the rhetoric of choice, they indirectly obscure not only the ambivalences surrounding the advancement of women in the male-dominated culture of IT, but also the continued systematic exclusion of low-caste and rural groups from the industry. Like the logic of "the global," the ideology of merit-based advancement appears to offer a compelling future for India precisely because of the ways in which its articulation in the everyday lives of IT professionals explicitly overlooks the specific conditions of its production in the history of India. Because of this separation, merit-based advancement as an ideology becomes not only a central feature of the culture of IT professionals in India, but among Indian transnational professionals in the United States and beyond as well.

IT Jobs (and the Private Sector) versus Government Jobs (and Politics)

The principle of merit-based advancement highlights the distinction between the IT sector and the private sector more generally on the one hand, and government jobs and the dirty business of politics on the other. The virtue of the IT industry stands in contrast with the government jobs that were the staple of the urban middle class prior to liberalization, which are viewed as bureaucratic jobs meant to stifle individual development while encouraging petty politics and inefficiency. Most of the professionals I spoke with articulated these distinctions in some form or another. Chandra, a thoughtful twenty-eight-year-old engineer working in Bangalore, explained, "The previous generation, they wanted a secure government job. That has been almost replaced by IT. That work culture was different. I have seen people frustrated with that work culture. With the revolution of IT, the amount of politics and bureaucracy is much less, although it is there. That has helped me grow as a person . . . You definitely get to know [a] lot of good people. Colleagues who are professionals—no unnecessary talk, no unnecessary business. They are sincere, and in the company of good people, you grow." Chandra's views are emblematic of IT professionals; he emphasizes the morality of a shift away from the work that defined a previous generation of India's middle class because this shift fosters the development of good people. By asserting the morality of the people in IT, Chandra also unconsciously reinforces, through a naturalized language of morality, his ascending position in India's new middle class: he is qualified, educated, and unwilling to dirty his hands in either the "unnecessary" business of politicking or the constraints of government-style bureaucracy.

Because India's history of reservations has been restricted to government jobs, the distinctions that Chandra articulates stem in large part from the acknowledgment that the private sector has remained free of such regulations. Government jobs, politics, and caste-based reservations are thus closely associated with one another not only in the minds of those I interviewed, but in the Indian public sphere more generally (Das 2000; Parikh 2001). The continuing debates over caste reservations in India's private sector reveal a deep and abiding tension between advancement according to "merit," which is associated with the virtuous private sector, and advancement according to the parochial categories of caste, which is associated with the backward public sector. The quota system of lower-caste reservations is commonly understood to account for the inefficiency and corruption of government jobs.[2] In contrast, IT and other private sector jobs, which have been spared such quotas so far, have been understood as embodying opposite and implicitly "global" values, including an emphasis on merit, fair competition, and efficiency.[3]

The IT industry in particular and the knowledge economy in general are deeply embedded in national debates surrounding the issue of reservations. The lack of reservations in India's private sector, and thus the apparent blindness to parochial matters of caste, contributes importantly to the perception of IT as a modern industry in which employees are proud to participate. In a workplace that regards merit above all else, the introduction of caste-based quotas appears to threaten not only the talent base of the company, as the leaders in the industry claim, but more fundamentally the abstract language of merit, premised upon the success of the individual, upon which the knowledge economy is supposed to operate. As the potential for the imposition of numeric reservations has become a political possibility, the CEOs of IT companies have begun calling for more sophisticated forms of affirmative action in lieu of numeric quotas. The tension between the ideology of the knowledge economy and government-mandated hiring practices became most pronounced after the resignation in 2006 of Pratap Bhanu Mehta from the prime minister's elite Knowledge Commission. In his widely publicized resignation letter, Mehta explicitly named this tension:

> The government's recent decision . . . to extend quotas for OBCs in Central institutions, the palliative measures the government is contemplating to defuse the resulting agitation, and the process employed to arrive at these measures are steps in the wrong direction. They violate four cardinal principles that institutions in a knowledge-based society will have to follow: they are not based on assessment of effectiveness, they are incompatible with the freedom and diversity of institutions, they more thoroughly politicize the education process, and they inject an insidious poison that will harm the nation's long term interest (Mehta 2006).

Mehta's words highlight the fundamental opposition between the effectiveness and freedom needed for a knowledge society and the parochial categories that are "insidiously" reified in the legislation of 2006. This set of discourses regarding the knowledge economy's deep disregard for "old" social stratifications such as caste in favor of more modern principles such as merit and efficiency importantly informs the ways in which knowledge professionals perceive the role of IT in shaping a new India. The implicit tension between government jobs and IT jobs (and, by association, the state and the private sector) pervades the discourses of work and merit in the IT industry. Within the everyday relations of the IT workplace, the roles of gender especially, but also of regional and caste identifications, are completely subordinated to the work at hand. Those who remain in the industry over time tend to share not only a particular set of highly valued skills, but also a language and a belief system that justify their class position, creating the illusion that anyone with the same talent and determination can achieve the same status, without regard to the (fairly uniform, elite) backgrounds that most IT workers come from (Upadhya 2007a). The ideology of purely merit-based advancement, when articulated in association with IT or the knowledge economy, presents a "global" India that is removed from the corrupt politics for which India is notorious and offers the opportunity for individual advancement free of class, caste, and gender biases. Belief in the virtuous system of advancement in IT firms provides an ideological alternative to the current political system, as well as an alternative to a fragmented cultural past, offering an ostensibly superior way for the nation to progress. The ideology of merit also supports the idea that those who remain in the IT industry are talented, moral individuals— capable of leading the nation forward in a desirable direction.

Subjectivities of Striving in the Knowledge Economy

How do individuals live out the logics and principles of the knowledge economy and how do these principles support the ideology of merit-based advancement? The narratives of success or failure that IT professionals articulate offer an inroad to understanding the internalization of the logics of the knowledge economy as a social process that makes these logics moral and virtuous. A thirst for learning and individual development, a tireless work ethic, and a willingness to adapt to change rapidly are hallmarks of the morals of the knowledge economy and K4D's implicit recipe for a nation's success in a global economy, but these principles only become meaningful when they are adopted by individuals. The value of merit in India's knowledge economy is not just a question of who does the job best, but who does the job best through personal striving, aspiration, hard work, and, finally, achievement. The flip side of this belief system is also accepted: failure or stagnation in the industry indicates a lack of ambition, talent, or some other personal shortcoming. In these ways, merit becomes the sole responsibility of the individual, who must produce an ever greater level of achievement in order to succeed, both in the immediate context of the Indian IT workplace and in the broader context of the knowledge economy.

Given this core ideology, IT professionals in all three sites I studied described IT as an ever changing field for which one must constantly train and learn to keep up. In India especially, many employees are simultaneously earning an additional certification or degree in addition to doing their jobs such that their entire lives revolve around working or learning for work. Women who leave their jobs temporarily to have families find themselves less marketable a year or two later because they are no longer up to date on the latest technology. But this rapidly changing professional landscape makes Indian knowledge professionals proud of their ability to constantly retrain to stay abreast of industry developments. Although women find the sacrifices they must make to be a hindrance in terms of their own families, most are proud of their ability to overcome these challenges and stay in the industry. For most, the need to constantly retrain and develop new skills makes the job desirable and challenging, fostering self-motivation and personal responsibility.

Parminder is a thirty-three-year old software engineer living and working in Mumbai and getting her MBA on the weekends. Soft-spoken but tenacious, Parminder described with pride the long and circuitous road she took to get into the IT industry, where she currently works at a senior level. She started out as a microbiologist and very painstakingly made her way into the IT industry through vocational coursework and constant job seeking. Throughout her interview, Parminder emphasized how much she learns as a part of the industry. For her, the ability to learn constantly is closely related to adaptability and independence. She sees the abilities to change and be independent as the most important factors for advancement in the industry. Parminder explains, "The only thing that one can ensure is to keep oneself upgraded and updated. Keep learning. As long as one is adaptable and equipped to handle the changes, I don't see any problem . . . You resist change the moment you do not know." She is proud of her hunger for learning, which she views as entirely responsible for her continued success in the industry.

Parminder's sentiments epitomize those of most Indian knowledge professionals, regardless of gender or age. Like Parminder, most of the knowledge professionals I interviewed were trained in something other than software or IT, and either took courses on their own to qualify for a position in IT or learned on the job. Vikram, a twenty-six-year-old engineer working in Mumbai, planned his entry into the industry in gradual stages. Articulate, well groomed, and confident, he framed his professional development in the terms of a personal journey. Vikram graduated with a degree in commerce, often considered to be less prestigious than an engineering degree, and took up work in the only job he could find after college—a BPO job that dealt with financial services. He worked as a call center agent for two years but quickly realized that the only way to a secure career with long-term opportunities was to switch into software. This was not easy, however—he had no technical background and he was aware of an oversupply of job seekers with the basic tech skills he could acquire through a vocational training institute. After much searching of local job listings, he noticed a demand for an unusual programming language—Lotus Domino—at a specific multinational firm with a large office in Mumbai. He also found out that workers with command of this language were in demand because there were so few of them; very few courses in this language were offered in Mumbai. Because the language was so specialized, these few courses were very expensive. So, Vikram began saving money to take one of those particular courses and eventually secured a position at the one multinational firm that demanded Lotus Domino. For Vikram, his entrée into software was an experience of personal growth through which he came to understand what he wanted and went about acquiring it through his own efforts to save, work hard (attending classes and working simultaneously), and maintain his focus on his ultimate goal.

Although Vikram comes from a financially secure family, his journey toward the affluence of the software industry, at least by his own account, was more circuitous than straightforward, and more based upon his own individual effort than the effort of his family, whom he described as "not pushy." Like Parminder, Vikram views his own mobility as a just reward for his ability to retrain and learn new skills, which he sees as fundamentally linked to embracing personal change. Because Parminder and Vikram have worked so hard to achieve what they have, and have overcome what are without a doubt difficult odds, it is easy to overlook the privileges that allowed them to educate and improve themselves in the ways that they did. As the principles of the knowledge economy implicitly presume a world of equal opportunity, Parminder and Vikram read their own continual learning not only as virtuous but also as something that anyone with drive can accomplish.

Indian knowledge professionals privilege a spirit of flexibility, innovation, and entrepreneurship both in their professional and personal lives. The self is viewed as an enterprising self that is challenged through constant change, especially through a flexible relationship to work. By opening themselves up to the vulnerabilities that change might bring, they also see themselves as possessing the necessary tenacity required to weather the tumultuousness of a global economy, and this tenacity folds nicely into pride in one's own accomplishments. Shirin, a twenty-five-year-old computer graphics specialist for an e-learning company in Mumbai, views the career ahead of her as one of constantly changing jobs in order to maintain a vibrant sense of self. Although she comes from a Muslim middle-class background where women seldom work outside the home, Shirin sees herself as an individual who must work in order to realize her full capacity as a person. "Change is permanent," Shirin says. "If you have to achieve something, you cannot stay in one job . . . it's very stagnant water." She goes on to say that in order to continuously seek out new jobs, she must continuously learn, and that it is only in that process of learning, gaining new skills, and expanding her horizons that she will feel she has accomplished anything. Other interviewees echoed Shirin's beliefs; among the most experienced professionals I interviewed, frequent job changes were viewed as an asset that fostered individual growth and experience.[4]

Constant change at work becomes more valued the higher individuals climb the ladder, but this aspect is more pronounced among men than women. Among men in senior positions, several expressed a feeling of being constrained or limited in the mainstream of the IT industry. Ashok, a thirty-six-year-old consultant working in Mumbai, explained, "You need freedom. You need it and I enjoy it. With an MNC [multinational corporation], controlling the stakes of the project is enjoyed by the front offices . . . Sometimes you feel your creativity is suppressed and your flexibility is curbed along with your freedom . . . It is a personal choice, but I want to experiment [with] certain things . . . I have a strong feeling of doing something on my own. The moment I know what is next, that will be my move." Although Ashok appreciates the "exposure"[5] he has received while working for a major multinational in Mumbai, he feels limited and believes that an entrepreneurial enterprise will be more ful-filling and challenging, leading to greater personal growth. Such a rela-tionship to work is emblematic of a knowledge society, where enterpris-ing individuals seek work that best fulfills their individual developments and desires. Dhiraj, a twenty-seven-year-old engineer in Bangalore, ex-pressed similar sentiments. When evaluating India's economic develop-ment, he linked its successes and limitations with his own trajectory and explained how he aimed to transcend those limitations through his own efforts:

> Most of the companies here are all getting small jobs and very few high-end technical jobs. You end up bored. Just the billing hours that you clock and you feel you have not done anything great. No-body wants to do something unique. People are happy with their rou-tine and their high salaries. These are not unique jobs. When I went abroad, it was an experience. They sent me as an expert, but I felt I was nowhere. I was working with a fifty-year-old person. He had such extensive knowledge that I could not open my mouth. We need to go [to] that extent if we are to be considered good.

Dhiraj's experience with working abroad had the effect of sobering what might have otherwise been an overly exuberant view of his own success in the IT industry, as well as the success of his peers. Moreover, this interaction with colleagues abroad awakened within him the ambition and drive to set himself apart from his peers in the IT industry in a quest for excellence that is simultaneously a pursuit of self-actualization as well as self-preservation: "So guys [here in India] are too happy [with mediocrity] and it may shatter . . . [But] I want to go into the managerial cadre. I am doing a part-time MBA in IIM Bangalore.[6] I do not want to be a regular manager, managing some folks or some billing of projects. I want to do something different, in the sense that I want to make a difference for myself and to get revenue for the company." Like many of the young men I spoke with, Dhiraj is proud of his success, but also sees it as his own personal responsibility to maintain that success. The only way to ensure constant upward mobility is through constant education and reeducation, which Dhiraj hopes will make him something "dif-ferent" from being "just" an ordinary IT manager.

In contrast with Ashok's and Dhiraj's restlessness and ambition, many women I interviewed were happy to remain in jobs with low levels of responsibility in exchange for less demanding hours and a schedule compatible with a family life. Several women, however, such as Nandini of Mumbai (chapter 2), Rani of Silicon Valley (chapter 4), and Shantha of Bangalore (chapter 5), expressed ambition and entrepreneurial spirit as well. The existence of these career women in the IT industry seems to prove, especially to those in the industry, that career advancement is available to all IT professionals, be they men or women, and thus helps to play down any alternative account of workplace dynamics. For both men and women, work was viewed as a space of choice and autonomy.

Successful Indian entrepreneurs serve as models for Indian technologists; they validate the model of a meritocracy, having lived out its logics in their own lives. At the time of our interview, forty-eight-year-old Suresh of Bangalore had recently sold his startup to an American company for a sum that could allow him to retire. When looking back on his long and diverse career, Suresh sees each career move as having led to the next, in a virtuous spiral that spelled out economic mobility and personal improvement. Starting out in the government sector in the 1980s, when the Indian IT industry had not yet taken off, Suresh shifted to the private sector when Wipro, now a multibillion-dollar conglomerate and a leader in India's IT industry, was a small startup with less than two hundred employees. As Wipro expanded and Suresh moved up the ladder, he gained a wealth of international experience while learning valuable skills and in-depth knowledge. When he left the company for an entrepreneurial venture with a few colleagues, he felt as though he was moving toward the next logical step in his personal and career development. Unlike many of his colleagues, Suresh is not convinced that the benefits of IT are "trickling down" and rather believes that the gaps between the rich and poor are widening. Yet, the IT industry has provided for him a path to personal enrichment and professional success that he thinks he might not have achieved otherwise. He explained: "The industry has changed my perception, the way I look at things, given me a lot of insight into international work culture, what international customers look for particularly in terms of quality, delivery. It has impacted my outlook, my thinking, and the way I approach some problems. We [in the industry] have gotten enriched because of this exposure. On the personal side, it has helped me to understand myself better. [If I had not been in the industry] my perspective would have been very different." Although Suresh does not see the IT industry as a fix for India's problems, he does identify strongly with the changes IT has brought to the country and narrates his own career trajectory as a benevolent one of personal and professional development, with his entrepreneurial successes representing the peak of this evolution.

Similar discourses of personal improvement and growth through the industry are especially prominent among women who have stayed in the industry for many years. Anu, a thirty-four-year-old project manager with extensive experience both in India and abroad, described her career as something that makes her happy and contributes to her growth as a person. Once the job stops giving her those things, she will stop working:

> I'm not stuck on anything. I don't see myself as being the CEO of some company. I may get there if I want to, but I'm not obsessed with position or power. I don't work for a company, I work for myself. I work for personal satisfaction. I should enjoy what I'm doing and be learning in the process. It doesn't matter in what—technically, managerially. But I need to grow. For me, that's more important . . . Right now, I'm still enjoying it. Right now, I'm still learning and growing. That's the reason it interests me. But if I come to a stage in my career and I feel that there's nothing much for me to do in this line, I'll probably quit.

Anu is a mother of two, balancing the demands of work and home, but she sees these multiple roles as enriching her and making her much more than "just a mother," a view echoed by most of the women I interviewed.

Anu's attitude to work, geared as it is toward personal growth and satisfaction, fosters a flexible relationship to that work—a relationship that is deeply invested neither in the firm nor in the work per se, but rather only in the individual enterprise of growth and improvement. Anu described to me how a flexible relationship to the workplace and the industry is essential to surviving and growing within the industry. Because Anu views the industry in this way, she projects it onto the success of the country as a whole, where not only does she advance competitively and according to her own merit, but India does as well: "I think the good thing about India is that we don't get hung up on things. We move on . . . Like for example, we lost a lot when we went into nationalization. We could have very well sat and cried about it . . . But we're still moving on, right? . . . You have to. It's a global economy now . . . If I lose my job in the IT industry tomorrow because China has picked up, what's the use of me cribbing? Maybe I should go grow potatoes somewhere. So, you have to have the attitude, and that isn't easy. And you have to have the guts." For Anu, her own ability to carry out her IT job with a high level of competence and dedication while still being flexible enough to do something entirely different with her life tomorrow is a reflection of a new India. Her own willingness to "grow potatoes" if Chinese knowledge professionals take over her IT job is closely tied to India's ability to "move on," which for now means competing in a global economy by providing a pool of Indian knowledge workers to meet global demand and improve India. Anu's viewpoint provides a stark contrast to an older popular conception of India as a culture and a place that endures all, rather than a place that moves with the times.

In these examples, we find that knowledge workers are subjectively committed to the ideals of adaptability and flexibility. Job seeking is not an insecurity of the market or a nuisance but rather a necessary step toward self-improvement. The necessity to retrain or change professions is not an occupational hazard but rather a challenge that ensures self-development and a competitive edge in the market. Knowledge professionals understand their experience as knowledge workers through the lens of individual choice and freedom. For them, the logics underpinning the knowledge economy provide the framework through which they imagine their own professional morality and achievement, which reflect the orientation of the industry as a whole and help to build a vision of a new India. Because the IT industry is so isolated from contact with other spheres of Indian society, it is almost inevitable that IT professionals should view their own success as emerging from their own personal strivings and not the class and caste privileges they enjoy. As the principles of the knowledge economy collude with the principles of merit-based advancement, they create a set of logics that promote a uniform disposition of individualistic striving as virtuous and exciting.

The Same for Everyone: Professionalism and the Ideology of Gender Equality

Central to the ethic of merit and personal striving is the belief that each employee is a part of a meritocracy that allocates rewards fairly. Not only is this fairness ostensibly good for women in the workplace, but it also reflects well upon the progress of the nation as a whole. The ways in which this ethic of professionalism has translated into more opportunities for women in particular are sources of significant pride. Indeed, the professionalism of IT becomes synonymous with the possibility of gender equality, which is thought to signal progress for women in India. The success of professional women in IT validates a professional ethic as a benevolent one, distinguishing the ethics of IT as progressive and moral. Shankar, a thirty-two-year-old man working in graphic design, explains: "When I see a girl working in these [technical] areas, I feel very happy for her and her family. Whatever I have seen earlier or in other parts of India, that situation was very different. Now girls take their own decisions, which is good for them . . . The lifestyle she can dream of has changed. Earlier they had to think only of working in a bank or government job . . . now they earn more than men!" For Shankar, the equal treatment that men and women receive in the IT workplace is a marker of progress for India as a whole, even though that progress is available only through IT. As a man, Shankar takes pride in the success of women around him, which he views as an indication of shifting social norms. Professionalism in the workplace, employees understand, leads to more opportunities for women and a shift toward gender equality in a society conventionally thought to be constraining in this regard.

Within the framework of a merit-based system, employees perceive advancement and change to be allocated fairly. Thus, even though the IT workplace may attract and retain only certain kinds of elite workers, IT's position as the global edge of the nation comes to be viewed as just and based on merit—and therefore beyond criticism. Francine, a twenty-two-year-old software programmer in Mumbai, took this totalizing belief in the merit-based system to its logical conclusion. When asked about her feelings about the persistently low ratios of women in management, Francine responded, "Maybe women just aren't as capable! I'm not saying that they aren't, but I'm just saying that if women are just as capable as men, then there should be no problem to get to [top management] positions! Nothing stopping them." Francine's unqualified belief in the fairness of the merit-based-system in her office leads her to speculate that low percentages of women in upper management might reflect a shortcoming of women themselves. Because Francine was still in her first few months in the industry when I interviewed her, her words reflect the reputation of the industry at large, as well as the ideologies operative within the workplace, rather than her own cumulative experience within the industry. Although this is a particularly dramatic example, demonstrating how far faith in merit-based advancement can go, the reasoning is similar to the views expressed almost unanimously among interviewees. Francine's words reveal that gender equality is not necessarily considered to be an overt aim of a merit-based system, but rather a happy side effect. As such, even if women do not advance as often or as quickly as men, the system is not to be blamed.

Parminder says that she has never experienced discrimination throughout her long career in IT, even though for the first several years of her career she achieved no upward advancement. She was working for a small firm with high turnover, and no other female employees, but she never moved up in the company or found a better paying job until almost seven years later. In retrospect, Parminder feels that she never got a better job because she was not confident enough—she appeared too sheltered and too unwilling to speak up. Still, Parminder sees this as her own shortcoming: "I was not as independent thinking, strong, as what I am now . . . I'd never been away from my parents, not even during my college. Never stayed in a hostel. Always in that protection. That shell [gestures her hands into an enclosed ball] . . . And somehow when I was giving my interview to the VP, he could get this out of me."

Parminder views younger workers entering the industry today as being much more independent than she was at their age, and she argues that through their high aspirations and expectations India is improving. Parminder is convinced that multinational technology firms maintain a sort of human interest at the core of their organizations, where anyone who suits a particular position will be given the opportunity to move up, and feels justified in this view because of her diverse experiences in IT, both in India and abroad. Most others I interviewed echoed her views. In a male-dominated industry with few women in upper management, professional women consistently agreed that all workers have the same opportunity to move up the corporate hierarchy without regard to gender, caste, religion, region, or family connections.

Professional women, thus, believe that they benefit from the IT industry's ostensible commitment to individual merit and professionalism. Moreover, their ability to adhere to such an ethic, with all of its ups and downs, attests to their own commitment to a professional meritocracy. Interviewees consistently attested to the idea that women employees are granted the same chances as men to move up the hierarchy, though the IT industry is still dominated by men. Good work is rewarded with more challenging work and promotions. Malini explained her own rise within the organization she worked for in terms of a merit-based, performance-oriented framework that I heard about frequently, especially among women in middle management:

> I was someone who was very mediocre in the first two years of my working life. And suddenly, something happened, and I woke up one day—it was around the time I got married—and I just started working very hard. In one year, it bore fruit, and I became a project lead. I worked harder and I became a project manager. Now I know that depending on my drive, I can go where I want. And I also know that depending on the consistency of my drive, it'll really shape the path of my life. So, now I know it's all about choices. If I take it easy for my baby, then I have taken it easy. It's a choice I have made. So, I think I believe that. I believe if you have the drive and the vision and you have a basic education in place, you can really go very far.

Once women subscribe to the idea that their own advancement and everyone else's is based purely on performance and hard work, it fosters the development of a framework of choice in all aspects of work, especially when gendered conflicts between home and work arise.

Aparna, a thirty-five-year-old upper-level manager working in the upper echelons of an IT firm based in Mumbai, typifies the attitudes and strategies of women managers when dealing with other women in the workplace. Aparna believes that the extra sacrifices that women must make outside the workplace in order to remain competitive in the industry are in fact part and parcel of the innate fairness of the industry. She spends extra time with new female recruits explaining to them that no exceptions will be made. When there is a deadline, everyone must work to achieve it, regardless of gender or responsibilities at home. "I briefed them . . . that it doesn't matter whether you're a lady or married or unmarried or have children," she explained. "If your colleagues are here, you're also here—no concessions."[7]

Aparna's own career choices over the course of her many years in the industry give her the authority to demand a "no concessions" stance from her female co-workers. She began in the financial sector, working on the Mumbai stock exchange, an extremely male-dominated arena, where she was conscious of her gender holding her back, preventing her from being taken seriously. In contrast, she has never felt that the software industry presented such obstacles. At the time of our interview, she held the prestigious position of delivery head in her multinational Indian firm—just one step below a vice president. Although she has gone through tough times, especially with regard to her personal-professional balance, the very fact that she has reached "the breaking point" so many times fosters a very particular sensibility toward her female colleagues, at once understanding and unyielding: "When I watch my female colleagues struggling, since I've got past that hump, I see what they're going through. I can feel it must be so hard. And the thing is—[even though] nobody expects it—you really can't make a concession. You've chosen to come to work. No one has forced you. You have decided that you will come and you will have to work like everyone else." For Aparna, then, the existence of a merit-based system in IT was proven by her own advancement within it. Her own management style reflects her belief in the meritorious and fair character of the industry, particularly with regard to gender.

Human resources personnel and upper-level male management concur with Aparna about the fairness of the industry. While they all agree that most women leave the industry after five or six years, usually to have children, there is a broad agreement that women do not face discrimination in IT. Still, many professional women I interviewed cited instances in which they were excluded from some networking opportunities available to men that perhaps would have helped them move up. More subtly, some female managers have experienced a reluctance to publicize their promotions among co-workers. In the case of Mamta, a twenty-eight-year-old engineer from Mumbai who later migrated to the United States, upper management granted her a promotion, but because the decision would be met with skepticism and jealousy among a predominantly male tier of management, the decision was not publicized to the team. Very quietly, Mamta assumed her new role, with none of the usual fanfare accorded such a step up. Despite these stories, almost all of the women I interviewed agreed that these biases were not a major obstacle. The perceived gender blindness of the industry was understood as an important part of what constituted IT as a good job for women, in contrast to other industries, such as finance or marketing, which are believed to have more overtly masculinist work cultures.

Under the surface of these assertions, however, lies a gendered segmentation of the IT workplace. This segmentation is seen not as a bias but rather was naturalized in gendered terms. Kala, a thirty-eight-year-old content writer for an e-learning company in Mumbai, explained, "There's a great divide—between content, writing, and coding. The writers and content people are mostly women. The coders are mostly men. It may not be written down anywhere, but these are the hard subjects and the soft subjects. Writing and graphics are the softer sides." Indeed, in the office in which Kala works, the disproportionate number of women surprised me until I realized that the engineers who write software code work on a different floor. All of the employees on Kala's floor work either on content writing or on graphic design. Similarly, within coding, there is quality and maintenance work on the one hand, and research and development on the other. Women who remain in the industry beyond the five-year threshold are much more likely to pursue quality and maintenance work, where the hours are more predictable and work is less stressful and deadline-driven. Indeed, quality and maintenance work provides an important space for women with significant work experience to continue their careers while maintaining a home life that is relatively free of stress. Because of the persistent demand for quality work from foreign firms, this type of work has not been feminized in terms of pay, and quality engineers are paid commensurately with their experiences. Still, men and women I interviewed viewed research and development work, the most male segment of the workforce, to be the most exciting, rewarding, and creative. In this line of work, deadlines are tight, pressure is high, and the hours are unpredictable. None of these kinds of segmentations, while transparent to most professional women I interviewed who had been working in the industry for more than five years, was viewed as evidence of a bias or an obstacle. Instead, this segmentation was considered "natural" and due to a combination of the choices that women make, as well as their own natural inclinations.

The Indian Economy as a Meritocracy

The belief in the IT industry's system of merit-based advancement has very specific implications for the ways in which IT professionals tend to think about economy and government in India. That is, most IT professionals view the economy and the government as opposing forces in India, wherein the free market becomes the benevolent driver of progress and merit, while the government and politics become obstacles to that progress, a limiting factor that prevents India from reaching its full potential. This set of beliefs is a key site for the production of neoliberal discourses in India, wherein a quest for merit is informed by an often erroneous understanding of the role of the Indian state in encouraging and fostering the development of the IT industry.

In 2004, when I conducted much of this research, the Congress Party had just unseated the BJP at the national level. With the change in government came a new financial administration led by P. Chidambaram, who raised taxes for the elite. This immediately affected IT workers, who felt that the move was just another sign of the backwardness of Indian politics. Mamta of Mumbai spoke about this at length, revealing an upwardly mobile perspective on how new forms of government taxation undermine individual efforts to accumulate wealth:

> They [the BJP] had done some good things for the economy, they were moving in the right direction, with the income tax structure and all that. Looking at the new income tax structure, I'm really like, 'Why the hell did Congress come?!' It's really a regression! . . . It's like we're moving away from what had started, with much more flat structures, and so it's going in the other direction. One point that [is] really pulling me down is the tax on every transaction of shares . . . The transaction tax is a great way for the government to earn revenue on each transaction, but it's like, you have killed that individual person who is doing their investments on the market. The daily trading that happens is getting restricted. There are a lot of people who do this individual kind of trading and that's how they earn their money . . . and you've killed that poor guy! Whatever they earn, that's their money! . . . It adds employment in the government to oversee it, and now it's just adding to the bureaucracy.

Mamta expresses frustration at the ways in which government policies trap and limit individual investors through an unnecessary bureaucracy. More significantly, however, her comments on the change in government policy reflect an abiding conviction on the part of Indian technologists that the government quashes a much-needed entrepreneurial spirit in India as a whole. The value for entrepreneurial spirit, a key component of knowledge economy discourses that hinge on innovation and self-reliance, is one of the many aspects of the culture of Indian IT professionals that coalesces in a fundamentally neoliberal view of politics and the economy, wherein a minimal state and a free market are thought to be the solution to all problems.[8]

Mamta's account of the new taxation structure and the emergence of new bureaucracy fits a larger pattern of IT professionals who believe that India's IT industry emerged without state intervention or policy. This discourse of the IT industry as a transcendent industry—one that goes beyond the pettiness of government—powerfully pervades discussions of government and economy. Despite well-documented evidence of extensive government policies that fostered and promoted the development of IT in India, including the Software Technology Parks of India (STPI) scheme in the 1990s, and the implementation of trade policies directed specifically at attracting foreign IT firms, IT professionals simply deny the importance of such policies.[9] Madhav of Mumbai, a thirty-eight-year-old general manager of a data-processing office, clearly articulated this belief: "No government can take credit for [the] IT boom. When it started, there was nothing. It moved on its own, from information and data. There was no government policy. These have come on in hindsight and then worked. Government could have done [a lot], but they did not." Madhav went on to explain the ways in which it is individuals who have used the energy of the IT boom to move up and expand their choices, but that this phenomenon could hardly be considered any kind of comment on the success of any political party or plan. Krish, a thirty-four-year-old Mumbai-based manager with significant experience abroad, takes the sentiment a step further to assume an explicitly anti-government stance. "Democracy means no morons should be around," Krish explained emphatically. "I think when they were trying to bomb the Parliament, that would have been the best thing that could have happened. IT has happened in spite of politics, not because of it." For Krish and others like him, acknowledging the long history of state intervention that made the IT boom in India possible would undermine the fundamental belief system that informs the industry's moral, economic, and political views: that free market capitalism (as opposed to government intervention) provides the most meritocratic, efficient, and profitable way to carry the nation forward.

The professionals I interviewed who were living in India expressed a generalized skepticism, tending toward antipathy, toward politics as a concept, and the government of India as a particular entity. Most of those I interviewed do not vote regularly, either out of explicitly stated apathy or because they have moved residences so much that they cannot register at the places they currently reside. The prevailing view within the IT industry supports the idea that when the economy is the prime driver of society (rather than the government), those with merit will naturally rise to the top and have more choices. Those improved choices, then, will benefit society as a whole, as middle-class people will not be driven only to careers that make high salaries.

> MALINI: When money, economy is driving the whole thing, I think . . . that India will take care of herself. I think so. You know, I know a friend of mine who is an environmentalist. And I think that's a great reflection of an Indian woman's education. She's a middle-class girl . . . so there are a lot of people like that also in mainstream India who will opt out to make a difference in areas that matter. Education, Dalits [untouchables], environment, all that. I think together, everyone will take it forward.

> SR: So, education, you're saying, doesn't just mean that people get out there to make more money; they do socially responsible things too.

> MALINI: Yes! See, when people have [economic] options, they have choices. Because, see, if you ask me, if my mom was rich, I think I would have done English literature. I wouldn't have done IT. But now, I'm in IT, and hopefully I'll be financially secure enough, and I think I'll let my child choose what she wants to do. If she chooses there, then you have one more thing in India taken care of. So, I think economy will fix the problem.

Malini's narrative exemplifies the kinds of benevolent spirals that most IT professionals expect of upward mobility. The expansion of economic opportunity opens up space for a more moral lifestyle, and, by association, a more just and open society. In these ways, Indian technologists utilize the discourse of a meritocracy within their industry to justify and promote their own position in a deeply divided society, as well as a particular set of attitudes about economy, politics, and society as a whole. These attitudes are powerful because they internalize the logics of the knowledge economy that stress individual achievement and performance while crowding out alternative discourses. The low number of women in upper management in IT is a result of the choices of Indian women, who can perform well and move up the ladder if they so choose. Similarly, anyone who tries hard to get an education and get into IT can move up the ladder with intelligence and hard work. By this logic, those who are successful in IT deserve it, while those who are not successful have earned their lack of success as well.

Globalizing Meritocracy as Political Discourse

In 2006, the expansion of caste reservations in government institutions of higher education was passed into law in the Indian legislature, sparking protests especially among medical and other professional students all over India. These protests lacked the fervor of the Mandal protests of the 1990s but nonetheless resulted in large gatherings, hunger strikes, and angry students articulating familiar phrases about merit and equality. The upper-caste medical students who became mobilized were admitted to medical school under the "general" (unreserved) category, which is far more competitive than the reserved category. These students see their OBC peers as lazier, less qualified, and liable to make bad doctors in the future. As one group of protesting students at the All India Institute of Medical Sciences (AIIMS) explained to the press, "Some are pushed up [given advantages] even if they can't cope with exams. They are always involved in everything from violence to drunken driving, because they aren't interested in studying. These days, some have been painting 'Proud to be an OBC' on their faces!" Another student explained his feeling of being marginalized: "The government refers to doctors, lawyers, engineers and the media as intelligentsia comprising 1 per cent of the population. . . . They would never dare attack a group of blue-collar workers because they are interested in votes alone. They think we can be ignored, but it is this 1 per cent that runs the country" (Pereira, Shankar, Singh 2006).

Meanwhile, in Silicon Valley, a parallel protest against the expansion of reservations in India was underway. Over five hundred professionals in the Bay Area gathered under the banner of Bay Area Indians for Equality and signed a petition addressed to the president of India, questioning his policies (Krishnaswami 2006). Their articulations were far more tempered than those of the AIIMS students. The focus was more on how the government arrived at the decision to implement the quotas, the facts and figures used to support the decision, and ultimately a concern for the effect that "thoughtless politics" has on an otherwise great nation (Bay Area Indians for Equality 2006). Because Indian professionals in the Bay Area are overwhelmingly middle class, urban, and upper caste, the policies hit close to home, and while they were unwilling to condemn reservations altogether or take direct hits at OBC students, their belief in the notion of "equality" and their belief that reservations are purely a result of dirty politics that are holding back a great country resonate deeply with their counterparts elsewhere in the world.

Almost two years after these protests, an e-mail entitled "Indian Version of an Old Story" circulated among Indians in India and the United States. This e-mail and its electronic genealogy provide insight into the depth of the animosity toward lower-caste mobilization among professional Indians, as well as the e-mail's resonance with the class politics of social justice all over the world. By the time the e-mail came to me it had been forwarded at least a dozen times, almost always with a line from the new sender: "Sad, but true." I present here the entirety of this e-mail:

An Old Story:
The Ant works hard in the withering heat all summer building its house and laying up supplies for the winter.

The Grasshopper thinks the Ant is a fool and laughs & dances & plays the summer away.

Come winter, the Ant is warm and well fed. The Grasshopper has no food or shelter so he dies out in the cold.
Indian Version:
The Ant works hard in the withering heat all summer building its house and laying up supplies for the winter.

The Grasshopper thinks the Ant's a fool and laughs & dances & plays the summer away.

Come winter, the shivering Grasshopper calls a press conference and demands to know why the Ant should be allowed to be warm and well fed while others are cold and starving.

NDTV, BBC, CNN [all major news networks] show up to provide pictures of the shivering Grasshopper next to a video of the Ant in his comfortable home with a table filled with food.

The World is stunned by the sharp contrast. How can this be that this poor Grasshopper is allowed to suffer so?

Arundhati Roy [an author and a progressive activist] stages a demonstration in front of the Ant's house.

Medha Patkar [an activist for indigenous groups in India] goes on a fast along with other Grasshoppers demanding that Grasshoppers be relocated to warmer climates during winter.

Mayawati [an Indian woman politician of low caste] states this as "injustice" done on Minorities.

Amnesty International and Koffi Annan criticize the Indian Government for not upholding the fundamental rights of the Grasshopper.

The Internet is flooded with online petitions seeking support to the Grasshopper (many promising Heaven and Everlasting Peace for prompt support as against the wrath of God for non-compliance).

Opposition MPs stage a walkout. Left parties call for "Bengal Bandh" in West Bengal and Kerala demanding a Judicial Enquiry. CPM [Communist Party-Marxist, representing India's Left] in Kerala [a state known for its Leftist social policies] immediately passes a law preventing Ants from working hard in the heat so as to bring about equality of poverty among Ants and Grasshoppers.

Lalu Prasad [another low-caste politician who was then the minister of railways] allocates one free coach to Grasshoppers on all Indian Railway Trains, aptly named as the "Grasshopper Rath [chariot]."

Finally, the Judicial Committee drafts the "Prevention of Terrorism Against Grasshoppers Act" (POTAGA), with effect from the beginning of the winter.

Arjun Singh [the minister of human resources in charge of the 2006 reservations] makes "Special Reservation" for Grasshoppers in Educational Institutions & in Government Services.

The Ant is fined for failing to comply with POTAGA and having nothing left to pay his retroactive taxes, it's [sic] home is confiscated by the Government and handed over to the Grasshopper in a ceremony covered by NDTV.

Arundhati Roy calls it "A Triumph of Justice."

Lalu calls it "Socialistic Justice."

CPM calls it the "Revolutionary Resurgence of the Downtrodden."

Koffi Annan invites the Grasshopper to address the UN General Assembly.

Many years later . . .

The Ant has since migrated to the U.S. and set up a multi-billion dollar company in Silicon Valley, 100s of Grasshoppers still die of starvation despite reservation somewhere in India,

AND

As a result of losing lot[s] of hard working Ants and feeding the grasshoppers, India is still a developing country . . . !!!

Within the IT industry, this e-mail was read primarily as a critique of politics in India, although the racist beliefs underpinning the setup of the piece are obvious. The numerous references to the most prominent Indian activists and politicians, and the marginalization of the virtuous Ant, who is forced to take his talents elsewhere—Silicon Valley, in this case—make it clear that the targets of the tale are those supposedly marginalized castes who are in fact marginalized because of their own inherent flaws. With minimal Internet research, the genealogy of this e-mail becomes extremely clear. Originating on the American conservative blog Right Truth (http://righttruth.typepad.com/right_truth) on October 20, 2007, the piece was originally an "American version" of the Ant and Grasshopper story that retold the political events of the civil rights movement, replacing "African American" with "Grasshopper" in exactly the way "Low Caste/OBC" is replaced with "Grasshopper" in the Indian version. Within days, there were multiple versions, all of which targeted the causes of the Left, painting the poor and disenfranchised as victims of their own laziness and criminality, and painting the privileged as virtuous and marginalized. Aside from the various American versions of the tale, there is an Australian version as well, targeting Aboriginals as "Grasshoppers." The proliferation of this story on the Internet and its eventual adaptation within the Indian context provide insights into the kind of politics that a belief in merit is complicit with, whatever politics individuals may individually subscribe to, and offer clues into the kind of worldview that is folded into such beliefs.

A long history of debates in both the United States and India surrounding the tension between merit and social justice has established well the tensions I wish to point to here (see, for example, the essays in Arrow, Bowles, and Duraluf 1999). In the case of Indian IT professionals, however, what sets them apart from the very obvious political agenda of the American version is their ostensible disregard for politics altogether. In the American version, the tone of the discourse puts the reader on alert immediately that the tale is a right-wing piece of rhetoric. In the Indian version, Indian IT professionals can safely bemoan the dirtiness of the political process in India that appears in the tale and still claim that they are apolitical and centrist in their societal views. Because the logics of the knowledge economy further support the development of an apolitical, individualized expert subject invested only in her own betterment, it is even easier for IT professionals to claim that politics is just not for them, and to feel all the more entitled to their dominant (and virtuous, moral) position.

The ideologies of merit that are carefully cultivated in the workplace emerge both from the importance of the concept to India's middle class as well as its resonance with principles of the knowledge economy that emphasize personal striving and achievement. Indeed, it is the convergence of these two aspects of merit that allow IT professionals to internalize the logic of merit and turn it into a key input for the cultural streamlining processes that transform what it means to be Indian—from an association with endless bureaucracy, inefficiency, and reservations to an association with striving individuals, a global competitive edge, and thriving capitalist business. The pursuit of individual achievement and excellence at work validates the managerial models of IT as purely based on merit, while concealing the kinds of exclusion that are already at work before employees even enter the IT workplace. By emphasizing an ideology of merit, the focus of personal and public life shifts away from concerns for society and toward concerns with the personal and the immediate, where the individual becomes entirely responsible for her own life trajectory. In this way, a meritocratic framework renders the particularities of "background" invisible without appearing to do so. When IT professionals leave the workplace, however, and reflect upon their own personal stories and trajectories, the extent to which their interpretation of individuality is already situated in their personal histories becomes clear.

NARRATIVES OF EMBEDDED SELVES

In a cozy flat in Bandra, a posh suburb of Mumbai, I am stretched out on a comfortable divan opposite Bharathi, a thoughtful technical writer in her mid-twenties. She sits cross-legged on the floor across from me, her eyebrows knitted together in deep thought as I ask questions. The tiny recorder between us bears witness. To me, Bharathi seems different from the colleagues of hers I have interviewed so far. She is in the IT industry, yet, as we have already seen in chapter 2, she is remarkably critical of the culture of IT. It is not completely surprising. A sociology graduate who studied law before realizing that her love for writing would be more lucratively channeled in IT, she has a more formidable set of tools for critical analysis of her social world than do her colleagues who have studied engineering exclusively. Now that I am interviewing her, asking her opinions and thoughts about working in IT, she is even more pensive than usual. In reflecting upon the colleagues she encounters in her field, Bharathi explains,

> And IT, well, I don't know. I think that environment just makes everyone a clone. You start thinking the same way. There's just that much range of a background you will encounter . . . It's not like a doctor, when you have patients from all different backgrounds. I will interact with an integrator, a software person, a graphics person. How different would that be? They still speak English, which means they have at least had a certain kind of education. You see them wearing the same jeans and t-shirt . . . Had I been a lawyer that would have been different. That empathy [for others unlike me] would have been much more. Now, from an IT field, my interaction with people is very limited.

Despite the popular perception that the experience of IT makes its employees more open-minded, Bharathi argues that the viewpoint of IT professionals is only becoming increasingly narrow. The popular perception of the industry as characterized by openness, communication, and dialogue seems dangerous to her: "IT was supposed to stand for communication—being able to speak another's language. But you are not. You speak the same language. And I mean language in the broadest sense, not just English . . . It's a class vocabulary. Even if they come from different places, it's the same class . . . You can almost rattle off someone's opinion without having to know them." Bharathi observes a uniform class culture surrounding her at work. She feels that this culture has narrowed her outlook on the world. She is frustrated by the complacency of a culture that presumes and produces individuals with similar interests, tastes, aspirations, and even interpretations. This similarity, according to her, trumps class or regional origins because, as she says, "it's the *same* class." Only a very few of my interviewees agreed with Bharathi's sentiments; most argued instead that IT offered them unprecedented "exposure," a term to be explored in the next chapter. Bharathi's claims offer a notion of IT workers as sharing a common culture that few recognize.

Yet, Bharathi's opinions about the culture of the industry are more than keen, albeit unpopular, observations. Her opinions are the basis of a deep-seated fear for herself. She is afraid of how an environment she considers to be suffocating might be affecting her own individual growth and development: "I can interact better with my client in America than I can with the peon who cleans my toilet. Why is that? And I feel that, at some level, is quite debilitating for my personal growth. When I can't carry on a dialogue with another human being, however different that person might be, that's really sad. While this person in Ireland who has something to say about my content, I can talk to him for hours! Which is probably bringing the world closer, but it's still estranging me from my own people." The lifestyle and status that IT offers her fails to fulfill her personal goals, and her criticism hints at far more subtle desires: an individuality she believes she possesses and wishes to develop. For Bharathi, this individuality is made real through independent thought and through the capacity to connect and relate to those outside her own social, economic, and political milieu. This kind of individuality, it seemed to Bharathi, was not encouraged or even recognized as valuable in her industry.

Bharathi's observations and fears raise a critical set of questions for analyzing the culture of India's new transnational class: Does the culture of IT and a "new" kind of Indian middle-classness produce individuals with a shared disposition of perceptions, attitudes, and ways of being in the world? And if so, what does this shared disposition look like? How might individual IT professionals, embedded in their certain backgrounds, incorporate the ideologies that the workplace fosters into their personal dispositions?

Notions of individual achievement share the rhetoric of individuality fostered in the workplace but are nonetheless articulated in ways that reflect the particularities of each person's background. The ways in which professional IT women especially tell their personal stories reveal a great deal about how the individual self cultivated in the workplace flows into personal lives, shaping and producing reinvented notions of marriage, family, and respectable femininity that will be addressed in depth in the following chapter. In this chapter, I explore the individual narratives of several IT professionals I met and show how various personal narratives offer us compelling insight into the kinds of possibilities for the production of the self that the IT industry creates, even as those new possibilities always interact with existing dispositions embedded in their gendered and classed positions.

Embedded Individualism

As previous chapters have suggested, the development of an individual self that strives for success and achievement in the context of the workplace is a fundamental part of the culture of the Indian IT industry and the broader knowledge economy as a whole. The development of this individual self plays a critical role in the streamlining of Indian culture and the production of appropriate difference as a sense of individuality develops in tandem with notions of "global" and "Indian" that are constantly being created and recreated in IT offices. In the context of knowledge for development discourses, the individual is the explicit agent of the knowledge economy—the individual will benefit the collective in an implicitly synergistic relationship.

Still, in social scientific thinking, most prominent theories of the individual focus on the tension between individual identifications and collective ones. In the context of globalization, scholars have suggested that new conceptions of the individual have emerged at least in part in response to a new global political and economic reality, wherein the individual becomes an independent "expert" actor who must manage risks by himself (rather than counting on the state) and craft his own path in the world, "disembedded" from the particularities of social or cultural context. For example, Ulrich Beck's influential characterization of reflexive modernization and the risk society centers upon the reconstitution of the individual as the most important manager of risks, displacing the importance of the family group and social class, which had previously absorbed such risk. This "individualization," as Beck calls it, is not a reference to fragmentation and isolation but rather to a new social form in which "individuals must produce, stage, and cobble together their biographies themselves" (Beck, Giddens, and Lash 1994). Anthony Giddens similarly argues that individuals have become "disembedded" from their local contexts and attachments; social relations are "restructured across indefinite time-space" (Giddens 1994). Nikolas Rose's Foucauldian conception of the individual emphasizes the ways in which the scaling back of the state and the expansion of the logic of the free market have had the effect of producing individuals who must increasingly rely upon themselves for calculation, thought, and planning (Rose 1999). In all of these conceptions, the fading state stands in for the increasingly irrelevant collective, and the individual, always rendered in the abstract, occupies a central, albeit singular place in a bewildering new world. Such influential accounts of the self-governing individual focus primarily on societal shifts occurring in "advanced liberal" contexts, namely Europe and North America.

Individuals who participate in the knowledge economy and imbibe notions of personal achievement and striving, while being able to conceptualize a future in many parts of the world, might appear to be quintessentially "disembedded" individuals, removed from the politics of the state and engaged entirely in personal, rational calculations. Yet, when we examine how IT professionals adopt the narrative of the self, we find that theorists of the "disembedded self" never refer to specific empirical settings. This oversight allows them to overlook the ways in which gender, class, and nation constitute fundamentally different kinds of individuals, even if these individuals are themselves embedded in a shared global political economy. Beverly Skeggs has argued that such abstract, disembedded conceptions of the individual obfuscate the extent to which the self being characterized is in fact a classed (and gendered) self—a bourgeois, implicitly masculine individual who emerges from a very specific, privileged social location in the global political economy (Skeggs 2004).

Studies in the South Asian context suggest that notions of individuality, especially in relation to the family, have a rich and complex history in the region, and that new ideologies of achievement circulating in the IT industry take shape in ways that reflect that history.[1] Theories of the self that pitted "individualistic" selves against "collectivist" ones continue to inform the cross-cultural training programs discussed in chapter 2 and essentialize the differences between the "East" and the "West," but these theories often vastly simplified a much more complex local cultural landscape. Milton Singer's influential work, based on fieldwork in Chennai in the 1960s, argued that "native" versions of individualism existed within the traditional culture of educated Smarta Brahmin communities—providing a set of existing logics and beliefs that could be compatible with capitalism. The growth of capitalism in the public secular sphere rested upon the compartmentalization strategies of these Brahmin men, who maintained a clear distinction between that outside sphere and the traditional sphere of home (Singer 1972). Mary Hancock has more recently elaborated upon Singer by underscoring the gendered nature of these compartmentalization strategies, examining the ways in which, by upholding tradition primarily through domestic ritual, South Indian Brahmin women assert notions of the self that underscore the subordination of the self to notions of traditional womanhood (Hancock 1999). New notions of individuality created in the context of the knowledge economy, then, necessarily take shape against an existing set of local conceptions of personhood, identity, and relationality.

The narratives of Indian IT professionals suggest that although the striving individual, overtly cultivated in the workplace, provides a key referent for narrating the self, individual accounts of the self and self-development are deeply embedded in class, gender, and family trajectories that already constitute the background of individuals before they enter the industry. It is clear that the knowledge economy produces individuals who are self-disciplined, educated, enterprising, and rational; they strive for creativity, flexibility, and autonomy in their professional and personal lives. At the same time, the self articulated by IT professionals is also a self that can serve to naturalize and authorize class privilege, even as it effaces it, and can enforce and heighten the importance of marriage and the family, rather than undermine it. All of these interactions are deeply gendered.

Embedding notions of individuality in their appropriate backgrounds deepens and complicates ungrounded notions of a particular kind of individuality fostered by a new global political and economic context, while also moving away from the idea that Indian selves are somehow inherently less bounded than Western ones. In the examples that follow, I contrast the various strategies through which IT professionals narrate and live out their individual selves. In so doing, I highlight the ways in which notions of individuality adopted from the workplace provide these professionals with the tools to refashion and reinvent the ways in which class, gender, and family constitute their backgrounds. Even as they strive to move beyond the particularities of their backgrounds, however, IT professionals remain deeply embedded within them. I highlight the notion of individuality (and the ways in which this notion is limited, bounded, and never absolute) in reference to expressions of independence and interdependence, self-actualization and personal development, and the pursuit of individual desires or "freedom" in relation to the expectations of the family.

"Not for the Money:" Wealthy Backgrounds and the Valuation of Hard Work

A small but significant proportion of those I interviewed came from upper-class families. For generations, business families were the only families that could claim wealth in urban India, as wealth could never be made from a salaried government job. Business families have constituted a particular culture, as running a business is the norm only in particular castes and communities. Wealth acquired through business, although admired, has never quite had the same virtuous cultural connotations that working a government job did. Business owners must often bribe, circumvent tax codes, and break the rules to make money. Indeed, such tactics are part of the game. For the dominant middle class of government workers, many of whom are Brahmins, business was seldom viewed as a viable career option because it was seen as not for them, mostly due to caste norms. Brahmins, who constitute the highest caste, are supposedly devoted to spiritual pursuits only, and the desire for money is supposed to be beneath them. In post-colonial India, Brahmins have historically been teachers, professors, or government workers. Because of entrenched caste norms, even as late at the 1980s, a wealthy

Brahmin businessman would have been rare indeed. Yet, in many ways, IT has shaken up these norms. People growing up in wealthy business families long for the ethical salaries and transnational exposure of IT jobs, while Brahmins who go into IT might be more open to entrepreneurship. And while IT constitutes an elite within India, the money that most IT professionals make does not compare to the money of a wealthy business family, creating complex layers of experience and desire among those who move from one stratum to the other.

Among my informants, most hesitated to reveal to me specific details about the class positions of the families they grew up in. Their insistence on their independence from their class histories was an important aspect of the narratives they offered me. Still, a few respondents eventually revealed their roots in wealthy business families. The stories of those from these wealthy backgrounds reveal the attractiveness of IT to ambitious young people who wish to cast their nets and ambitions wider than the family business, despite a potential cut in income. I also heard a theme that emerged clearly among interviewees from almost all backgrounds—the insistence that they are *not* in IT for the money, a discourse echoing Brahminical tenets for living a virtuous life. This insistence is achieved through a narrative of the individual self as hard working, driven, and, in some cases, desirous of serving society as a whole. The disavowal of economic motivations, although common among IT professionals, is particularly pronounced among those few informants from wealthy backgrounds and reveals the extent to which notions of individuality imbibed at work operate against an already existing background of class privilege.

Shubha, a software engineer I interviewed in Mumbai who first introduced me to the importance of the word "background," comes from a Marwari business family in Mumbai's suburbs. Her parents run a lucrative pharmaceutical business and were dismayed by Shubha's decision to work in IT. A daughter working in this industry was a step down for them, not a step up. After avoiding discussion of her parents for much of the interview, Shubha finally explained, "I do come from a very different family background than most of the people who would work in my company . . . like, many of them *have* to work . . . I really didn't have to work for money, I really didn't. My parents could afford to give me anything I wanted . . . and the amount of money I make [in IT] is nothing compared to the amount I would make if I put the same amount of effort into our business. There's just no comparison . . . So, it was just crazy for my father. He was like, 'Why are you doing this? You don't have to!'" Shubha was hesitant to explain to me this aspect of her background. She knows that it sets her apart from her peers, and she indicated that she purposely tries not to bring it up around her colleagues. For her, the decision to go into IT stemmed partly from her personal drive and partly from her desire to distance herself from her family:

> For me, the major reason was independence, wanting to work on my own. I've been a fairly ambitious person throughout . . . I was academically very good in school. I was a board rank and my name was in the top ten in the city in my tenth standard. So I've been a very brilliant student. I don't think I'm intelligent; I just work very hard. I am by nature a slogger. So, that sort of fuels you into thinking that you should get ahead . . .
>
> You see, my mom and my dad and my brother go to the same office. Family business. It was something I never wanted. My father has never been able to understand that . . . He always takes it that I don't want to be with them, but it's not that. I want to be with people, and at [my] work[place], you're always meeting people your age, and at work there's that fun associated with that. In business, I only meet people my dad's age and you are—well—it's different. I didn't want that and I don't miss that.

In contrast to Bharathi's account of the IT workplace being a place of mind-numbing uniformity and complacence that inhibits individuality, Shubha's narrative describes the IT workplace as a space that can fulfill her individual desires, remove her from the restrictions of her family, and allow her to craft a new independent sense of self, even though it means choosing a less lucrative path than she might have.

Shubha's decision to work in IT opened up opportunities that went far beyond the experience of working in a high-tech Mumbai workplace. When the opportunity to live in the United States temporarily for work arose, Shubha was determined to grab it, despite the very vocal objections of her conservative family. While most of my respondents, even those from otherwise protective and strict families, enjoyed encouragement from their families when the opportunity to go abroad came up, Shubha's parents strongly discouraged her from going to the United States. She fought them and eventually prevailed. Her stay abroad was exuberant for her. "I loved my seven months over there [in Minnesota]," she explained. "For me, it was just amazing. I've been pretty protected with my parents. *Very* protected, actually. So, it was like me spreading my wings and I just had a blast." While in the United States, Shubha lived on her own like most other IT workers, taking care of her own apartment without domestic help, and this distanced her even further from the everyday experience of her class position in India. Shubha explained, "I used to live in my apartment alone for a lot of the time and I had roommates coming and going, which was a big pain, but I used to do everything . . . My mom would be like, 'Oh, how are you doing this and that, cleaning the toilet?' But you just did it. You don't think, 'Oh my god, I'm cleaning my toilet.' You didn't think of it as a moral issue." Even in the short space of seven months, Shubha assimilated to the norms of suburban life in the United States, an experience that put a hard-won distance between her own sense of what was normal and her family's. When her triumphal stint in Minnesota was over and she returned to India, she agreed to marry, but her reference points for a good mate had changed. After screening and rejecting several potential grooms from business families, who would have expected her to quit her job and join the family business, she reconnected with a man from Mumbai with whom she had worked while living in Minnesota. Also an IT professional, he did not come from the same caste community, nor did he come from a business family, and for Shubha, choosing him also meant opting out of the expectations of business families altogether. Although her parents were initially resistant, they eventually approved of the match.

Once Shubha had married, her parents gave the couple a flat in an expensive part of the city, something they could not have afforded at such a young age from their IT salaries alone. Still, Shubha's everyday professional life has changed the group of people she interacts with, and made her less allied to her family's particular community. Although Shubha's father wanted for her the lifestyle typical of wealthy urban women from business families, who spend their days shopping or at parties, Shubha spends long hours at work in IT. For her, the relative hardships of the industry, and the relatively low compensation she receives, have nonetheless won her independence from her family and the lifestyle that would come along with being part of the family business. Now, most of Shubha's friends work in the IT world, and these social and professional connections help to make Shubha even more closely identified with ideas and pastimes common to other IT workers. Through her interactions with an IT workplace, then, both at home and abroad, Shubha fashions a story of herself that is rooted in striving and individuality, but its unique character is made possible by her preexisting class privilege, which came with both opportunities and obstacles.

While Shubha's everyday life is more similar to the lives of her peers in IT than of her parents, her class background provides us with important insight for understanding how she has forged her particular story of her own individuality. Shubha's desire to work in IT was defined not by economic considerations, but rather by motivations toward independence and a separation from the world of her parents. Her talent as a student formed the basis for her ability to make these decisions. Once she made the decision not to join the family business, and defied her family to travel to the United States for work, she opened up space in her relationship with her parents to marry a person of her own choosing, a decision that, once again, took her away from her family's expectations. Still, she benefits from her parents' wealth by living a lifestyle that would not be available to other young IT couples, including a fully paid for apartment in a posh neighborhood and a safety net of financial security beyond her husband's means that is unavailable to most of her peers. Shubha's decisions, although bold, do not fundamentally detract from her otherwise secure life odds; rather, they underscore her ability to claim to be a hard worker driven by the motivation for independence and self-actualization rather than by a naked pursuit of economic gain. The ways in which she pursued this lifestyle have worked in precarious cooperation with her family; had her parents ever forbidden her from making the decisions she did, she is not likely to have pursued her own will so strongly.

While a drive for individual independence in itself provides a virtuous justification for disavowing economic gain among some informants, another type of narrative coming from those who grew up in wealthy business families underscores the virtue of IT as an industry with the potential to serve the world. Personal development and individualism are important here but are in service of a larger good. Here too, economic motivations are secondary. Rani, a twenty-eight-year-old Silicon Valley engineer moving into product development, works at a powerful company I will call Surge. While Rani's life trajectory took her away from India for the long term, her narrative bears important parallels to Shubha's. Like Shubha, Rani explained her career in IT as one that she pursued for the sake of her own self-actualization. More importantly, Rani explained that she expected to have a major impact on the world through the field of technology. Raised in a wealthy business family, Rani never had the drive to forge a career for herself, or indeed to work at all while growing up. While in college, however, a major Indian multinational identified her as someone with aptitude in the field, and after that she became more and more committed to the notion of a career. Through work, she met and later married her husband and moved to the United States with him in 2000. Since she has been in the United States, her vision for herself and her career has expanded and matured, as she has pursued her career more and more seriously. Rani feels that her work will someday have a major impact on the world, even as it actualizes and transforms her as an individual. "What do you think of cell phones?" she asked me early in our interview. I said I thought they were useful. "No, I mean, do you think it's a great thing? How has it changed your life?" I told her that it had certainly made life more convenient, but that it had downsides too. In response, she explained the scope of her vision and ambition for herself: "I have a different perspective. I feel it is a great technology. The thought of being able to talk to anybody, all my dear ones, even someone who is so far anytime, even if you are hiking or on the road. When I want to make an impact on the society, it is to create an invention, a technology like this, something that would eventually make a difference to all the people in the world." Rani's narrative, like many of those I interviewed, maps out a compelling story of personal development and drive in which the IT industry plays an actualizing role, and that actualization is heightened through migration. Economic need has little to do with it; indeed the substantial salary she earns at Surge can be viewed even more effectively as a secondary motivation *because* of the class privilege she grew up with. Rani explained, "When my husband says, 'If I have this much money, I will retire,' I reply, 'Do you think we work only for money? We also work for development—for contributing to the society' . . . I want to find out something that makes quite a difference to all. And that's coming from someone who never had such a dream earlier."

Like Shubha, Rani outlines a path of self-discovery and actualization through her work, but, importantly, her individuality is deeply tied to her relationship with her family. Her family background did not pose the kinds of obstacles it did for Shubha; rather, her family supported Rani's decision to pursue a career in IT because it was a respectable career, even if members of her family did not prompt Rani to pursue IT themselves. Indeed, her closeness with her family is quite central to Rani's account of her own drive and success. Her mother's motivation played an especially prominent role in Rani's narrative:

> [When I entered IT] I was not really motivated by technology or any of the latest advancements happening in this field. It was more of my mother's passion to see me leading in whatever I am doing that made me achieve what I have done today. She wanted me to lead everywhere; even if I ever stood second in class she used to be sad. At that time when I had to opt for a career, this was the number one career that I could have gone to, and I felt it was ideal . . . I never neglected my family. Were it so that I had to make anybody in the family unhappy [in my career pursuits] I would not have stirred out [of the home in the first place]. That is the kind of value I would like to carry on.

Rani asserts her individual development and ambition through a particular discourse of virtue—she aims to contribute to society even as she makes her family proud. Her constant invocation of the family echoes the "family comes first" narratives of most IT women I interviewed, to be discussed in depth in the next chapter, and hints at the ways in which Rani's particular background—her class background, as well as the expectations of her mother—shapes her particular articulation of individuality. In saying that she is not in IT for the money, she relies upon her preexisting class privilege, the moral support of her family, and her vision to help society through technology in a modified version of knowledge for development discourses.

Although they live in Mumbai and Silicon Valley, respectively, Shubha and Rani invoke notions of individuality that are similarly embedded in the class privilege they were born into, such that the position and feelings of their families profoundly affect the ways in which they imagine and actualize their life trajectories. Although both clearly articulate individualized desires and choices, most obviously in their choices of careers and partners, they also enhance their own symbolic position by disavowing the financial incentives that the IT industry provides because these incentives are actually a step down from lifestyles they were born into. In the way they met their spouses—at work rather than through an arranged process initiated by their families—the examples of Shubha and

Rani also hint at the important ways in which their navigations of individuality might be producing new gendered norms, even as these navigations are embedded in the context of class and family dynamics. The gendered aspect of the decision to marry becomes all the more clear when examining the stories of two single women, Shilpa and Devika.

Single and "Settled"? Women Navigate Marital Norms

About one-third of the professional IT women I interviewed were single. Many of these women were young enough that they were not yet experiencing serious pressure from their families to marry, but a number of women—those over the age of twenty-six or so, expressed the feeling that they were "late," and that parental and societal pressure was mounting. The various ways in which both young and old women navigated the convention of marriage, still paramount in its importance for women especially, provide an important lens through which to understand how they craft their individuality. Most informants tend to accept implicitly that the decision to pursue a relationship at work or in college (commonly known as "love marriage") signals individuality, while going through a more conventional matchmaking system through the family (commonly known as "arranged marriage") signals a kind of capitulation to "traditional" norms. This stark dichotomy, however, belies the complexity of the choices underpinning how, when, and why professional women marry or do not marry. Indeed, some of the most complex narratives of individuality come from women who have crafted their stories as single women, well outside the love marriage/arranged marriage dichotomy, even as they are always implicitly in conversation with these norms.

At the age of thirty, Shilpa is typical of single professional IT women who project themselves as "settled" in their marital status and narrate their life trajectories as a result of individual decisions and circumstances that moved them away from their class and family backgrounds. I met Shilpa in her apartment in Koramangala, an affluent suburb of Bangalore known for its profusion of tech companies. Shilpa's place is just a short walk away from Koramangala's posh mall, the Forum. Unlike many single women in the industry, Shilpa lives on her own, occasionally visiting her family, whose members live a few hours away. Her flat was neat and modest, populated with shelves of books, simple furniture, and a small television. From the outset, it was clear that Shilpa was practical and grounded—she does not spend time or money on expensive clothes, outings, or other similar activities that seem to be emblematic of IT professionals. Indeed, for a woman of her means and freedom, Shilpa seemed to me to live a rather austere lifestyle.

Shilpa is one of only three women in my sample (of sixty living in India) from a rural or small-town background who has stayed in the industry more than five years. Shilpa's personal transformation over the course of her career possesses a fundamentally different character from her counterparts coming from urban middle-class backgrounds. Shilpa is among a small but significant contingent of IT professionals who come from small towns. Although many IT professionals and human resources personnel use employees like Shilpa as evidence that IT employs "rural" people, Shilpa grew up in a financially secure household that relied upon a stable government job (rather than agriculture)—a situation similar to her urban peers. Yet, Shilpa's upbringing was worlds away from the vibrant metropolis of Bangalore. She grew up with no television, radio, or exposure to city life. Although her sisters are both highly educated, and one of them continues to be a practicing doctor despite marriage and children, by Shilpa's account their knowledge of the rapid changes taking place in urban India is limited, at best, even today. Shilpa got into an engineering college in a small town a few hours north of Bangalore and landed an IT job before she even graduated. She was the first in her family to move to the city for a career, a move that caused some trepidation for her family, despite their pride in her success. At first, she lived as a paid guest in a shared accommodation in Bangalore, a common arrangement for young single women working in Indian cities with family elsewhere. Many years later, she moved into her current living situation.

Shilpa's expectation to marry shaped her initial foray into her career. She says that she did not see herself as a career-oriented person when she began working. She did not even find software work to be very challenging or interesting, so she just completed the work allotted to her and went home on time. A mediocre performer, she never stayed at work late and assumed that she would quit working once she was married. Over time, however, her relationship to her work shifted. Under the mentorship of a new manager in a new job a year later, Shilpa started to work long hours, began loving her work, and became a star performer. Slowly, the satisfaction she derived from her work started to change the way she viewed herself: "I'm a perfectionist, and the project was interesting. It was amazing. It was tremendous. I felt as if I can do anything. Up until then, I hadn't really used my skills. Then, I moved to the next project, with the manager who had worked with me before this project. He saw a huge change in me, because I was taking responsibility for everything. He was amazed. He didn't expect it from me at all. Even my relationship with my colleagues changed. They looked to me to check over things." When her colleagues started to look at her differently, and she continued to succeed in each subsequent project, Shilpa began a virtuous spiral of promotions and high expectations, where her work got her a promotion, and thus more confidence and drive, which would earn her another promotion. This process has been continuing over the last several years in an upward trajectory that has made her more invested in her job and her personal development on the job. Simultaneously, it seems she has become less invested in her old expectations of herself, especially with regard to marriage.

Shilpa's growing excellence at her job was not the only factor shaping this shifting sense of her own individuality. Indeed, interpersonal interactions in the workplace also have played a critical role in informing how Shilpa has decided to view herself and her future. Shilpa spoke at length about a romantic friendship that she had developed with a colleague at work, and how the end of that relationship affected her. Having experienced the relationship completely on her own, outside the purview of her family, Shilpa dealt with its end by turning to an even more autonomous view of herself: "Actually, [the relationship] made me change a lot. You cannot take anyone for granted, whoever may be the person. However close—husband, wife, son, daughter, sister, friend, anybody. No one can be taken for granted. Now, I don't get attached, I keep a distance, though I may do good things for them. But emotional bond, I keep it as minimal as possible." Her experiment with choosing a potential mate had the effect of moving her away from the expectations of her family and perhaps away from the expectations she had of herself to marry. Shilpa has moved toward a more self-consciously individualistic view of herself as independent and completely self-sufficient, a view that Shubha and Rani never quite came to adopt themselves. At the age of thirty, Shilpa is past what is generally believed to be a suitable age to be married, though she still sees marriage as something she might want. Unlike the former incarnation of herself, however, she does not view marriage and family as her singular aim in life. She wishes to be financially independent, whether or not she marries, and she wants to be able to continue to support her parents. Too distant from small-town life and involved in work to agree to a match of her parents' choosing, and too cautious to date someone of her own choosing, Shilpa remains suspended in an uncertain individuality growing out of her own family background as well as her own personal experience.

As with many of her peers, Shilpa's interests have turned toward continuing her education within the field, and later expanding the scope of her work to include philanthropic goals. Echoing discourses of constant growth and personal change so common within the IT industry, Shilpa believes that continuously improving oneself is the key to success in IT. She has nurtured an interest in business education outside of work, meant to spur her rise into management. Over a couple of months, she read a book assigned in MBA courses that she borrowed from a friend, and she believes that the knowledge she derived from the book made an immediate impact in her work. Shilpa also speculated about getting out of IT and entering the nonprofit sector, a prospect she found extremely appealing on moral grounds. For the time being, however, she has resigned herself to the fact that there is no money in it, and that she still wishes to make a good salary in order to be able to send money to her parents, as she has been doing for many years now. Shilpa cannot completely disavow the economic incentives of IT as Shubha and Rani do, yet she still asserts virtue and respectability by supporting her family and expressing a desire to work in the nonprofit sector.

Notions of merit and individual accomplishment fostered in the IT workplace have importantly shaped Shilpa's narrative of herself. Still, those discourses became meaningful in her own personal life through their interactions with previously existing gendered expectations surrounding marriage and family, as well as her distance from her small-town family and the set of experiences with which she grew up. The experience of the industry has fostered a particular set of desires, expectations, and decisions that have accompanied the attainment of financial independence and a place in India's cultural elite. Shilpa's experiences in the workplace have made her family less able to relate to her everyday life, which has in turn made Shilpa feel more independent and removed from their expectations, freeing up space to set new expectations for herself. The sense of self that she has cultivated is deeply skeptical of middle-class narratives of the family and women's place in it—narratives that are dominant even in the seemingly open-ended IT sector. Shilpa does not reject the centrality of family in these discourses altogether. Indeed, her continued attachment to her parents and her insistence on continuing to support them financially figures prominently into her career plans, present and future. Certainly, she derives a sense of moral virtue and respectability from this arrangement, even as she postpones marriage and lives on her own. Shilpa's refusal of marital norms, or perhaps her inability to fulfill them, opens up new and complicated futures that may fit only uneasily alongside respectable Indian middle-class ideals, but Shilpa is able to gloss over these inconsistencies, however thinly, by grounding herself in her individual accomplishments.

Devika offers another example of a single, professional IT woman whose navigation of marital norms figures prominently into her sense of self and the life trajectory that has resulted from it. Unlike with most of my other informants, I did not formally interview Devika. Instead, I became close to her during my time living in Bangalore and I was in touch with her over a number of years, reconnecting with her each of the three times I returned to Bangalore between 2004 and 2008 and electronically in each interim. When I met her in 2004, she was a human resources professional at a small Bangalore firm, and she was the person her boss turned to when I requested his help with getting me in touch with employees for interviews. Devika became my contact person for the dozen or so interviews I conducted at that firm, and each time I met her we spent more and more time together. I found her to be warm, welcoming, articulate, and thoughtful. Plump and always looking slightly disheveled, Devika was the social butterfly of her workplace, always in touch with a wide circle of friends and colleagues and always willing to help others. Devika's experiences and dilemmas offer insight into yet another mode of individuality that has come of age in the IT workplace—one that appears to operate on a logic similar to those of her peers, even as it stumbles upon new and unforeseen dilemmas. Her single marital status figures prominently into her everyday navigations of work, family, and her social life, yet these interactions, in stark contrast to the practical, grounded Shilpa, provide insight into how a very different background and set of experiences can lead to a completely different sense of self derived from the IT industry, even in the same city.

Devika grew up in faraway Orissa, the only daughter of well-educated, well-respected urban parents. She performed extremely well academically and left Orissa to come to Bangalore for her degree, staying on to work in the field of human resources after college. Even at the age of twenty-six, in comparison to Shilpa, Devika seemed to belong to another generation altogether. She spent her leisure time at upscale malls, spent liberally on clothes, shoes, and outings, and rarely cooked. Devika's sparsely furnished Bangalore apartment was often strewn with clothes and open packets of snack foods, offering the impression of a person who was always just stopping by home. Although she never spoke of romance per se, she was clear that arranged marriage would be a last resort for her. She seemed to hide her life in Bangalore from her faraway parents, as if the city was her space of independence. She often said that she felt constrained in her hometown, as if all eyes were upon her because the community was so small. Had she desired, she could have long since returned to Orissa, even for work, but she avoided this option at all costs and was postponing the question of marriage as long as possible, an extension facilitated by her distance from her parents and home.

When I met her, Devika was coming out of a traumatic romantic relationship while fending off the demands of her parents that she marry someone they had arranged for her back home in Orissa. A few months later, when the relationship had ended completely, her parents beckoned her home for an arranged marriage yet again. This time, it seemed she could no longer put off the proposition. She quit her job in Bangalore, left for Orissa, and informed me that she would very likely be married in the next two to three months.

Several months later, I reconnected with Devika electronically and was surprised to find her back in Bangalore. She told me that she could not stand to marry any of the potential matches that were presented to her and had come back to Bangalore as soon as she found a new job. In January 2007, when I was back in Bangalore for research, I caught up with her again. Now working for a high-end American multinational in a more technical position, Devika seemed to have regained her emotional composure and seemed as confident as ever, or so she led me to believe. Several months after our meetings in Bangalore, however, when I reconnected with Devika electronically, she was again heartbroken and, this time, deeply in debt. Another terrible breakup with a man she had loved had cleaned her out financially, leaving her alone and unable to turn either to her family in Orissa or to her colleagues in Bangalore for help.

As a young single woman living in Bangalore, Devika was financially on her own feet when I met her in 2004, although she hinted on occasion that she borrowed money from her parents at times to stay afloat, suggesting that she spent almost as much as she made, if not more. Her work opened up for her a lifestyle and a circle of friends that allowed her not only freedom from parental authority, but also freedom for the personal development that she values. Her financial independence, however, bears an ambivalent relationship to her personal autonomy. While her work has certainly opened up a freedom for her that she could have never experienced otherwise, her financial independence has complicated her life course in ways she could have never predicted and perhaps never desired. She takes for granted financial independence, rejects conventional relationships and marriages, and chooses to forge a path driven by individual desires and ambitions, be they for the perfect mate or the ideal job, however difficult that path may be. This was made possible by Devika's well-paid job and position, as well as her freedom from financial responsibility toward her family and her freedom from their direct or indirect supervision of her everyday life. Yet, her choices have not been able to win her the long-term stability she seems to desire. At the same time, she is keenly aware that she has always had choices, however poorly they may have turned out for her. Her financial independence gave her the ability to reject marriage, but the process of choosing her own mate has turned out messier than she anticipated. Distanced from her family, Devika rejected the dominant norms of femininity and family, whether consciously or unconsciously; even as she might wish for the stability of arranged marriage in the midst of her personal turmoil, she forcefully rejects it in practice.

Devika's spending patterns, job satisfaction, class background, and leisure practices line up closely with the prototypical IT workers that Bharathi dubs "clones." Yet, Devika's quest for a special individuality, as well as her distance and independence from her family, creates myriad possibilities for life experiences that differ sharply from the normative experiences of the industry, especially with regard to the shaping of gendered selves. Devika's brand of individuality expresses itself through her romantic relationships, in which she invests herself mightily and with full faith each time, viewing such relationships perhaps as an alternative to the sensibility she grew up with—a rejection (however unconscious) of the dominant mode of femininity she sees around her. Neither Shilpa nor Devika have married, yet Shilpa's life possesses a quiet, pragmatic stability that she reinforces through her austere lifestyle and her support of her parents. Although she perceives immense experiential distance between her own everyday life and her parents' small-town existence, Shilpa strives to maintain contact with them through frequent visits and financial support. Despite not having married, Shilpa maintains an individuality that is bounded by notions of self-control, family values, and virtue. Devika, in contrast, is from an upper-class urban background and seems to be constantly running away from her family, making no attempt to justify or moralize her lifestyle. Where one heartbreak was enough to caution Shilpa against romance, Devika moves from one heartbreak to the next, ostensibly looking for love, even as she rejects the stable options that her family continues to present her with. Despite the striking contrasts in their experiences as single professional IT women, however, in both their cases it is clear that the imperative to marry in their twenties (and their unwillingness or inability to meet that imperative) has played a very prominent role in shaping how the ideologies of individualism promoted in the workplace have translated into their everyday lives. The stories of Devika and Shilpa show us not only the abiding centrality of gender, age, family, and class in understanding how individuality becomes real to professional IT women, but also the specific creative strategies through which young women deal with the imperative to marry, an imperative that the advent of the IT industry has done little to change.

Gendered Ambitions and the Making of a "New" Respectability

The imperative to marry and forge a particular kind of virtuous individuality, embedded both in the family one is born into and the family one creates, takes on a very different shape in men and women. Masculine narratives of the self assert individuality not only through the actualization of inner potential, but also often through a reassertion of conventional gender roles in the workplace and beyond. Feminine narratives often begin with an emphasis on the ways in which women's inner potential is unlocked by the workplace, and then move subsequently to the ways in which women's lives are deeply informed by expectations that balance family and home. I turn now to the stories of Madhav, a thirty-eight-year-old single man, and Mamta, a twenty-eight-year-old married woman, both high achievers and in higher management positions. Madhav and Mamta tell compelling stories of the actualization of their individual selves, but their gendered subjectivities shape their life outcomes in divergent ways, providing insight into how gender shapes the ambition, trajectory of upward mobility, and conception of the balance between family and work among IT professionals.

Madhav works in upper management in a data-processing firm in Mumbai, having moved between software engineering and data processing throughout his career. Like Shilpa, Madhav also comes from a small town—what he termed a "humble background" (in contrast with the "ordinary middle-class background" that most respondents claimed). Relative to women, a larger proportion of men working in the IT industry come from small towns, since it is more acceptable for men to pursue careers far away from their families, so Madhav's story is less unusual than Shilpa's. Still, Madhav's narrative made clear that he beat the odds he was born with by joining the IT industry and attaining the level of status and affluence that he has. In a lengthy narrative peppered with numerical reports on his achievements at each stage of his career, Madhav explained to me the many risks, wrong turns, and seized opportunities it took for him to arrive at the place he is today. His story turns on a Horatio-Alger-style belief in the value of merit, hard work, and a bit of luck. When I asked him if the industry had changed him into an ambitious individual, he responded emphatically, and in a way that highlighted his preexisting passion, drive, and hard work: "[The industry did not change me.] No, the drive was present in me. Previously [when I entered the industry], people were not engineers. They might have had science or arts background. But we had the drive and the passion to work. That passion is missing now [in the current generation, who are driven by money]. We were driven by something different."

Here, Madhav articulates an observation that echoed the feelings of almost all the men I interviewed who have worked in the industry for a decade or more: before IT became so widespread and lucrative, those working in the industry worked without expecting a reward, while today, youngsters entering the industry are driven too much by monetary considerations. In these types of expressions, which are typical of men who came of age in the industry, we find another version of a virtuous individual who disavows financial motivations. But in contrast to the narratives of women like Rani or Shubha, the male disavowal has little to do with family background and more to do with asserting masculine agency. While many women I spoke with also scorned the overt pursuit of material gain, they did so in other ways—by belittling call center workers, for instance, or by placing limits on consumption, discourses to be explored in depth in chapter 5. Men like Madhav, however, saw themselves as virtuous for having worked hard simply for the sake of the work, rather than for any material gains. Considerations of family seldom enter into such narratives, which center around male agency and ability in a competitive environment, a narrative that gels nicely with the principles that drive the knowledge economy. Now that he is successful, Madhav explains that these virtuous motives, refined and reinforced over years in the industry, continue to make him an exceptional worker: "Even today, I come in early. While my office timing is from 9 to 6, I drop in at 8:30. I have that intuition of working. I know that I will get more files today, next day there are more . . . I am on the floor, standing behind people, taking final output data. I can identify a problem that they cannot identify. I teach them on the job . . . They keep wondering how I stand there and manage to find a mistake. That is what drives me. People know that Madhav will ask."

Madhav's account of his own individual drive for self-improvement and actualization is complemented by his exemplary surveillance of those working under him, many of whom are young women from poor or lower-middle-class backgrounds. Indeed, the narrative of virtue that Madhav articulates centers upon his management of those who work under him, and his ability to foster their development into independent individuals:

[In my previous job] I knew each and every person. People came and spoke things which were very personal, about husbands, parents. In fact they could open up [to me]. I had confidence-building exercises with them and it worked. I am proud of that . . . Some boys give their whole salary to families. There is a direct bank credit and their ATM cards are with parents. People just take Rs. 200 or Rs. 300 per month for pocket money. One boy confided this to me. The pocket money he got was not sufficient for him. I gave him additional projects and ensured that the money for this additional work will not be deposited in [the] bank along with [his] salary. It was paid separately as conveyance. Payments are also accounted when given as cash payment, and we made it between the tenth and the fifteenth [of the month] since people tend to spend their regular salary income by the tenth. People were really happy . . . With respect to their family, change was positive as it [the extra money, outside parental control] gave them an identity.

Madhav's pride comes not only from his personal accomplishments in his own career, but also in these small differences he can make in the lives of those working under him. His account of his own influence over them in giving them "an identity" also helps to illuminate his own sense of individuality and accomplishment. Certainly some of the women in upper management I spoke to took pride in their ability to mentor younger women coming up the ranks, yet Madhav's account contains within it a paternalism that feminine stories of mentorship and support lacked; his wisdom and insight gives those youngsters working under him financial freedom, which Madhav believes gives them an identity.

Madhav's relationship to his family and their expectations of him seem to figure quite minimally into his own understanding of his individuality. The inevitable speed of technological advancement validates his decisions in his personal life, and his trusting father concedes to his son's decision not to marry:

> I wanted to have a career. When I moved out of [my village], I thought I will also get settled. That's what we call it. I thought, by [the age of] twenty-five, I should settle. When I came [to Mumbai], I was already twenty-five or twenty-six. Before I knew it, I had already worked for two and a half years. Then Pentium I[2] came. By the time I left my first job, Pentium II came. When Pentium IV came in, I had already put in nine years in this industry. Changes were fast. There were opportunities which could be taken only if I remained single without too many responsibilities . . . Dad stood by me. He said, "If Madhav wants it, he will have it. He is supporting us. We have a son." He believed you should do whatever you want as long as you do it with your money and as long as you understand your worth.

Madhav's self-assurance is informed by an approving, benevolent father who values his son's contribution to the family as much as his ambition. Unlike the ambivalence that single women express, the sense of individuality that Madhav describes is relatively unfettered by cultural expectations of marriage. Indeed, his continued support for his parents and the paternal relationships he fosters in the workplace provide him with ways to embed his individuality in a larger social context while still maintaining himself as the primary agent in his story. By *not* marrying and taking on "too many personal responsibilities," he is able to be a good son *and* an excellent worker, a confident narrative of the self that women like

Shilpa and Devika find more difficult to assert. Madhav explains his success in the industry as resulting from the drive that was already present within him—the drive with which he broke into the industry, beat the odds, and is now occupied in the work of uplifting both his family and those who work under him.

Women who are as successful as Madhav explain and live out their individual stories very differently. Mamta, a twenty-eight-year-old manager with significant experience abroad, provides a striking contrast to Madhav, showing how successful women from urban, middle-class backgrounds who outwardly conform to dominant notions of femininity also subvert those notions by drawing on their own experiences. Mamta carefully accommodates and negotiates dominant norms, even as her actions and life trajectory challenge such norms in important ways. Like Devika, Mamta was among the dozen or so of my informants with whom I maintained a close personal relationship over the years of my study. I formally interviewed her in 2004, but by that time I had already spent a great deal of time with her at work, in her home, and in leisurely settings. When I first met her in 2003, on a pilot study, she was twenty-eight. She had already worked in Europe and the United States and was rapidly rising through the managerial ranks at the educational technology firm she worked at in Mumbai. Mamta is tall among Indian women, built lean, with a ready smile and probing eyes. Unlike many of the women I met, who later told me that they dressed up to meet me for the first time, Mamta wore a comfortable ordinary *salwar kameez* (a long tunic with pants that has become a ubiquitous dress for women in India), *chappals* (Indian-style sandals), and slightly-too-large spectacles to meet me—no designer jeans, brand-name tees, extra make-up, or even contact lenses, which I later found she usually wears in lieu of glasses. In the years that followed that first meeting, Mamta served as an indispensable source of support, personal connections, and encouragement during my subsequent work in Mumbai. Aside from a formal interview I conducted with her in 2004, I visited her in her home very often, eventually got to know her husband, and, later, when her son was born, I met her parents and her new baby. When she moved to the United States in 2006, I reconnected with Mamta and her family.

Mamta is a typical transnational Indian professional, and perhaps ideal in the sense that she fulfills many kinds of competing dominant expectations at once. She is ambitious, hardworking, and extremely talented in her work. Her work has taken her to Europe and the United States on multiple occasions and as a result, even on our first meeting, she displayed a kind of quiet, self-assured cosmopolitanism that is the privilege of the elite. She maintains strong connections to her family and her husband's family, and comes from a "typical middle-class" background—her father worked a steady government job that offered the family enough for a comfortable standard of living in urban Gujarat, albeit with few luxuries. Mamta was not raised in a family that expected her to work, but, from the beginning, she wished to be independent, financially and emotionally. Rather than finding her spouse through the "arranged" system, she too chose her husband herself. As with Shubha's husband, Mamta's husband, Dev, comes from a different linguistic, class, and educational background from herself. Yet, unlike many others, Mamta did not focus on her choice as an act of rebellion or rejection of her family's norms. Rather, it was a matter of course in her personal development that was not to be overly romanticized or discussed. Instead of living off of a credit card, as do many of her peers, Mamta is relatively conservative with her spending. She dresses modestly, pools her money with her husband for expenses, and rarely goes out to eat, preferring home-cooked food and good books to fancy restaurants, bars, and multiplex movie theaters. Politically, Mamta would describe herself as progressive, but she believes that progress for India is occurring through the economic growth and "exposure" that industries like IT are bringing to India's citizens. Disgruntled with the new progressive tax structure imposed by the Congress Party when it took over from the BJP in 2004, Mamta seems to believe largely in open markets, free trade, and a free exchange of information, like many of her peers.[3] She is unusual, though, in that she makes it a point to vote, a practice that most other interviewees did not share. Mamta is thoughtful and careful in speech and displays artistic flair in her love of painting, photography, and graphic design.

Despite her position in the economic and cultural elite of the nation, Mamta's unselfconscious individualism and deeply pragmatic outlook on everything from culture to women's issues to IT have prompted her to make decisions that might be considered unconventional, even subversive. When I interviewed her in 2004, Mamta was one of just two professional women I met in India who were willing to move abroad permanently, even though almost all of them expected or desired to live abroad for a short period. Unlike most others, Mamta did not believe that emigration out of India would be threatening to her cultural identity or that of her children. She refused to romanticize Indian culture in India and refused to accept the generalizations that are made about life in the United States, her destination of choice. Mamta used her extensive work experience in the United States to speak out against nationalist claims about the superiority of Indian culture and the privilege of India as a space of authentic belonging:

> I have been born and brought up in India, but if you ask me why we celebrate Navratri [the festival of the goddess], I couldn't tell you because I've heard nine different things and I don't know which is right. So, that's the same anywhere . . . There are things that are distinct to India, like closeness to family, camaraderie with neighbors . . . There's a network. [But] I've seen that happen abroad also. I really think it depends on who you are and where you spend time and with whom. I have interacted with my clients who have been married for years, not divorced ten times like you see in the media. And they have their grandparents and their family close by and they go there. My friend who just called up, she's a single mom. And she's made her house in such a way that her parents can stay with her. So, it's like the basic family values are going to be the same . . . And if you think the guy's going to do more work around the house just because he's American, I don't think so. The perception that guys do more work there is not right, I think. A lot of it has to do with women too! And I don't think there's some culture in the U.S. that says, 'Go out and have sex at fourteen.' No! It's the media saying it, I don't think that's the culture.

By refusing to make the usual generalizations about American culture, and by focusing on the people in her experience who have shown her a different view of both India and the United States, Mamta rejects nationalistic stereotypes in a subtle but powerful way. In so doing, she participates in cultural streamlining by rendering "things distinct to India" as attainable anywhere—as values she feels confident she can create in her family anywhere she pleases. This perspective opened up opportunities for Mamta that many women like her would have shied away from. In forging her own individual story upon a cultural landscape that rejects dichotomies and divisions that most of her peers take for granted, Mamta is also participating in cultural streamlining processes, rendering "family values" as normal and universal, even as they are also fundamentally "Indian."

After the birth of her son, Mamta switched jobs, opting for a higher position at a different multinational company in Mumbai. I was out of touch with her for some time, but about a year after I saw her in Mumbai in 2005, she had arrived with her husband and son in the United States, having accepted a senior-level liaison position that could be converted into a permanent U.S.-based position. Mamta's move to the United States could be considered radical among her peers; her husband left his job in India to accompany her to the United States, and at the time of our meeting in 2006 he was on a dependent visa, looking after their child during the day while Mamta was at work. Of all the women I interviewed, Mamta is the only person whose husband followed her in a permanent move. While it is common for women to accompany their husbands to the United States for similar opportunities, it is still extremely rare in the IT industry to see a move like Mamta's. Yet, it is clear that for some who rise high enough in the managerial ranks, such a move is possible.

Mamta enacts a gendered individuality even as she remakes and re-forms it. She lives a responsible, grounded lifestyle, remains committed to the welfare of her husband and son, and yet pursues an individualized path of achievement justified through her own personal beliefs and experiences, most of which have taken shape within the IT industry. Her parents are supportive of her decisions, but they seldom figure prominently into her account of her decisions or beliefs. Still, Mamta invokes the importance of family and has made her career moves such that her family can stay together no matter what. In these ways, Mamta's life trajectory is instructive for understanding the individual possibilities that open up as a result of women working in well-paid, high-status positions. Her privilege within class hierarchies and her ability to articulate an acceptably feminine version of individual desire and ambition allow her both to reshape gendered expectations, at least within her own sphere, and to renegotiate the meaning and location of Indianness. Mamta provides only one kind of life trajectory emerging from the pursuit of this kind of embedded individualism. Several other women I interviewed managed to strike a balance between an ambitious career and a kind of respectable femininity that was committed to the family, but Mamta was perhaps the most successful at this.

Individuality as Situated Class Practice

When Bharathi complained about the uniformity of class dispositions in her industry, she seemed to tap into a deeper truth than she realized. The superficial markers of uniformity she cited—speaking English, wearing jeans—might prevail only among a certain subset of her friends in the IT industry. Yet, the uniformity she sensed was a desire she herself shared—a desire for an individual life story driven by personal desires and ambitions. Bharathi's desire for personal growth and development through her personal and professional life tapped into a shared desire that centrally constitutes the disposition of the Indian transnational class. Growing out of an industry culture that places top value on individual merit and achievement, the notion of individual development and actualization is a key aspect of the disposition that is cultivated in IT workplaces, and it is this notion that powerfully shapes the ways in which the ideologies of the IT industry spill into the personal lives of IT professionals.

Yet, the diversity of narratives used to articulate individuality suggests that the selves fostered in the heart of the knowledge economy are never the disembedded, rational individuals that globalization theorists such as Beck, Giddens, and others propose emerge in response to a generalized deterioration of the collective or the state. At best, such accounts might reflect masculine accounts of agency in advanced industrial contexts, and, as thus, should be regarded as restricted to that context. As Indian IT professionals encounter and incorporate notions of individuality in the IT workplace, they do so as individuals embedded in class and family histories who are beholden to gendered imperatives. Against already multilayered backgrounds, the experience of the IT workplace opens up new possibilities for forging a novel sense of self, but these possibilities are always shaped and constrained by preexisting backgrounds. Still, the consistent focus on individual development and achievement is at odds with other characterizations of Indian modes of being that emphasize collectivity, fluidity, and openness—characterizations that dominate both the anthropological literature on selfhood in India and in cross-cultural training modules referenced in the workplace (Hall 1976; Hofstede 1980). Accounts of individual drive and development serve to reshape, re-form, and sometimes reauthenticate notions of what is "Indian," as the individual—in this case the privileged IT professional—

becomes the agent for streamlining notions of what is "Indian" into something transportable and able to be reproduced in the private sphere by individuals. In this way, embedded individuality sets the stage for cultural streamlining. At the level of the individual, notions of what is "Indian"—associated with such practices as being sheltered in the family, supporting one's parents financially, and accepting "arranged" marriages—are made flexible and rendered compatible with an individualistic take on the world. At the same time, these navigations are deeply embedded in the gendered and classed subjectivities of those making these navigations.

Perhaps the clearest arena in which Indian IT professionals reauthenticate Indianness by highlighting its compatibility with individual development is the arena of the family. In private lives that are ostensibly separate from the workplace, IT professional women in particular forge a shared notion of the "good family" as one that naturally grows out of empowered individual choices, while potential tensions between them are effaced or glossed over. Embedded individualism sets the stage for the most intimate forms of cultural streamlining that occur in the home, through delicate gendered "balances" between work and family.

GENDERED "BALANCE" AND THE EVERYDAY
PRODUCTION OF THE NATION

In the summer of 2003, India found a new heroine. She was neither
a movie star nor a politician, neither a beauty queen nor an ath-
lete. Nisha Sharma was just another bride in Delhi, anticipating
the day of her wedding. But, extraordinarily, just hours before
her wedding, Nisha called it off. She reported her would-be husband
to the police for violation of India's largely ignored anti-dowry
act. The groom and his parents had demanded an exorbitant payment the night before the wedding as dowry, apart from the substantial money and household goods that Nisha's parents had already promised as gifts to their daughter and future son-in-law.
Although illegal, such demands, which are not uncommon among
urban middle-class families in India, are seldom opposed. Nisha,
however, enraged by the humiliation caused to her parents and
herself, called the police.

Overnight, Nisha became a celebrity, occupying the limelight of
the Indian media for several weeks. While her groom-to-be spent
what was to be his wedding night in jail, she was surrounded by
media attention. *Rashtriya Sahara*, a Hindi newspaper, headlined
her front-page story with "Bravo: We're Proud of You," and her
family was subsequently flooded with proposals from prospective
grooms who said they would be honored to marry her without
dowry (MacRae 2003). Women's groups lauded her; political parties wooed her to be a spokesperson. Internationally, she received
coverage on the BBC and in most major newspapers in the United
States. The TV program 20/20 covered the entirety of her story at
the height of its international visibility, focusing on Nisha as well
as the dozens of "copycat" incidents that occurred throughout
India following Nisha's story. Most coverage of the incident viewed
it as a sign that social attitudes in India may be changing, and

that Nisha's actions were an indicator of important progress for Indian women. International and domestic media coverage, however, tended to gloss over a critical point in explaining how the "Nisha moment" became possible: twenty-one-year-old Nisha Sharma was a software engineering student. When she sent her fiancé to jail, Nisha did not speak of simply choosing a new groom to marry, as she might have. She told reporters, prospective grooms, and political parties alike that she planned to return to her studies (Amanpour 2003).

Nisha Sharma's story suggests that the choice of a high-tech education over marriage in contemporary India has been validated, at least under some circumstances. The country and the world lauded her courage not only in standing up against regressive social practices, but also for choosing the path of education to channel her future energies. Her actions also seemed to reflect an admirable blend of individual and family-oriented motivations. Her rejection of the marriage served to preserve the honor of her family, which was compromised by the last-minute demands. At the same time, the various media accounts of her story suggest that Nisha made the decisions she did out of her own individual initiative and sense of self-preservation (she did not want to be a part of a family that made unreasonable demands, which she thought might foreshadow her future life). Her ensuing choices, reported months after the incident, reinforced the respect of the nation: Nisha agreed to marry another groom of her parents' choosing—a software engineer, incidentally—and was pictured in all her bridal finery in the press. It was unclear whether she had returned to her studies, as she had announced initially, but Nisha's defiance of dowry convention had already won her such mainstream appeal as a youth role model that her story was subsequently included in a social studies textbook in New Delhi (Pandey 2004).

Nisha displayed an admirable initiative that validated a particular kind of femininity—one that is not submissive, but rather confident and professional. Just as importantly, however, her personal choices ultimately upheld the sanctity of the Indian family. The phenomenon of the Nisha moment speaks to the appeal of a new kind of Indian femininity that is driven by individual motivations and convictions, but also unwavering in its support and orientation toward the family. The model of *respectable femininity* that Nisha's story presents—gutsy, professional, and yet distinctly "Indian" in its prioritization of family—contains a deep resonance with the ideas of domesticity, respectability, and family articulated by the professional Indian IT women I interviewed. Nisha's decisions are held up as exemplary for the nation precisely because she stands up against "backward" traditions while also standing up for her family.

Respectable femininity, and the kind of family it supports, comprises the crux of a streamlined, transnational notion of Indianness. By "balancing" the desires and motivations of the individual with the duties and obligations of the family, professional women produce a notion of Indianness that draws upon older notions of a sacred, feminized domestic sphere while also engaging in the progress of economic and social development. Partha Chatterjee has famously described the importance of the gendered division between the outer and inner spheres in the context of the Indian nationalist movement (Chatterjee 1990). New gendered "balances" recreate older strategies of cultural preservation that seek to prevent the feminized private sphere from becoming *essentially* Westernized. Since it is women who are responsible for this task of cultural preservation, efforts to "balance" work and home effectively possess deep cultural valances, and a successful "balance" participates in the everyday production of a new Indianness. Their location in the private sphere also makes these strategic gendered "balances," which are solidified primarily in the home, particularly amenable to the lifestyle of a transnational class. Because the notion of the good Indian family is situated entirely in the private sphere, it can be upheld and reproduced anywhere, even as India remains a privileged site. Because it is constituted through the decisions of individual women, professional IT women themselves tend to view the preservation and renewal of the Indian family as compatible with their own actualization and empowerment, even though there are clearly tensions that appear in women's everyday lives. Cultural streamlining strategies that begin in the workplace are subsequently realized through gendered "balances" in the home that fold a multiplicity of potential meanings of Indianness into culturally loaded navigations that fall upon the shoulders of women.

In this chapter, I examine how professional IT women conceptualize themselves as particular kinds of workers who are symbolically at the helm of the family, and, implicitly, the nation. To reproduce, and in doing so, reinvent and *achieve* the good Indian family, professional women must strike a delicate and much-valued "balance." It is this "balance" that lies at the heart of a "new" Indian culture: an appropriate difference that can be showcased to the world. Striking this balance allows for the enactment of respectable femininity, a critical symbolic performance in which professional women strive to participate. The reiteration of the word "balance" among my interviewees conveys a sense of careful tightrope walking that reveals the necessarily tricky space these women inhabit, even when their narratives seem to naturalize and normalize these balances. However delicate, this sense of "balance" governs the values of many areas of family life, including work/life priorities, moralities of consumption, and the rules by which women must abide when interacting with the world outside the home. The notion of the "right" balance comprises the dominant model of femininity in India's transnational class and thus acts as a form of symbolic capital (see chapter 1).

In another sense, the term "balance" conveys the position of IT women in a contemporary discursive universe of urban, working women. Especially with regard to consumption and interactions with the outside world, professional IT women position themselves as situated somewhere "between" a bank worker and a call center worker; they emphasize— sometimes vehemently—their differences from both of these kinds of working women. In so doing, they forge a unique symbolic position for themselves in which they incorporate the logics of the knowledge economy into their intimate, everyday lives while reinventing the culture of the nation.

Professional women draw upon deeply resonant notions of the family, even as they reconcile those meanings with notions of individual achievement imbibed from the workplace. The notion of prioritizing the family can take myriad forms—from prioritizing family over work, to supporting parents financially, to avoiding a corrupting materialism in order to uphold the emotional bonds of family life. These ways of articulating and upholding the family are supported not only at home, but also at work in a surprising synergy with the IT workplace, where the private world of the family is reinforced, encouraged, and renewed. The IT workplace seeks to empower women (see chapter 2), but it also allows space for women to make choices that prioritize their families over their careers. Professional women perceive these choices to be driven by individual desires and personal morality, reflecting the extension of the logics of the workplace to the sphere of the domestic. The result of these navigations is a sense of family that is distinct from other, less cosmopolitan imaginings of the Indian family, while also being distinct from non-Indian, "Western" families. In making these distinctions, professional IT women reproduce the "appropriate difference" forged in the workplace in the intimate space of the family—a difference that can claim to be "global," while still being rooted in ostensibly "Indian" values.

Through gendered "balances" in the sphere of the domestic, then, the realm of the family becomes the ultimate realization of cultural streamlining and appropriate difference. "Good" families can assert a particular version of "Indianness" as normal, taken for granted, and transportable. By asserting the normalcy of the Indian family, Indian IT professionals also assert a cultural identification that is distinctive and moral—a progressive improvement on an already superior sense of Indianness.

Family First, Job Second

As the high status of women in the IT workplace has become established, the "time bind" between obligations to work and obligations to home has become an important factor in women's lives. In contrast to public sector jobs, in which many urban Indian women have been working for decades, IT jobs require long hours and sometimes employees must work from home or on the weekends. The divide between work and home is blurred; a woman's job begins to impinge on her family life. In a society where this kind of time bind for middle-class women is relatively new, questions about the priorities between professional and personal lives arise.[1] Interview data suggest that women consistently choose to be career oriented, but rarely at the expense of family life, which is almost always privileged over the stimulation or even the salary a woman may receive from her job.[2] Most women describe themselves as "not too ambitious" and view a career as something supplemental to a married life with children. They admire other women who "rise up" in the company hierarchy, but often think of these women as having sacrificed something crucial or as being "aggressive." In these narratives, we find some continuity with nationalist conceptions of women as the protectors and nurturers of Indian culture—for these women, the role models are not the women who gave up their families for success, but those who manage to balance the two, most often by sacrificing the climb up the company hierarchy.

The clearest articulations of prioritizing family over career came from young women who were relatively new to the IT industry as they explained to me their goals and aspirations for their future lives. Gautami, a twenty-six-year-old graphics specialist, has been working for about five years. Her movement between several areas of the high-tech industry complements Gautami's impressive academic background. She began with a commerce degree, moved into IT through vocational training for job prospects, and has since been in positions that have ranged from teaching computer programming to public relations and graphic design. At the time of our interview, she was managing a team of graphic designers who design the illustrations for Hewlett-Packard printer manuals and using her substantial income to back her parents and siblings financially. Gautami's plans for her future, however, hung largely on her parents' opinion that it was high time that she married. Despite the stimulation she gets from her job, Gautami was very clear that from the moment she marries her priorities will change. She said that she would love to be a housewife, care for her in-laws, and look after her kids. If her husband allows her, she will continue to work until she has kids, but not afterward. Later, she explained, "Around thirty-five, forty, when you're rising up the ladder, I think I'd prefer to settle down with my family and my husband . . . Because ultimately, it's your family for whom you're doing it. And if they're not happy, it really doesn't make any difference, so it's better that you spend time with them and make them happy rather than earning money and money and money and nothing else." Gautami clearly expressed that the stimulation she enjoys from work is ultimately linked to her support of a family—her parents and siblings for now, and her own husband and children in the future. As such, when climbing the ladder becomes a purely material pursuit that does not benefit the inner well-being of the family, it is no longer necessary.

Women of Gautami's age who are ready to shift their own career trajectories based on the expectations of their future husbands respond to prevailing attitudes among men of the same age. Several of the IT men I interviewed who were looking to marry were clear in their expectation that their future wives would have their priorities in order. At the same time, they value the professionalism and efficiency of women in IT, a quality that they expect to translate into the domestic realm. Dhiraj of Bangalore, who was engaged to be married at the time of our interview, explained this expectation in a matter-of-fact manner during our conversation:

We [IT guys] like our job[s]; if she is like me, she too will like working. [That] is the general [line of] thinking. I should be considerate and give her the comfort that she needs. It is not like [the] Indian working style of olden days when the women had to come back home and do all the work . . . I feel that IT girls are managing their houses much better when compared to middle-class girls who are teachers, small-time job holders, or government job holders. They may have more ego, but IT girls know the problems and how we struggle to get things done. [They] understand . . . the importance of money. They are much better in comparison to girls in other professions.

Before I met my fiancée I was looking at all sorts of options. I used to meet around five to ten girls at a time, some from IT and some from non-IT, some typical homemakers. I wanted an employed girl. Not from the finance angle, but for her to have her space. She can go until she can manage [to work and take care of our family]. She should not be too enthusiastic about working. She should be a secondary income earner. Not sit at home and sit idle. There are other constraints. Some onsite assignments you can take your family; if she cannot work what would she do in a new place? If she is employed, it helps. I feel there are a lot of changes happening. I have seen a couple of guys. All my classmates are married to employed girls from IT and they are doing great. Doing very well. That is what one wants eventually from life.

Among the married professionals I interviewed, men were almost always the primary breadwinners. In the few cases they were not, as in the case of Shantha explored below, this fact was concealed from extended family and colleagues, albeit thinly. These outcomes emerge from ostensibly shared understandings between young men and women concerning the gendered division of labor in the home and the subordinate position of women in the marital relationship. The primacy of the woman as mother and protector of the domestic sphere is not fundamentally transformed by her employment in a lucrative global industry; rather it is enhanced in unexpected ways.

Geetha, a twenty-six-year-old engineer in Bangalore who was expecting her first child at the time of our interview, expressed clearly the ways in which she had to navigate between her husband's expectations and her own desire to work, and how the forthcoming child made it dubious that she would be able to continue. In an account that echoes Dhiraj's idea that women should work, but not too much, Geetha eventually decides that she will give up work to follow her husband's wishes and take care of the family, albeit hesitantly, and hopefully, on a temporary basis:

> Ladies' career—you cannot say. They have a lot of things in their life. Getting married, having kids, bringing them up, and simultaneously working is a problem. You won't be either dedicated to your family or to your job. It'll be a fifty-fifty kind of thing. It's hard. . . . And he [my husband] doesn't encourage that, basically . . . Earlier, he was kind of skeptical about [my working]. He said, like, 'I think that'll spoil our family life.' . . . I stayed at home for some days and I was getting very bored. I told him this and he said, 'Okay, if you're interested and you get a job, fine.'
>
> But this is only until the baby. [In any case,] I don't like putting the baby in a crèche and going for job and all that . . . But then, we'll see. My parents are here and local, so that's kind of an advantage. That's the reason I'm thinking that maybe after the baby is a year or so, it's possible [to work again].

Geetha's situation reveals the extent to which professional careers for women have not transformed the gender division of labor in the home, and that in marriage men still largely expect women to remain in charge of the domestic sphere. While women often comply with those expectations, albeit with reservations at times, the notion that the moral choice is to prioritize family over career never comes into question, even for Geetha as she tries to imagine her life as a working mother.

Women who have remained in the industry more than five years, and who have stayed on through marriage and children, express much more complex views on the dilemmas balancing the demands of home and work, going beyond the navigation of the gendered division of labor in the home and hinting at the more symbolic aspects of these balances. Human resources personnel I spoke to agreed that the five-year point is a critical benchmark at which managers determine whether a female employee will pursue a long-term career in IT. More than a third of the interviews I conducted in India were among career women who had crossed that mark. For the most part, these women overwhelmingly say that they have no ambitions of rising beyond a certain point in a company's hierarchy, and this is true even among the most successful women I interviewed. Still, a few women I interviewed had made what they described as very large sacrifices in terms of family life in order to make a successful career. Even these women, however, use various tactics and strategies to uphold the appearance of a wholly fulfilled family life while downplaying obvious tensions.

One such woman was Shantha, an ambitious manager working for a large American multinational in Bangalore. Unlike most of the women I interviewed, Shantha's husband's income is erratic; although educated, he does not work in a high-tech field, and for most of their eight-year marriage Shantha has been the primary breadwinner in the family. Shantha has a six-year-old daughter, whom she never took time off work to spend time with, even when she was a baby. Shantha admits that her work "gets under [her] skin"; she thinks about work constantly, comes home late at night very frequently, and even mentioned an instance when her husband caught her talking about a project from work in her sleep. To compensate for her absence at home, Shantha pays a full-time, live-in domestic worker, Kirti, who has lived with them since her daughter was born. Shantha claims that Kirti is part of the family—she eats with them, travels with them on holidays, and is paid handsomely. Shantha's mother-in-law also lives with them and acts as yet another parental figure in Shantha's daughter's life. Shantha's success at work has earned her the begrudging respect of her family, all of whom are based in Bangalore. Though she is fully aware of the extent to which they gossip behind her back, she says that no one dares question her. Whether they disapprove of the extent to which Shantha embraces Kirti in the family or her late hours, Shantha says, "[I have become a kind of] goddess in the family. Not the acknowledged goddess, but people think twice before questioning me." Shantha's confidence in making such a statement suggests that her economic power has indeed translated into other kinds of power within her household, even if this power is not as openly acknowledged as it would have been had she been a man with the same level of success at work.

Although she feels deeply tied to an Indian cultural identification at a personal level, Shantha realizes that her status as a bearer of culture in the family is tremendously compromised. She understands that most women continue to prioritize their families over their work, and that this choice is the one that is coded as "Indian." This "choice" has persisted strongly, despite all the recent changes, among women of her generation and beyond. Shantha explains: "This husband of mine says, 'You're not fit to be an Indian. You don't have your family priorities right.' But I think that [those priorities are] very clear for a lot of people. That traditional role playing. To a large extent it is still maintained. In spite of the fact that you work so much, you will still find houses like ours to be exceptional." Women like Shantha, who play what would conventionally be a masculine role—that of a breadwinner who is committed to a career above everything—find it difficult to enact respectable femininity in their everyday personal and family lives. Because she does not put family first and work second, she is unable to become a convincing symbol for a renewed national culture centered on the family. To a large extent, Shantha has internalized the individualized logics of the IT workplace, but the ways in which she brings those values into the home do not allow her the symbolic power to achieve the dominant "good family" model. She must constantly defend her unconventional choices and their impact upon how her family might be perceived by others. To this end, she does not reveal the true financial situation of the household to anyone, nor does she leave space for her family to criticize her.

The "balance" that women must work out is not restricted to the private domestic sphere. The IT workplace also places a clear value upon respectable femininity that may serve to naturalize, justify, and even valorize "not so ambitious" women by diverting attention away from a glass ceiling. Management practices, especially in Indian corporations, seem to offer informal but nonetheless systematic "concessions" for women, which vary according to their marital status and familial restrictions. Firms value female employees, especially those that stay on beyond the five-year mark. This is because these women are much more loyal than men, who are likely to switch over to another firm for a higher salary at any time. Personnel in human resources and upper management explained to me that the high demand for IT talent means that young professionals are constantly on the lookout for more lucrative opportunities, making for very high turnover. Women are much less likely to leave a firm that they feel comfortable with. As one human resource manager said, "Women are much more reliable. If they come back after marriage or after having a kid, they will be the most loyal employees you can ever have. You can count on them."

It is not surprising, then, that firms tend to make an effort to accommodate women wherever possible, even though in training women are told that there will be no special concessions for them. Some "exceptions" that were mentioned to me during interviews include allowances for married women with children to go home earlier than their teammates on the night of a tight deadline, or escorts home by male coworkers on a late working night. Such arrangements highlight the acceptance and support for professional women who enact particular forms of femininity. The lack of concessions for most single women can be viewed, then, as a penalty. For example, Bharathi of Mumbai, who is single, expressed frustration at the extent to which her job has taken over her life. She regretted her inability to say "no" when her boss asked her to work overtime and frequently worked through the night to meet ever tighter deadlines. Yet, in the same firm, in the same division, thirty-six-year-old Kala, a married mother who, like Bharathi, is also a content writer, explained that she rarely stayed late, and that management generally understood that she needed to be at home with her family. In at least two of the five firms in which I interviewed multiple people, it seemed clear that in most cases women with families were more able to set clear boundaries with management about their working hours, while single women more often complained about endless demands from work. This dynamic serves the industry well by retaining experienced employees and pushing unmarried employees, who tend to be younger, to work very hard. Most IT professionals accept this naturalized give-and-take understanding because they perceive these dynamics to be driven by personal choices and ambitions (or lack thereof). Furthermore, the special understanding granted women with families also helps to cloak a glass ceiling in the garb of "choice" and Indian womanhood, such that women themselves are fairly convinced that the odds are not stacked against them.[3] Indeed, the vast majority of the women I interviewed believe that the low percentages of women in upper management in IT reflect the choices that Indian women make for themselves and their families.

Interviewees working in Silicon Valley expressed the work-home balance in gendered terms that were very similar to their counterparts in urban India, suggesting that the prioritization of family over work for Indian women retains a symbolic value indicating "Indianness" and family, even (and perhaps especially) in the diaspora. In particular, women in Silicon Valley who are faced with the decision of whether or not to move back to India find that decision deeply entangled with career sacrifices they are already making as Indian mothers living in the United States. Lakshmi, a thirty-four-year-old engineer working in Silicon Valley, expressed the difficulties she faces when balancing her professional and family lives, and how the move back to India, which her husband has already decided will be best for the family, further challenges these difficulties to a point that she may no longer be able to bear. For Lakshmi, her work is a part of her—something that gives her meaning and motivation. Despite this, she put boundaries on her career climb after she had children, declining offers for managerial positions and keeping her hours to a minimum. Her decision to continue working, however, has led to vocal opposition from her mother-in-law, who feels it is not right for her to be going to work when she has children at home. Lakshmi's own mother, who also lives in the Bay Area, has supported Lakshmi's career through these difficult times, filling in with childcare when needed. Although Lakshmi's husband has already accepted a position in Bangalore, she finds herself pulled in opposite directions. While Lakshmi feels that the imperatives of Indian motherhood require her to move to India for the sake of keeping the family together, she is hesitant. Her predicament is heavy with cultural meanings. If she decides not to join her husband in India, choosing to pursue her career and life in the United States instead, her status as an Indian mother will be in jeopardy. If she agrees to go, she will have sacrificed her present career for an uncertain future in which she may or may not find a job. Yet, she feels compelled to choose the latter option in order to uphold her Indianness by being a good mother, a dilemma she expressed pointedly in her interview. She explained, "I'm now caught in this conflict . . . One side of me says that I should put aside my wants and preferences and make it work for the family. But the other side of me says, if I'm not okay with this, how efficient am I going to be as a person? . . . How am I going to make it work for my kids?" Lakshmi is similar to her peers in Silicon Valley who articulate a range of attitudes concerning this dilemma. Several of the women I interviewed had already scaled back their careers for family considerations. In some cases, this choice was a wholehearted one, while, in cases like Lakshmi's, it was an ambivalent one.

Most other women who experience the stimulation and respect of a well-paid, high-status job "choose" to prioritize a home life in the final analysis. Such a choice displays their individual virtue and respectability as representatives of a new and upcoming modern class in which women work in privileged workplaces. At the same time, the choice to prioritize family over career, while interpreted as an entirely individualistic decision, also works to produce a new India, where the culture of the middle-class family still lies at the center of its cultural superiority. Shantha is respected for her work and for her success, but she cannot quite convert her economic success into a respectability that supports the reinvention of the good Indian family. Although older notions of middle-class status and national culture, which highlighted the importance of a woman devoted entirely to the domestic realm, are being modified in important ways through the IT industry, this reshaped notion of respectable femininity is always in conversation with its older discursive counterpart. The "option" to stay at home and take care of husband, children, and in-laws is always the invisible norm that women relate themselves to. Those who reject the conventional notion of a respectable woman's place as being in the home reject it explicitly, though they cannot ignore its potential influence on their choices. Most women inhabit an ambiguous space between a new, reshaped notion of respectable femininity that includes home and a "safe" job that is still entrenched in global networks, and an older vision of idealized feminine domesticity. In the course of these navigations, the nation is imagined and reimagined. The cultural streamlining of transnational "Indianness" and the production of the "appropriate difference" of the Indian family—as superior, and yet "normal" and universal—occur in close cooperation with the individualized, gendered "choice" to prioritize family over home.

The right "balance" of work and home, however primary, works in concert with other gendered "balances," which together govern the production and stabilization of a "new" transnational Indianness. I turn now to the ways in which family virtue surrounding consumption practices constitutes another important aspect of these private cultural processes, considering the importance of the figures of the bank worker and the call center worker in constituting the status and the respectability of the IT professional.

Consumption without Materialism

The recent influx of cash and consumer goods in urban India has made what were previously luxury items—a car, a microwave oven, foreign cosmetics—into necessities for the upwardly mobile classes. Indeed, global consumer goods have become critical markers of status among India's new middle class (Rajagopal 2001b; Lakha 1999; Fernandes 2000a). A critical value of respectable femininity and the "good" Indian family, however, is the avoidance of materialism. How, then, do IT women and their families engage in the consumption practices that have made them the darlings of marketing experts and foreign companies around the world while still managing to renounce materialism? In the previous chapter, we saw that some individuals disavow economic motivations for working in IT, and this denial allows them to access other moralities, namely the intrinsic value of hard work, individual drive, and service to society. In many ways, the various discourses surrounding consumption, materialism, and the family elaborate upon these values. Professional women situate moral, high-status consumption practices against the opposite extremes of the bank worker, who comes to symbolize a conservative, Indian, working femininity, and the call center worker, who comes to symbolize an impulsive, Western, not-so-respectable working femininity. Consumption patterns that uphold, reinforce, or add status to the family are acceptable and do not signal materialism, while leisure practices that spend money irresponsibly, outside the purview of the family, signal an unacceptable morality. This unacceptable morality—a capitulation to materialism—is marked both by call center workers living in urban India and by those living in foreign locales.

Some professional women identify the ability to spend freely as central to their identity as women working in a highly paid, competitive industry, one that allows them freedoms that other working women in India have never had. Asserting this ability, then, is not only acceptable but also desirable. Seema, a forty-year-old technical writer in Mumbai, explained the importance of impulsive spending and consumption to her own identity by explaining how she sees herself as fundamentally different from women working in a government bank. For decades, public sector banks have been a large source of employment for middle-class women, especially in Mumbai. The stereotypical view of the female bank worker is that of a bank teller—a woman who arrives at work at 9:30 a.m. and closes her books at 5:00 p.m., having done more or less the same thing every day. She makes a decent income, which she contributes to her family. Seema feels she has something special as an IT worker that her counterpart in banking could never have: "She [the bank teller] knows that, okay, I can only spend 10,000 rupees in a month. So, in the family income chart, her place, her income, her expenses, is very definitely marked. She's not the kind of person who would suddenly book a flight to Bangalore for the weekend because her friend is getting married. No, she won't do that. Whereas I would do that . . . Not that she's not making good money, but that she would have planned everything. Whereas I may not have a job tomorrow, so I can be a little impulsive." Seema never questions the respectability of the bank worker, whom she regards as committed to her family, careful in her budgeting and spending, and long-term in her life planning. But Seema clearly takes pride in her own ability to spend impulsively and partake in a lifestyle that she assumes other professional women do not have.

Malini echoes Seema's sentiments on the importance of consumption and vocally advocates materialism as a way forward for the nation, especially in terms of conspicuous consumption. Quickly, however, her thoughts turn to other kinds of consumption, and she questions her own Indianness:

MALINI: India needs money. I think materialism is good. That's what I think. Because it's pathetic the way we think. You know, "I don't need a fridge, I have a black and white TV." I mean, come on! That's all crap . . . Somewhere along the line, we've gone and made a virtue out of our poverty and I think it's time to stop doing that . . . But then, if your question is whether I'm very Indian, I don't know. I don't know what Indian is. Is it being ritualistic? . . . See, I'm not very religious, but my husband is . . . But then, when there's a festival, I cooperate completely. I go the whole hog. I do the *puja* (worship of the deities), I do the cooking, I do the whole thing. But, if that's Indian, then, yes, I'm Indian. But, then I also [go to] pub[s]. I also go out with friends. And when I've gone with my husband, I've gone to the beer bars and seen the women dancing. So, that's me.

SR: Are those things un-Indian?

MALINI: That's a good question. Isn't it? Isn't a woman going to a bar and throwing money? Isn't it un-Indian? At least, that's not the way a Hindu woman would be.

In this dialogue, the question of Malini's own Indianness as a woman becomes quickly entangled in her assertion of materialism as the way forward for India as a country. She is confident that getting a nicer fridge and a color TV is crucial, that what Indianness means can and should change to accommodate that. Once she comes to behavior, however, she sees her own actions as mutually contradictory; she wonders whether her taste for pubs and beer bars might undermine the Indianness she enacts during festivals.

Malini's conclusion to my query about what "un-Indianness" is provides a way of beginning to understand the slippage between Indianness and Hinduness in and among those of India's transnational class. Malini is no supporter of the BJP, but as she reflects upon her own personal behavior, she puts forth the assurance of her Hinduness when she is unsure about the meaning of Indianness. Her comment suggests that Hinduness at least, if not Indianness, provides a clear set of values against which she ultimately measures herself, and that at least Hindu norms demand her propriety as a woman. In her earlier explanation of Indianness, she detailed her participation in Hindu practices and festivals, suggesting that for her Indianness and Hinduness were (almost) interchangeable. In the end, her actions as a woman are evaluated through the yardstick of religion, but they are read, importantly, through the nation. Malini's comment is one of the few clues from interviewees in India and Silicon Valley that suggest the centrality of Hindu religious belonging in constituting what it means to be Indian. Among interviewees in South Africa, however, Hindu religiosity becomes an important indicator of belonging to a transnational sense of belonging to India that is dynamic and living. While religiosity in its transnational incarnation will be explored further in the next chapter, Malini's narrative provides insight into a seemingly apolitical assertion of Hindu Indianness during a moment of strong Hindu nationalism: Malini strongly disagrees with the tenets of Hindu nationalism, yet her articulation of appropriate materialism, tied at its heart to her notions of respectable femininity, is strongly informed by a Hindu morality.

Malini's hesitations around the "Indianness" of consumption practices occurring outside the purview of the family resonate strongly with the ways in which most women I spoke to reject the morality of materialism, associated with call center workers and life abroad. Like Malini, most women seldom view the acquisition of luxury goods that enhance a family's comfort or status as a problem; rather, it is gender inappropriate behavior that makes a woman unable to uphold the culture of the nation. Geetha of Bangalore articulated these distinctions clearly. For several minutes she denounced the onslaught of materialism in the new India—the lavish monetary spending of youth on parties, pubs, and clothes. She explained that this kind of spending was wasteful and should rather be put toward charitable causes, such as orphanages or helping the poor. I asked her if it was not quite normal to want a better car or a nicer house or a bigger TV once you are earning good money. Geetha immediately responded, "That's enhancing your comforts . . . That's not a problem . . . If you have money in abundance and you don't know how to spend it, okay, you can have a luxury life. Okay, why should you suffer, being in a hut or something? So, if you have money, invest in yourself, that's not a problem . . . It's momentary things that don't help you." In Geetha's logic, the "momentary things" are exactly those things that are associated with promiscuity or deviance, occurring in places that are beyond the purview of the family's supervision. These "momentary things"—pubs, parties, and clothes—undermine the cultural superiority of the Indian family and thus Indianness itself.

Geetha's comments are a thinly veiled critique of call center workers, who epitomized the immorality of materialism for many of my informants. Pooja, a twenty two-year-old software engineer working for a major Indian multinational in Mumbai, spoke of call center workers as a primary cultural threat to urban India. When I asked her how she felt about some of the major changes that she sees happening in large Indian cities, Pooja immediately spoke of call center workers. She described them as kids who have dropped out of college to make money and are too young to handle handsome salaries responsibly.[4] To Pooja, the availability of highly paid call center jobs to teenagers was pushing urban India too much toward a Western model of education, wherein parents relinquish control over their children when they turn eighteen. At that age, Pooja said, people do not have the maturity to act responsibly and will waste money on the wrong things, rather than saving it as they should. Because they often do not have the foundation of college to stand on, these young people will not be able to make wise decisions or set appropriate boundaries for themselves. When I asked her why we could not just leave them alone and let them have a good time, Pooja replied emphatically,

> They are the future! They are India's future . . . They have to be controlled, they have to be taught, they have to be told about these things. That's the potential danger that metro India is facing . . . I

don't know what kind of culture, what kind of education they'll be able to give their children . . . If these people are behaving so rashly today, what will their next generation be? If we compare what our parents did and what we are doing, imagine what our next generation will do. But today, they are fine. We have good money, we have parties, we have fun, we have drink, we have everything. What's the thing that will happen next?

Here, we see a glimpse of a moral panic over the actions of call center workers, who are seen as young and immature in the eyes of a twenty-two-year-old IT professional who has been in the industry less than two years. What sends Pooja into a panic is not their salaries per se (although she is certainly alarmed by the financial freedom call center workers experience), but the fact that she views them as spending their money outside the purview of family control. In the final lines of her quote, "they" shifts inexplicably to "we," and the slippage between her and the call center worker she might have been under slightly different circumstances becomes more apparent. Also interesting in this narrative is what Pooja does *not* say. Pooja is concerned about a deep kind of Westernization that lies beyond parties, money, and drinking—a feared promiscuity that will irrevocably violate the Indian family in future generations.

Professional IT women express the morality of consumption that lies at the heart of shared notions of the good Indian family most often in explanations for wanting to remain in India in the long term, rather than moving abroad, as their professions may permit. The aversion to the materialistic life found abroad is almost always articulated in connection to the familiarity, security, and emotional bonds of a loving family in India. Parminder of Mumbai, for example, decided to return to India from Singapore, turning down a permanent job and a higher standard of living. She explained that to her, an emotionally rich family life in India was preferable to the emptiness of a more affluent life in Singapore. Similarly, Anu, a thirty-four-year-old manager also in Mumbai, spoke of her decision to return to India from Dubai after a prosperous two-year stint as signifying her disregard for money after a certain point. Having plenty of facilities and clean roads was not fulfilling for her; earning money could not replace her extended family. Through these decisions, both Parminder and Anu have shored up their sense of Indianness. By choosing to return to their families, and thus to India, these women reject the materialism that characterizes the West and embrace the "family values" they support in India, a theme that was particularly pronounced among the narratives of professionals who returned to India from abroad.

For returned professionals, the excess of consumption available in the United States was often one of the most important indicators of a life-style that has become drained of all culture. For Ram, the boredom of his children, prompted by a culture of materialistic acquisition in suburban California, triggered his thoughts about moving back to India in the first place. Ram explained, "My four-year-old came and told me he was bored. He just had a birthday party with thirty kids and gifts filling all of one room. Four days later he came and said he is bored. That was not the childhood I was used to . . . I wanted him to have more basics. Initially [when we moved to California], it was good. I had a lot of my college friends. Suddenly there was déjà vu, the same birthday party, [the] same thirty guests, [the] same gifts . . . It was just getting too much. All the same holidays, no sense of community, no identity." It is precisely Ram's belief in a better childhood—one that revolves less around generic holi-days, birthday parties, and gift giving, that made him consider the pos-sibility that a more culturally rich life for his kids could be had in India.

Even among women currently living in Silicon Valley, concern with how materialism could potentially undermine family values was a com-mon sentiment. The anxiety around raising kids in the United States often focuses upon the consumer goods that will inevitably flood their lives, and thus keep them from knowing the value of money and hard work. Chitra, a twenty-eight-year-old engineer with a young child, ex-plained well the quandary that the experience of immigration, and the upward mobility that comes along with it, presents in raising a child. Chitra explained that having grown up in a middle-class context in India where she had to fight tremendous odds for every minor step up, she is happy now to be able to offer her child small luxuries without having to think about it. At the same time, she does not wish to spoil her child. She explained, "I will not give him anything on a platter—he has to earn. But as far as that is concerned, the fight is not so much [for him.] . . . I bring him more toys than I ever had, and I do not feel guilty. But [when he grows up], a Mercedes? No. Let him earn it. Show your ability to climb into that. This is the value I will pass now—not as an Indian woman, but as any sensible woman. That is cross-cultural." In this statement, Chitra streamlines Indian culture by rendering moralities of consumption as "normal" and as something that can be reinforced anywhere. At the same time, she sets limits to consumption through the invocation of a sense of moralities and values anchored in private family life.

Such sentiments resonate deeply with the ethics of consumption and family that most IT professionals I interviewed expressed, whether in India or Silicon Valley, even as the reference points for appropriate and inappropriate consumption shift across these locales. While Seema, Geetha, and Pooja in India are concerned with differentiating themselves from bank tellers or call center workers, striving to avoid the moral pitfalls of materialism, and achieving a femininity that supports high-status consumption, Ram's and Chitra's anxieties about consumption draw a clear line between the consumption they see as appropriate and that of mainstream American culture. All of these sentiments associate a virtuous morality with an implicitly Indian, Hindu family in which good women oversee the consumption of the domestic sphere. Some types of consumption contribute to the status of the family and are thus virtuous, but once that consumption becomes "materialistic," either by association with an empty life abroad or with the inappropriate behaviors of India's call center workers, it no longer works to support the consolidation of the good Indian family.

Just Enough Freedom: Navigating "Exposure" and Promiscuity

In order to enact a respectable femininity in service of family and nation, professional women must respect a set of boundaries that delimit how they travel between the private sphere of the home and the public sphere of work and leisure in their everyday lives. Here too, strong notions of appropriate, positive "exposure" available in the IT workplace, and inappropriate behaviors and actions that undermine the family, set up the terms of the delicate balance that IT women must strike. As with moralities surrounding consumption, the bank worker and the call center worker set up the discursive extremes between which IT women navigate, and the potential promiscuity of the call center worker is associated with deteriorated morals found in foreign locales. By asserting the value of "exposure" to the outside world and avoiding the dangers of promiscuity, professional women ensure their symbolic value as actors at the helm of cultural globalization in India, incorporating only the positive aspects of the "global" workplace while rejecting the negative aspects.

Most IT women I spoke to in India agreed that they experienced a kind of "exposure" to the world that bank workers did not. This experience, they felt, set them apart from bank workers and other professional women, both in India and in the world at large. Gautami, for example, hinted that bank workers have limited horizons, especially in comparison to herself and her colleagues in IT: "See, someone who is working in State Bank would never have the opportunity of meeting people all over the world. And she would be doing that normal routine kind of a job . . . but we are totally different. We have deadlines, we have pressures. It's not a routine job kind of a thing. You have something new to look up to every day . . . For them, responsibility is finishing off the cooking. For us, cooking is also a responsibility, but finishing off our deadlines at [the] office is also a responsibility." Gautami echoed the sentiments of many professional IT women that bank workers were less aware of what was happening in the world compared to IT women. Because women bank workers are tied to insular routines and their families, and do not interact with the rest of the world, Gautami and most others I spoke to said they could never envision themselves in bank jobs—that working in a bank would make them fundamentally different kinds of a people than they wanted to be. As Mital of Mumbai explains, "I actually had an aunt who said, 'Hey, join State Bank of India, you can have a house, you're paid well.' But still, there's still something missing. They [bank workers] don't have a sense of the world. Definitely they're better than the ones sitting at home. Probably because they're going out and meeting people . . . those women are working, so that's good . . . But for my generation, for me, it's not challenging enough, I guess . . . There's that image factor that 'I'm associated with the IT industry and I'm adding a lot of growth to India.'" What Mital refers to as the "image factor" recalls the attraction of the industry for most of my informants. Women especially believe that the "exposure" to the world that the IT industry provides is one of the most critical reasons for being in the industry—one that exceeds its financial benefits. As Geetha put it, "Everyone has a craze for this industry. They're being paid well also, so everyone wants to get into this . . . [but] it's not only money. The kind of exposure they get here is much more—exposure to the world. It's a worldwide kind of thing." Upon closer examination, however, it becomes clear that the kind of exposure that IT provides is attractive precisely because it occurs within prescribed limits that do not require women to "expose" themselves too much, as they might in other industries. As Mital reflects upon the advantages of IT for women, she explains the ethical nature of the exposure it provides for women:

> Modeling has glamour. But people do wonder about models, like what kind of a woman is she going to be? I don't mind going out on a date with her, but I wouldn't want to marry her. Probably. But IT is not like that. Because you have to think. Maybe that's the difference. Because you're actually using your brains, not your body. You just get the job done. Maybe that has something to do with it. Like, so many non-beautiful women join IT . . . It's definitely a lot better than other fields. Like, I have a friend with an MBA in marketing. And [in the business world], women are just not taken seriously. You have to sleep around with your boss to climb. But see, in IT, you don't put on a show in the office. You don't dress up, even. It's very casual. It's what you do in front of the computer that counts. In other fields you have to put on a big show, wear the right thing, say the right thing. In IT, it's not like that. You can be yourself.

Mital's reflections hint at the limits of exposure—interacting with the world is positive, but in the end, these interactions cannot interfere with the enactment of a bounded, respectable femininity, which includes clear limitations surrounding sexuality. Mital is also able to pinpoint how, compared to other professions, IT jobs come to be compatible with other dominant expectations of Indian femininity.

The ways in which sexual limits are set, reinforced, and enacted in the IT workplace become clear in the narrative of Meena, a thirty-year-old manager in Bangalore working in an American multinational. Meena describes how she and her IT colleagues assert this particular style of femininity for their foreign colleagues in an interesting counter to Mital's claim that women do not "dress up" in IT:

> We like shocking the Americans who come over. We just declare a sari day, and you have all these Indian girls walking around with open *palloos*![5] You should see the open mouths! And you see all these bright colors—red, yellow, green, and all these lovely girls with their eyes made up. And in India, it's allowed. You can come to work that way on a sari day. And we do it purposely. We do it just to shock them

[laughing] . . . They just love the Indianness, you know? . . . I've had a lot of colleagues from the U.S. say, "There's such a nice blend here. You don't have these too aggressive women, but at the same time, these women are serious about their careers. But they also know how to look like women." . . . I think Indian women are very good at that . . . I think you just need to look like a woman and dress like a woman and talk like a woman. It's okay. When it comes to the job, just be professional about it . . . you just do what you have to do, enjoy the money you make, enjoy the exposure, and go home in time.

In this account, Meena spells out the ways in which the IT workplace provides the arena for a positive "exposure" that allows women the opportunity to work in a professional environment while reshaping a specific kind of Indian femininity for themselves and their American (male) clients. The sexual undertones of her narrative suggest a kind of flirtation with an admiring Western male gaze, but the sexuality on display for this gaze is self-consciously professional, competent, and ready to go home to be with the family on time.

Both call center workers and foreign locales provide professional IT women with the outer boundary of "exposure"—too *much* freedom, associated with a deterioration of values that can no longer uphold the family or the nation. Within India, the moral panics surrounding the consumption patterns of call center workers is closely linked with their potential promiscuity in the minds of my interviewees—both men and women. Several interviewees articulated moral concerns with call center workers, especially in the areas of gendered behavior and sexuality, reflecting the perceived moral threat of call center workers to the essence of the Indian family.[6] For example, Anjali, a twenty-five-year-old technical writer in Mumbai, said that because call center workers work night shifts, and girls and boys work side by side, they are seen as morally questionable. Even Malini, who views call centers more positively as a part of a globalizing India, says that call centers are seen as pushing old value systems too far and thus are not respectable. She narrated a recent instance of a clogged drain in a major call center near Electronic City that was allegedly caused by a backup of used condoms in a bathroom.[7] Malini said the story raised many eyebrows and further confirmed the suspicions of respectable people that questionable morals circulate in call centers' working environments. In this way, women working in call centers appear to flout the conventions of middle-class domesticity by working at night for high salaries. In itself, this is perceived as a rejection of behavioral norms, and by association, sexual norms.

Foreign locales serve as a foil for the sexual morality of urban India. While many accept that raising a child in an Indian metropolitan area like Mumbai or Bangalore today may present as many moral and psychological challenges as raising a child in the United States or in the United Kingdom, most insist that there are still important differences. Aside from the preoccupation with a materialistic life, several interviewees regarded Western foreign locales, like the United States or the United Kingdom, as places with "too much freedom." This sense of "too much freedom" is almost always linked to sexuality. Shubha of Mumbai, who spent several months in the United States for work in 2002, explained that she enjoyed her experience immensely, but that her freedom from the constraints of family and "Indian culture" led her to make sexual choices that she later regretted. In reflecting upon whether she would ever be comfortable raising a child in the United States, Shubha referred to her own experiences in the United States and India.

SHUBHA: I know I'm quite blunt to say this, but there are certain things I've done that I really, really regret. I wish I had not had this particular relationship with this one person.

SR: Was that in Bombay?

SHUBHA: No, that was not in Bombay, it was in the U.S. Because I was alone and had freedom. And then if my daughter wanted to do something, all this would come back to me and I would be like, "Oh my God." But how do you stop them? Indian culture, the control is to stop these things from happening.

SR: Does it work?

SHUBHA: I never had the guts to lie, but people lie and things happen here also. So, I don't know. It really depends on the nature of the child . . . But in my case, my parents would never let me go out with a guy . . . there was this guy I liked in college. And if we managed to travel by auto back alone, it was like, wow, a big thing. You just die to be alone, do things alone . . . [But still,] I'm not sure how comfortable I would be to raise my kids in the States. Because things are so much more open there. I'd probably be worried that "Oh my god, has she lost her virginity already?!" [laughs]

Even though Shubha regretted the restrictions she had growing up, she is unwilling to relinquish them completely when it comes to her own (unborn) children and feels that she would have more control over her daughter's sexuality if she raised her in India.

Similarly, Anu's conviction that her daughter would be better brought up in Mumbai than elsewhere springs from her belief that teenage pregnancies are much more rampant in the United Kingdom and the United States. Her sister-in-law, who works for a state welfare agency in the United Kingdom, told her how commonplace thirteen-year-old mothers are there. Anu expressed deep fear at the prospect of her daughter becoming pregnant at thirteen and felt that keeping her in India made it much less likely that would happen. I asked her if there weren't many mothers in India who were only thirteen—perhaps even more than in the United States or the United Kingdom. Her response makes transparent the importance of class in Anu's understanding of nation and morality: "Yes, there are [thirteen-year-old mothers]. But not so many. Well, there are, but that's another thing. That's because the parents have got them married, not necessarily out of choice. They're forced into it. Child marriages here are in the slums . . . But that doesn't happen in—well, we don't do that to our daughters anymore. So, at least, we try to give them the best." Here, Anu demonstrates the ways in which respectable morality is tied not only to a larger notion of India and Indian values, but also importantly to class, which makes real the kinds of boundaries that both Shubha and Anu articulate. The important thread running through all the narratives women articulate is the idea of the "right" amount of freedom—not as much as abroad, where your sexual and leisure behaviors might indicate a rejection of family and thus a loss of culture, but not as little as in earlier Indian generations, or, implicitly, those less-educated and less well-off Indians today who cannot exercise these freedoms. This "right" amount of freedom informs the "appropriate difference" of the Indian family—cosmopolitan due to appropriate levels of "exposure" to the world, but also restrained and grounded in a cultural identity that maintains the sanctity of a woman's sexual purity. Although the line between not enough freedom and too much freedom is hazy in many cases, the line is clearly acknowledged by IT women across a range of ages, regional backgrounds, and attitudes as a limitation. As Beena, a thirty-year-old project leader in Mumbai, said in a discussion of the sexual permissiveness of cultures abroad, "It's better to grow up in a restricted society than in an unrestricted society."

The Intimate Nation

Professional IT women occupy a symbolic position that enables them to creatively produce and stabilize the "good" Indian family as a primary marker of Indian culture. While these women play an active role in shaping this position, the boundaries within which their navigations take place are demarcated in highly specific ways. Women bring lessons about individuality, hard work, and personal choices learned at work into the private sphere of the home, which strongly influence dominant new notions of the family. These incorporations mean that the "good" Indian family also values "exposure" to the world and a professional, highly competent femininity. Integrating these values in the private sphere signals a break from a "backward" past in which women stayed at home, and is even set apart from a perceived past generation in which women worked routine, insular jobs, such as those in the government banking sector. At the same time, long-standing associations between the domestic sphere and national culture continue to resonate deeply for professional women and their families, providing a set of normative beliefs and practices that women consistently refer to.

It is no coincidence that in the context of a mobile, stabilized transnational Indian professional culture the family is the ultimate site at which cultural streamlining takes place. Because of the family's relative autonomy from the larger society in which it exists—whether in economically polarized Indian cities or culturally diverse locales abroad—claims to have a good Indian family can travel effectively, provided all the gendered balances are just "right." Even in India, the families of IT professionals do not necessarily have to celebrate festivals traditionally (which most cannot do because of their hectic schedules), or speak a particular language (especially when the lingua franca of many of their lives is English), or be familiar with any "local" Indian practices (especially since most IT professionals live far away from where their families have lived historically). To assert a "good" Indian family, all that is needed is the imported logics of the knowledge economy (which contains an implicit class privilege) to be melded with existing resonant notions of the domestic, private sphere as the core of an essential Indian national culture. This balance is a fundamentally gendered one that reinforces a symbolic position for highly educated professional women who must model respectable femininity to produce and uphold an improved notion of Indianness. It is a "balance" that can be stabilized, transported, and generalized, supporting cultural streamlining processes that naturalize such balances as constituting the "core" of Indian culture in a way that is meaningful and appealing to an audience of Indian professionals around the world.

Largely absent from these accounts of a reimagined notion of Indianness in the family is a clear conception of how religion informs the family, if at all. Malini's invocation of her Hindu identity, when she could not define her Indian identity, hints that identification as Hindu is important. Yet, the diversity of practices associated with Hinduism and the relative silence of my informants on questions of religion and religious identification, especially in India, raise questions about its relevance to transnational meanings of Indianness. To examine how Hinduness becomes an implicit part of the culture of India's transnational class, I turn my attention next to South Africa.

WHEN THE PRIVATE IS TRANSNATIONAL

Deterritorialization, whether of Hindus, Sikhs, Palestinians or Ukraini-
ans, is now at the core of a variety of global fundamentalisms, including
Islamic and Hindu fundamentalism. In the Hindu case for example . . . it is
clear that the overseas movement of Indians has been exploited by a
variety of interests both within and outside India to create a complicated
network of finances and religious identifications, in which the *problems
of cultural reproduction for Hindus abroad have become tied to the politics
of Hindu fundamentalism at home.*—ARJUN APPADURAI, "DISJUNCTURE
AND DIFFERENCE IN THE GLOBAL CULTURAL ECONOMY," *MODERNITY AT
LARGE* (EMPHASIS ADDED)

What is the role of Hindu religious practices in constituting the
culture of India's new transnational class? Beginning with Appadurai's observations, a well-developed literature suggests financial, ideological, and political collaboration between urban,
middle-class Hindus in India and upwardly mobile Indians in the
diaspora in support of the Hindu Right (Hansen 1999; Rajagopal
2001a; van der Veer 2004). Yet discussion of religious practice
seemed distant from the dilemmas of cultural reproduction that
my informants in India and Silicon Valley discussed with me. Men-
tion of religious belief and practice arose sporadically, and even
when it did, the beliefs expressed by my informants were certainly
not consistently supportive of the politics or ideologies of the
Hindu Right.

In this chapter, I attempt to tease out the complex interconnections between the processes of cultural streamlining I identify
throughout the book on the one hand, and the collapse of Hindu
and Indian identifications into a singular, monolithic, ahistorical
identity on the other hand. I do this by briefly exploring discourses
of Hindu religious beliefs and practices among informants in India

and Silicon Valley, and then focusing in depth on experiences of Indianness among professional IT women in South Africa. I argue that the various discourses of belonging to India among South African Indians offer important clues about the centrality and prevalence of a particular form of Hinduism in constituting a sense of authentic Indianness in India's transnational class. The common thread across locations in expressions of religious belonging is the translation of place-bound, community-specific Hindu practices into apolitical, individualized, modular practices that can be transferred easily across borders and adopted by those in the diaspora who lack the regional and community identifications that define the diversity of Hindu religious practice in India.[1]

Transnational Hindu organizations that aim to propagate and raise awareness about Hinduism play a key role in adapting Hinduism to global conditions of mobility and diasporic belonging, and this trend becomes extremely clear in the South African case, where such organizations essentially function as the link between South African Indians and notions of an emergent India and a transnational Indian culture. Like individualization and discourses of the good family, practices of Hinduism among Indian IT professionals in divergent locations are strategically homogenized to produce, reinforce, and promote an idea of Indianness that cannot be separated from Hinduism. It is the notion of the inextricability of these two identifications that is shored up in the upwardly mobile diaspora, and that has had the effect of fueling right-wing Hindu movements in India, especially in the 1990s.

Individual Practices, Practical Spirituality: India and Silicon Valley

My informants in Mumbai, Bangalore, and Silicon Valley were predominantly upper caste Hindus.[2] Two Muslim informants in Mumbai, two Christians in Mumbai, and one Christian in Bangalore were the only departures from that norm. Yet, few of these informants discussed the practices or beliefs of Hinduism explicitly in thinking through their notions of culture. "Indian culture" was much more readily tied to a "good family" than to anything explicitly Hindu. In India, those who did touch upon their religious or spiritual beliefs tended to explain them without regard to a particular place or community, but rather with reference to a broad, decontextualized philosophy, or small, personal practices. There was significant continuity between these expressions of religious belonging and those expressed in Silicon Valley, although among a few respondents in the latter group, especially those born in the United States, some recognition of the importance of specific rituals and community functions was also deemed important.

Especially among men in upper management living in India, identification with Hinduism was expressed through an interest in Hindu philosophy, often thought to be compatible with science and technology, and a long-term interest in developing a spiritual self through self-directed study and reading. In these accounts, we find the motivated, curious individual seeking knowledge, a conception of the individual that resonates both with the ambitious individualism fostered in IT and ancient Hindu notions of self-inquiry especially for men who have completed their worldly duties (Dumont 1980 [1960]; Heesterman 1981). For example, Ram of Bangalore explained that he has developed an interest in Hindu philosophy. He feels that within this philosophy lie deep reasons that explain social and economic divisions and unities he sees in the world around him, and he believes that, in some sense, those who understand Hindu scriptures have already figured out much of what plagues humanity today. His engagement with Hinduism, then, occurs mainly at the level of individual scholarship and inquiry directed toward improved understanding of the world around him. Similarly, forty-eight-year-old Suresh of Bangalore, who is a successful entrepreneur, has his sights set on a retirement that allows for time for spiritual inquiry. When asked how he envisions his future life, he responded,

> Maybe I will do one more [entrepreneurial] venture. And then quit. I have certain things which I wanted to do which I could not do . . . for various reasons and I want to pursue those . . . I want to learn and understand Hinduism. It has got a rich wealth of knowledge and wisdom. Born and brought up in this country, I have no idea of the scriptures. I am absolutely ignorant. I want to acquire at least .00001 percent of that knowledge. Start learning Sanskrit from the beginning . . . Just more for knowledge['s] sake. It is a big ocean and I want at least a little taste of that.

For Suresh, the philosophies of Hinduism, which he feels he ought to understand, have felt distant from his adult life as an IT professional. He looks to retirement to close that distance somewhat, but again, his engagement with Hinduism will be personal and self-directed.

Others in India draw upon philosophies of Hinduism to explain the world around them. In these articulations, Hinduism is a flexible philosophy that is open to individual interpretation, while more narrow interpretations of Hinduism that dominate many communities are overlooked. Anu of Mumbai, in explaining why she did not wish to move out of India, interpreted Hinduism as a philosophy of individual freedom that pervades everyday life in India:

> The beauty about living in India is, especially, being a Hindu, is that Hinduism doesn't enforce anything on you. So, you pick what you want and you make your own religion, basically. And you decide what you're going to do—how often you're going to pray, whether you're going to pray or not, whom you're going to pray to, what you believe. Do you believe in God? What is God? All those things. And that can only come in India . . . The sense of spirituality, accepting people the way they are, not forcing your views on others . . . And all that can happen only here. I can't get that kind of freedom anywhere else.

The freedoms that Hinduism offers, in contrast to the sexual and material freedoms that informants perceived the United States and Europe as offering, are desirable and proper. For Anu, Hinduism is important in her life because of the subtle infusion of its philosophies, as she understands them, in her everyday life. Although this philosophy-infused lifestyle is, for her, specific to living in India, it is not connected to specific rituals or practices that she must adhere to. Furthermore, for Anu, as for all of my informants in India who spoke of religion in any way, a Hindu identification was not connected to political support for a Hindu nationalist party, since most informants declared no interest in politics. These articulations suggest that Hinduism remains an important source of identity and belonging for IT professionals, but that Hinduism as they understand it is largely decontextualized and depoliticized.

Respondents in Silicon Valley offered a little more of a range in their understandings of Hinduism and were often more explicit about the inextricability of Indianness and Hinduism from one another. Still, Hindu identifications remain tied to personal practices and are explicitly transferable, able to be practiced anywhere in the world, precisely because religious practices take place primarily in the private sphere. Lakshmi of Silicon Valley, who had doubts about moving back to India, explained that she wished to pass on to her children small, personal religious practices, such as lighting a lamp after bathing in the morning, and the importance of faith in a higher power. For Lakshmi, these practices were more important to her than conformity to other vague notions of Indian culture that she herself rejected. Lakshmi says that she wishes to teach her children the importance of having a spiritual core that they could turn to in times of trouble, and she felt that this sense was something she could pass on to them regardless of whether they grew up in the United States, India, or elsewhere. Lakshmi's articulation of Hinduism was quite typical of immigrant women I spoke with in Silicon Valley, and it sits uneasily alongside studies of North American Hindu culture in the United States that have shown affluent Indian Americans to be invested in a regressive form of Hinduism—a form that idealizes a mythic Vedic civilization and is no longer practiced in India today (Lal 2003; Mathew and Prashad 2000).

Second-generation Indian Americans in Silicon Valley were slightly more explicit in their pronouncements of the importance of Hindu religion in upholding Indianness in the United States. Their articulations might find some resonance with the ahistorical form of Hinduism that many scholars have found being practiced in the United States in the name of "culture." Neetu, a thirty-one-year-old hardware engineer who was born in the United States to Indian immigrant parents, understands the conduct of *puja*—ritual worship of deities—and the celebration of festivals to have been a key part of her upbringing. As a child, community religious life was important, and she wishes to offer the same kinds of religious resources to her child. In Neetu's narrative, her understanding of "Indian culture" is deeply entangled with Hindu religiosity, which governs beliefs and lifestyles at once. In reflecting upon those things she wishes to pass on to her young daughter, Neetu explains:

> Having our children know our language is important. Knowing about the basics in Hindu mythology and religion [is also important]. Obviously, there is going to be some loss when I think of what my mom passed on. [But] I am hoping I can pass on what my mom passed on to me. I want to share my beliefs with my children. Eventually when they come to be teenagers, well, my point of view for example, if you have an Indian [mother] who is very close to her family and very much believes in Indian values and religion or whatever, she is also wanting [her daughter] to go by the book . . .
>
> So [as far as Indian values go,] sense of family it is a big thing, and

also knowing about, well, learning about Indian history, basic principles of Hindu religion. You learn a lot about Indian values through Hindu mythology.

For Neetu, Hindu values are inextricable from Indian values. Hindu mythology informs properly Indian practices that must be negotiated between parents and their teenage daughters. Although Neetu is quite flexible in her beliefs about what these factors will all add up to mean in terms of her own daughter, for her being Indian and being Hindu are closely tied together.

All of the informants I spoke to in Mumbai, Bangalore, and Silicon Valley felt aware of, tied to, and invested in the idea of a rapidly rising India on the global economic landscape. Yet, Hindu religious practice or identification was seldom the primary link that forged that sense of belonging. When Hindu identification did appear as important for informants, however, it was always a version of Hinduism dissociated from "local" regional or caste practices that are more typical of how most in India understand and practice religion. Instead, IT professionals assert a "globalized," streamlined version of the religion that could be practiced anywhere, even as India may remain the privileged location for its realization. Although an existing literature on Hindu nationalism strongly suggests that the urban middle class in India was largely responsible for the rise of Hindu, non-secular notions of India, these attitudes never became explicit among my informants in India and Silicon Valley, offering at best an ambivalent, underspecified understanding of the importance of Hinduism in constituting the culture of India's new transnational class. Yet, clues about how Hinduism circulates among transnational Indians abound; the version of Hinduism that emerges is individualized yet transferable, and surprisingly uniform in its distance from ritual, its emphasis on family values, and its insistence upon the inseparability of Indianness and Hinduness.

South African Indians in the IT world offer a very different picture of these trends and clarify in important ways the centrality of Hinduism in transnational Indian class culture. For the remainder of the chapter, then, I turn to the South African case, which makes explicit the types of cultural streamlining that take place in Hindu religious practices that attract affluent Indians to a vibrant, living sense of belonging to a transnational notion of India.

Navigating Hinduism and Indianness in Post-Apartheid South Africa

At a meeting of a Tamil women's group in the Indian township of Chatsworth outside of Durban, South Africa, I am seated with a group of women discussing a recent event the group had organized. Some of the members of the group have never met me before and are curious to know what a woman with an Indian name and an American accent might be doing there. A young Indian man, a visitor to the group who is assisting them with a printing order, asks the question that many others are wondering: "So, what are you doing in this country?" Upon barely listening to a cursory answer from me, the young man launches into a diatribe about crime and corruption in South Africa. "If you see the whole of Africa," he explains, "we in South Africa are the only part living in like a civilized society, but it's just a matter of time before we go that way. That's why I want to emigrate. To the U.S. Soon, I'm making plans." Suddenly, his attention turns to India, which seems to be the next logical step in his lecture. "India is the world's next economic superpower, you know. The future is there. They have been developing so much, economically, especially on the tech side. And you know, they have these 'person of Indian origin' cards now, so we can apply for those if you're less than four generations removed from India. We could become residents there!" A middle-aged woman, an active member of the group who has been silent so far, chimes in with a grimace, "But really, where are we going to go live in India? I don't know about that." Others nod and agree sympathetically. "But then," the same women perks up, "maybe we could live in Bangalore!"

This exchange, which took place in 2008, has become increasingly typical of attitudes among South African Indians, a group of over one million descendants of Indian migrants who have been residing in South Africa with little direct connection to India for as much as seven generations. The exchange reveals the many dimensions through which South Africans of Indian descent call upon their Indianness, as well as the ambivalences surrounding such an articulation. While many South African Indians feel strongly about their sense of exclusive belonging to South Africa, others identify even more strongly with a specifically South African Indian identity—a minority identity that came into being initially under an apartheid system and was remade in the post-apartheid cultural crucible of Mandela's rainbow nation. This minority identity, however, made as it was during a long history in South Africa, does not necessarily imply participation in, or even awareness of, the hegemonic cultural politics of the transnational Indian class that is the subject of this book. Patterns of interconnectedness between South Africa and India have been historically uneven, and feelings of connectedness to an Indian homeland among South African Indians are diverse and difficult to classify. Yet, there exists a strong and growing voice—one that bubbled up in the context of this meeting of deeply religious women devoted to Tamil language and culture—that is profoundly aware of a rapidly changing India. This voice wishes to participate in this phenomenon by staking a claim to membership in it. The desire to claim such membership arises in the context of a confluence of factors: a growing desire to reconnect with "roots" among post-apartheid South African Indians, the availability of finances for travel or emigration to do it, and, finally, a wish to flee a country in which Indians increasingly feel alienated (Hansen 2005; Padayachee 1999).

This confluence of push and pull factors has led a growing number of upwardly mobile South African Indians, especially those working in the emergent IT sector, to embrace a connection with a transnational circuit of Indian culture through travel to India, religious practices, and a gendered language of morality and respectability that places the family first for professional women. Yet, this was not the case for all Indian IT women I interviewed in South Africa. For many, a sense of belonging to India is an abstract question of "origin," restricted to a designated "cultural" realm of life and empty of broader meanings. For others, an awareness of a changing India that has gone "global," and thus is no longer the imagined, Orientalized India that was supposed to be a space of cultural and spiritual purity, has undermined their belief in India as the authoritative source of their Indian cultural belonging. For them, South Africa's version of Indianness is the only one that is meaningful. There are some women, however, who actively embrace and participate in an everyday sense of belonging to a transnational Indian middle class that is almost indistinguishable from those articulated in Bangalore, Mumbai, or Silicon Valley. Among upwardly mobile women of similar class positions and heritages living in the same country, why might some identify with this hegemonic class culture and others not?

Interviews with South African Indian professional women reveal explicitly those dimensions of India's transnational class culture that are only implicit among individuals whose belonging is already a given by virtue of their geographic and class positions. I have been arguing throughout this book that the culture of transnational Indian professionals is defined by not only class position and a certain "global" lifestyle and set of attitudes afforded by their participation in the knowledge economy, but also by certain moral and cultural expectations that seek to remake Indian culture. The South African case elaborates on this point in an important way: the professional women who are able to articulate and identify with a transnational Indian class express their connection to India primarily through a religious idiom. Indeed, the centrality of Hinduism, and specifically a transnational, de-ritualized, context-free form of Hinduism, is what finally differentiates women who participate in this class culture and those who do not. The ways in which South African Indians "mobilize" Indianness more clearly reveal the multiple layers that constitute an authentic sense of belonging to the hegemonic class culture described in this book, precisely because their belonging is *not* a given, but rather something that is crafted and mediated at an individual level.[3] Narratives of belonging in South Africa also serve to underscore the extent to which "Indian" as a transnational category is only available to those with a certain class background.

Situating the South African Indian Experience

South African Indians have had an uneven pattern of interconnection with India as a homeland—one that was at first mediated through colonial relationships, later interrupted and controlled by the apartheid regime, and finally, in recent years, asserted through a global cultural circuit that disseminates new forms of religion, culturally marked goods and services, and ideas about a rapidly changing India. These shifting patterns of interconnection and influence have produced a diversity of idioms through which South African Indians experience and articulate their feelings of connection to India, and it is only some of those articulations that find resonance with the hegemonic culture of a transnational class.

The end of apartheid in 1994 elicited an ambiguous reaction from South African Indians, and the majority voted against Mandela's party, the African National Congress (ANC), aligning mostly with the White National Party that represented South Africa's apartheid past. Although many Indians were involved in the struggle against apartheid, which counted all "non-whites" as part of the black majority, the majority of the Indian community was fearful of the changes a black government would bring for them (Desai 1996). Elsewhere, I have argued that the end of apartheid and the triumph of a "rainbow nation" imaginary signaled a shift in the terms of a racial state. In the post-apartheid multicultural South Africa, South African Indians have now had to express their difference in "cultural" terms rather than self-evidently racial terms, an expression that has been profoundly gendered (Radhakrishnan 2005). In the realm of cultural production, South African Indian women play a key role in learning, preserving, and performing classical Indian arts, such as dance and music. In the media, representations of a multicultural nation must include a brown-skinned woman wearing Indian clothes to be politically correct. Even in politics, the activities of Indian political parties, while deeply male-dominated, have a large and vocal contingent of women.[4]

In these ways, South African Indians maintain a distinct, though deeply racialized, relative position in their society, and although the terms of this form of national belonging remain tenuous in a post-apartheid world, they are constantly being renegotiated to fit a shifting sociopolitical scenario. In recent years, more than a decade after the end of apartheid, even the ambivalence that South African Indians have felt toward the "rainbow nation" appears to be transforming into an increasing alienation of the sort I was exposed to at the meeting described earlier. The leadership of Thabo Mbeki has fostered a new emphasis on "African Renaissance," a notion that asserts South Africa as a distinctly African nation and differs in important ways from Mandela's more inclusive rainbow nation. These shifts have compounded the sentiments of many Indians who have felt "left out" of South Africa's transition to democracy.

Such cultural and political trends within South Africa have coincided with the increased visibility of Indianness as a transnational culture associated with upward mobility, the economic powerhouse of India, and an ancient, moral, and timeless culture. Thanks to a more open economy and increasing levels of upward mobility in the community since the end of apartheid, exchanges between India and South Africa have intensified. South African Indians are participating in explicitly "Indian" cultural experiences that connect to contemporary India in increasing numbers, where, previously, very few had active ties to India of any kind. The global boom in the Hindi film industry has made Bollywood virtually main-stream in South Africa, and beyond that, South African Indians have become a key audience for Bollywood awards ceremonies, live perfor-mances, and guest appearances for movie stars (Rajadhyaksha 2003). Moreover, especially since the 1990s, South African Indians have become targets of global organizations, such as the Vishwa Hindu Parishad (VHP) and the Global Organization for People of Indian Origin (GOPIO), which seek to draw upon the significant financial and political resources of the indentured diaspora to channel funding and resources to India for vari-ous aims (Hansen 2002; Lal 2004). Such organizations have helped to rekindle interest in "origins" among South African Indians and have coincided with the upward mobility of Indians that makes it possible for them to explore those origins through travel. Today, many South African Indians make the trip to India, which is often viewed as a kind of pil-grimage. In acquiring what Thomas Blom Hansen has called a "diasporic disposition," which he links to "upward mobility and the search for mid-dle class respectability," South African Indians have increasingly become integrated into a larger circuit of Indian diasporic cultural practices and meanings, despite their peculiar and isolating history (Hansen 2002).

The heightened interest in Indian culture and belonging, alongside economic mobility, has produced the desire to participate in high-status forms of cultural production that distance South African Indians from a working-class history. During apartheid, Indians in South Africa were associated with a particular working-class culture, marked by distinctive food preferences, patterns of speech, and segregated residences. These associations were particularly pronounced in the townships of Chats-worth and Phoenix, outside of Durban, where South African Indians are most highly concentrated. These townships were designated as Indian areas under the apartheid Group Areas Act and formed a physical buffer between the white city center and African townships. Although insulated and isolated, these townships also became important sites of South Afri-can Indian cultural production, political activity, and community build-ing (Desai 2002; Hansen 2000; Maharaj 1996). With increased economic mobility in recent years, many successful Indians have moved out of these townships, either to live in more affluent suburban areas or to pursue more lucrative employment in Johannesburg. There remain vast and perhaps growing class divides among South African Indians, who are also culturally divided along the lines of linguistic heritage and religion, yet the visible upward mobility of many Indians has led to a refashioning of South African Indian identity in the public sphere that distances itself from its working-class history and asserts instead an upwardly mobile, middle-class position. Uniform representations of Indianness in the multicultural imaginary of South Africa as a "rainbow nation" further legitimize these assertions (Desai 2002; 1996).

As more and more South African Indians are able to have lifestyles commensurate with those of their counterparts in industrialized countries, the idea of participating in the transnational culture of professional Indians becomes a highly visible and attractive cultural option for many, as it is able to knit together a deeply felt cultural and often religious identification with a newer economic and social position. At the same time, a sense of belonging to India helps to validate feelings of alienation in South Africa.

Religion as the Mediator of Authenticity

Religious life among South African Indians very often forms the basis for cultural life. While most South African Indians identify themselves as Hindu, a large percentage are Christian while still others are Muslim. In this sense as well, there is much greater diversity among Indian professional women in South Africa than in India or California. In the context of this diversity of religious practices, those women who identify closely with Hinduism, and particularly a transnational brand of Hinduism that has appeared in South Africa since the 1990s, tend to articulate religious and spiritual life as their primary link to India. Thomas Blom Hansen has called this form of Hinduism "a 'modern', 'globalized', diasporic and 'thin' notion of Hinduism as the emblem of a shared civilizational identity" (2002, 5). In contrast, although many Christian and Muslim women express a tie to India as a homeland, it is a faraway homeland—one that is not related to their personal lives or experiences. In these cases, the sense of belonging to India is expressed strictly in terms of gendered family priorities in which family comes first, perhaps a legacy of Indian women's roles in South Africa historically. As I will show, however, Hindu women who view India as a space of authentic religious experience travel there for this experience. In so doing, they develop new ideas about what India is and feel that they participate more wholly in the changes taking place in contemporary India. By participating in a transnational Hindu religious movement, they can be recognized by other Indians elsewhere in the world as one of them, thus asserting their Indian identity on a global stage.

In South Africa, one of the most visible transnational Hindu movements is the Sai organization, led by the guru Sri Satya Sai Baba, who is based in India. In the teachings of this tradition, the elaborate rituals of Hinduism are simplified dramatically, and the core of the teaching centers on service to humanity and living a moral, ethical life. The specificities of practicing Hinduism are minimized to a set of simple principles, making them easily compatible with a more Western lifestyle. Dubbed the "global guru," Sai Baba has created an organization whose base in India and elsewhere is largely urban and middle class (Weiss 2005). Sai centers are common in South Africa and have large congregations from a mix of class backgrounds, with a large professional contingent. During weekly "services," *bhajans* or devotional songs are sung and simple *pujas* are performed. Special festivals and occasions are marked with appropriate Hindu rituals as prescribed by the teachings of Sai Baba. Many Sai centers in Chatsworth engage regularly in community service activities, offering mobile medical clinics to underserved communities and preparing and distributing food in poor areas of Durban. For Sai devotees around the world, the ultimate religious experience is to visit Prashanti Nilayam, a large ashram in South India that is the headquarters of the Sai organization and the permanent residence of Sri Satya Sai Baba. Sai organizations in South Africa regularly organize group trips to Prashanti for those who can afford to go. Many devotees also go on their own, usually with their immediate families. The purpose of these visits is not only to be in the divine environment of Prashanti, but also to have *darshan*, or divine sight, of their guru. In this way, the Sai organization sets up a clear relationship with India, where India becomes reestablished as the fount of spiritual and religious life to be connected with for purposes of pilgrimage and personal renewal.

Aside from the Sai organization, other important Hindu religious organizations that set up a similar relationship between devotees in South Africa and specific locations in India include the Divine Life Society and the Hare Krsna movement. Of the women I interviewed, however, not one was involved with Divine Life, and only one was actively involved in the Hare Krsna movement. Yet, eight of the twenty-two women I interviewed were actively involved in the Sai organization. I had the opportunity to participate in several gatherings, activities, and services of the Sai organization, which offered me a much more informed view of the ways in which people feel engaged in the organization as well as in their Hindu religious identification.

Hindus in South Africa who are not a part of these transnational Hindu organizations have very often grown up in tightly knit communities in which religious practice, especially in its ritual form at temples, was a key component of collective life. Hindu respondents discussed going to "service" on Sunday at the temple in the same way that Christians might discuss going to church, even though Hinduism has not conventionally been a congregational religion in India. In my ethnographic work, I found that strong communities formed sometimes over generations around particular temples or places of worship. At these temples, collective ritual celebrations, perhaps passed down from the nineteenth century, are practiced in ways that are seldom seen in India today.[5]

As one of the key concerns of this book has been to illuminate some of the interconnections between the ideas of India as a Hindu nation, especially as envisioned in Hindu nationalism, and of India as a "global" one, the South African case offers an important opportunity to think through these relationships. Scholars such as Peter van der Veer and Steven Vertevec have documented and theorized the important ways in which the diaspora in the United States and the United Kingdom has played an important role in fueling religious nationalism in India (van der Veer 2004; Vertovec 1997). In the U.S. context, Vinay Lal has argued that the forms of Hinduism practiced there help to preserve a conception of India that is "largely derived from texts and practices of remote antiquity, which supposedly furnish us with a version of Hinduism in its pristine state." Lal argues that the Hinduism of Indian Americans "displays the most retrograde features" of the religion, unlike "homeland" Hinduism that continues to evolve (Lal 2003). Many of these observations may apply to the South African case as well. Like American Hindus, South African Indian Hindus are heavily involved with VHP activities and sometimes even take an active role in defining a "global Hinduism," such as in the widely circulated publication *Hinduism Today* (Rai 1995). Yet, because of the peculiarly uneven history of interrelationships between India and South Africa, among South African Hindus there exists a diversity of beliefs and rituals, only some of which have emerged in conversation with India itself. Transnational Hinduism of the kind practiced in the

Sai organization benefits from the constant back-and-forth interactions with India, such that members of the organization are inserted into a set of transnational religious exchanges that offer them the opportunity to belong to a transnational class of Indian professionals. Temple- and community-based Hinduism, of the type practiced in many of the old temples of Durban, offers less of this kind of opportunity and was a form of Hinduism rejected by many of my interviewees as patriarchal, limiting, and difficult to adapt to the busy lives of dual-earning couples in urban South Africa.

For South African Indians, Hindu religious practices and beliefs authenticate a vibrant, living sense of connection to India as a homeland. The various forms of Hinduism found in South Africa offer to their adherents divergent ideas of India as well as divergent modes of belonging to India. On the one hand, transnational Hinduism such as that practiced within the Sai organization offers the opportunity to engage with India in a cosmopolitan way that is also tied to an ancient, timeless, spiritual culture and, as such, is very compatible with the logics of preservation and change that define the transnational Indian professional ethos. Relative to other forms of Hinduism, transnational Hinduism deemphasizes everyday ritual, encourages service to humankind, and offers a location within India where adherents can travel for spiritual upliftment and renewal. Devotees who travel to the ashram can sing familiar songs, follow the same disciplinary rules and dress code, and share in a large, vibrant religious community that nonetheless is well adapted to a contemporary lifestyle. On the other hand, Hinduism based in Durban's Hindu temples is closely associated with the particular local community and its practices. As such, these temples do not necessarily offer the same opportunity to mediate a living sense of belonging to India.

Religious practice thus plays a critical role in authenticating South African Indians as a part of a transnational community of Indians. In India and Silicon Valley, work in the knowledge economy secures belonging in this transnational class, which then opens up specific ways in which to remake traditional notions of family and Indian culture. Although the vast majority of those who make up this transnational class are upper-caste Hindus, their religion is implicit. In South Africa, with its subaltern diaspora, we see clearly the ways in which religion acts as the ultimate lynchpin of belonging to this transnational class of professionals. The other aspects of transnational Indian class culture implicitly presume a particular conception of Hindu belonging.

When Indian Women Are Professionals in South Africa

In the communities in Durban and Chatsworth where I conducted field-work and interviews, young Indian women from middle-class families go to college for professional degrees of some kind, usually in accounting or finance. Unlike in India and Silicon Valley, in South Africa few Indian women have technical educational backgrounds in engineering or computer science, which remains a white male-dominated domain in South Africa.[6] Those women working in the burgeoning IT industry work in a range of administrative, technical, and management capacities, while very few are actually programming code. Still, Indian women working in the IT realm are relatively highly paid professionals, often making more than their husbands do, and they frequently feel a sense of belonging to a global knowledge economy. They have ample opportunities to travel, and most of the women I interviewed had traveled to India at least once, sometimes for work, but more often out of interest.

Perhaps the greatest difference between South African Indian women working in IT and their counterparts in urban India and California lies in their class histories. Many of the women I interviewed grew up in poor, working-class or rural families, which was a common position for South African Indians a generation ago. Although some women did grow up in what they characterized as middle-class surroundings, most did not. As such, the economic privilege they experience as adults is new for them and the expectation of domestic femininity was often not imposed upon them. Most of these women, unlike many women in India, always expected to work outside of the home for a living, as there has been a long history of Indian women of all classes working outside the home in South Africa.[7] In India, although most professionals I spoke to grew up with few luxury goods, they were relatively elite in the context of their society, and, for most women, working was a choice, not an economic necessity. Politically speaking as well, the old Indian middle class has always been the implicit audience for state policies and ideologies. In dramatic contrast, South African Indian professional women grew up in an apartheid world that purposefully limited their economic opportunities and sought to exclude them from political life as members of a subordinate group. In this sense, the dramatic social and economic transformations that these women have experienced in their adult lives make them at the outset of a different "background" from those who belong most easily within the transnational class of Indians.

Given this diversity, how then do South African Indian women express their sense of belonging to India and in which cases do they identify specifically with India's new transnational class?

AUDREY: INDIA AS ORIGIN

Audrey is a thirty-five-year-old corporate marketing manager for a major South African bank. Based in Johannesburg for the past thirteen years, she has climbed rapidly up the corporate ladder in the financial services industry. Having completed her MBA two years before her interview with me, Audrey spoke to me as a person approaching the peak of a successful career that has offered her not only a dramatic break from what she characterized as her conservative upbringing in Durban, but also the opportunity for travel and global engagement that she never could have imagined growing up. Audrey is a typical example of professional women I met who have a strong sense of being South African Indian, an identification to which they attribute a number of their own "traditional" attitudes and behaviors. Yet, as a Christian, Audrey has little sense of India as a vibrant, contemporary place. For her, India is the place of her ancestry, but not a place that she sees as associated with a "global" future, either for herself or for her family.

Much of Audrey's narrative centered around the traditionalism of her "Indian" views on the family. In this regard, Audrey sounds hauntingly similar to some of the professional women in India I spoke to who lead double lives: successful professional woman by day, traditional Indian wife and mother by night. What is distinctive here, however, is that she attributes her very traditional home life to the expectations her husband had been raised with in a Hindu family. Religion serves as a thread in Audrey's story in which her husband's conversion to Christianity has helped to make him progressive to some extent but has been unable to reverse his fundamentally conservative, patriarchal upbringing, characteristics that are inextricably linked to being Hindu in her mind. Audrey also saw me as an Indian familiar with the attitudes of Hindus; she assumed that I would be able to understand and perhaps condone the actions and attitudes of her husband because of my understanding of Indian culture, generically defined, and of Hindu culture specifically:

The people at work would not recognize me if they saw me at home. Because as soon as I leave work, then I have a different hat on. When I go home, I'm the traditional Indian woman that takes care of her family . . . They rely on me, they're totally dependent on me. Sometimes it's frustrating because of time. I'm highly pressurized . . . I've been married twelve years this June and my husband is also very traditional in the way he sees me. There's some part of him that does understand that I'm, well, my own person. I can say that . . . I used to be actually very afraid because when I first got married my husband used to never allow me to wear pants anywhere. I couldn't cut my hair, I couldn't color my hair, it was really bad.

So, I had to really fight, but the struggle was actually more like, well, I'm very spiritual. I'm a Christian, I was brought up a Christian. My husband was raised a Hindu. I'm sure you must have come across this. But when I met him, he had already converted to Christianity. *It is that cultural thing. That's Hindu culture as well, about women's roles and stuff like that.* And his mom never worked. Neither did mine. So, [what I was doing] was actually radical. So, there were a lot of obstacles that came in our way, but we've actually grown. I have grown as a person, my family has grown. He's changed [emphasis added].

Audrey relates her personal transformation to the transformation of the Indian community around her, in which women have started playing more prominent roles in public life. She feels ambivalent about some of these changes, as she wonders if the new generation, born into a democratic South Africa and brought up in a world with seemingly limitless choices, has gone "a bit too wild" in moving away from the older ways of respecting elders, dressing up for festivals, and being committed to a single relationship throughout one's adult life. In expressing all of these anxieties, Audrey sounds uncannily like upwardly mobile women in India who are concerned about the onset of a deteriorating Westernization that has arrived along with globalization in India.

Yet Audrey is very different from her South African Hindu peers in expressing these anxieties. Many of the Hindu women I interviewed in this age group made observations quite the opposite of Audrey's. Hindu interviewees tended to be surprised at the extent to which their young children embraced Indian cultural and religious activities, especially during festivals and weddings. For many, their own children seemed more concerned with this cultural dimension of their lives than when they themselves were growing up in apartheid South Africa. Indeed, Audrey's narrative of moving away from the collectivity, respect, and traditionalism of Indian family life speaks directly to the democratization of South Africa and the integration of South African Indians into a wider sphere of sociocultural experience. Her narrative also reveals Audrey's distance from the increased intensity of interchange between South Africa and India in recent years. This distance, which stems from her distance from South African Hindus, prevents her from becoming aware of either a "global" India or a transnational group of Indians who have transformed what Indian culture means to the world at large. The kind of status she might gain through association with that culture is also lost to her, as her own community does not value it in the way that Hindu religious communities do.

Audrey has never traveled to India, but when I asked her how she felt about it, her response revealed the extent to which India remains a static location of ancestral belonging to her, rather than a place that she belongs to in an everyday sense:

> There's a strong linkage for us to India, although we haven't been there. That we are very proud to be Indian, the fact that our forefathers came here and made a life for themselves. My dad's mom, she came here with her brother. They ran away from home and got on the ship and came down to Cape Town and then into the Natal to work on the sugarcane plantations. But then they opened up a jewelry shop, lived together, and they were very successful. She's still got her brothers, nieces, nephews in India. Next year, we want to plan to go. We want to go and see them. We do feel very strongly for Indians all over the world because we have that bond. There's still a connection to each other. Like, my mom's sister went to England. I think she's there about thirty years now, and her kids and all are there, but when they come home, it's like they're home! South Africa is home for them.

Audrey is unusual among South African Indians for claiming that she has existing relatives in India that she knows of. Yet, being proud of being Indian is disconnected from any contemporary sense of belonging to India, except as it positions her within South Africa. She plans to go to India, but the trip would not be a pilgrimage. She feels connected to Indians all over the world, but only through the lens of South Africa.

Narratives like Audrey's are typical of many upwardly mobile South African Indian women who have identified themselves as Christian for their entire lives. They like the idea of being Indian, but these ideas are informed neither by a living sense of interconnection with India as an authentic space of belonging nor by Indians with histories different from their own.

SHALINI: AMBIVALENT AUTHENTICITY

Shalini presents a very different articulation of Indian identification, one that is informed by travel (both to India and other diasporic locations) and identification with Hinduism. Yet Shalini's personal trajectory, which has not conformed to expectations of respectable femininity, and has not included any involvement with transnational Hinduism per se, has left her with ambivalent feelings about her connection to India. Indeed, her recognition of the changes occurring in India and the increasing wealth and visibility of Indian cultural life leads her away from a strong identification with her Indian heritage. For her, the contradictions entailed in producing and participating in a "new" version of Indianness are too much to overlook.

Shalini works in upper management with a multinational technical and financial services firm. In her early forties, Shalini has a grown daughter, with whom she constantly compared her own attitudes and experiences throughout our interview. In her college years, Shalini was involved in the anti-apartheid movement, and she now feels a commitment to the democratic ideals of the new South Africa. She is proud to be South African, but her Indian identification is strong for her, although she speculated that it might be even stronger for her daughter, who enthusiastically celebrates Indian festivals and enjoys Indian movies. For Shalini, growing up as an Indian woman carried with it a host of oppressive associations from which she distanced herself in her adult life. She found herself questioning the norms and beliefs of her community from a young age:

> You sort of conformed to certain things, but because we were exposed to a lot more and we were aware of what is going on politically, we challenged a lot more [than my daughter does today]. So though you were maybe forced into certain situations like to dress Indian and to follow Indian customs, you also challenged them; you had an awareness that there is something that is more important, something that

is not right . . . although you were brought up with it, you were forced into a situation where you had to question it. You sort of went into it kicking and screaming.

Shalini left her daughter in Durban with her parents to pursue a career in Johannesburg, an unusual and gutsy decision for women from her community. While the distance she felt from Indian norms of motherhood and respectable femininity explains in part how she was able to make such a decision, this distance also allowed her to continue to identify with aspects of being Indian that remained meaningful to her. She explains the unique aspects of being Indian in South Africa, a sentiment echoed in almost all of the interviews I conducted:

There is always an open door policy in the Indian homes and your food is prepared. It was a generosity that Indian family and the extended Indian families celebrated that is very difficult [from] white culture. In the white culture, if you are coming, I cook two people's meal or you bring something. I find generosity within Indian people to be a lovely policy. Whether it is food, whether it is sleeping on the floor, whatever, you have like semi-family and the support system . . . I think being Indian is particularly nice because you can count on your family's support without sort of feeling bad about it.

Shalini had married young and divorced after a ten-year marriage that made her feel like "a piece of furniture." As a single, divorced parent, clearly, she has found important and meaningful the interconnectedness and community of South African Indians. Yet, when she sought out similar meanings in India to extend and deepen her feelings of identification with India as an adult, she was disappointed.

For Shalini, "[Going to India was a] journey to see how comfortable I am just to go to my roots." She said she did feel a sense of comfort, being in a country of people who looked like her and wore familiar clothing. She identified with the religious life of the temples. Indeed, it was her continued identification with the Hindu religion that motivated her to visit in the first place. But in her search for a simple, spiritual place, she found people in India to be caste and class conscious and overly willing to forget about the values she thought were distinctly Indian—respecting elders, relying on family, staying away from smoking and drinking—in favor of a life of partying and fancy clothes in a country somewhere else.

People living in India, in the cities, I mean—I don't want to generalize —they are trying very hard to become American in the clothes they wear, the food they eat. Instead of going and trying to see what your culture is and how comfortable you are. That just did not do it for me . . . you had to be rich, you had to have a title, you had to be someone. I always thought that India is a lot more simple, that people are lot more simple, more accepting. They [Indians in India] had struggled a lot more [politically and economically, compared to South Africans]; I would have just expected it to be a lot more of people embracing other people.

Shalini's experience of India, which she found to be dramatically at odds with her expectations, was informed in part by her political identification as a part of the anti-apartheid struggle. Her Orientalized preconception of India was overlaid with her desire to find a kind of democracy and equality in the place of her heritage. This search was more important to her than visiting temples or exploring her religious identity in India. Once she encountered rigid social hierarchies that disappointed her expectations, it made her other experiences less appealing. In all, Shalini's trip to India made her feel more committed to the cultural mix she identified with in South Africa. She explained, "I came back feeling at a loss. But then, I thought, I belong here, I am a South African and even as an Indian I maintain some of my things—food and language and all that. I am a South African. It is a nice fusion of being Indian and South African. I get both aspects of the culture because the African culture is different, and that's the best part in some of what we do." Shalini has also compared her own articulations of Indianness with the Indian diaspora in Canada and the United States. These experiences led Shalini to conclude, "Indians are trying very hard to maintain their sort of Indianness whether in the form of language, having cultural things, temples. I often wonder whether that upbringing has taken us and made us more Indian." All these interactions, however, have left Shalini feeling far less invested in an unchanging and timeless cultural authenticity.

Like several other women I interviewed, Shalini asserts a partial identification with India as an authentic place of belonging and with the growing visibility of a transnational Indian professional class around the world. Her Hindu identification and upbringing provide her with a certain set of cultural expectations of India, and her upwardly mobile class position allowed her to explore those expectations through travel. Yet, her experience in South Africa, particularly her involvement in the anti-apartheid movement, had transformed her expectations of India. When the social realities did not coincide with what she expected, the presence of familiar temples and even a kind of visceral comfort in her surroundings could not compensate for it. Shalini remains ambivalent and divided in "mobilizing" a sense of belonging to India that exceeds her South African identification.

RANESHNI: INDIA AS BOTH "GLOBAL" AND "AUTHENTIC"

Raneshni, a thirty-five-year-old sales manager in a Durban-based software distribution company introduced in chapter 1, was typical of professional women I interviewed who belonged to a transnational Hindu organization.[8] Her experiences with religion, family, and travel to India closely coincide with the expectations and norms of India's transnational professional class. For Raneshni, her tie to India is a religious one at its core, so passing on a particular set of Hindu moral and ethical values to her children is of prime importance to her. Through her belonging to the Sai organization, she articulates her Hindu identity in a religiously neutral language centered on faith and human values. She explained, "Religion is a big thing. I think that's something you get from the time you can talk . . . and that's what makes Indians strong, in my opinion. That's a very, very big thing. And then comes everything else with that . . . I think because of religion, everything fits into place and everything makes sense to me . . . I realize that you have to do the right thing, you have to be honest . . . and if you don't do those things, you will face the consequences, life will teach you the hard way." Raneshni sends her children to a special school run by the Satya Sai organization, where they are taught the religious and moral principles through which to live their lives, while gaining an excellent education.

Like most other South African Indian women who expressed their tie to India primarily through Hinduism, Raneshni viewed India as the place where Hinduism was practiced in its most unadulterated form: "I've been to India three times. I went first after I got married; I was about twenty-five. My mother and I went. Because of Prashanti [the ashram and headquarters of Sai Baba]. That was my main calling to go. So, the first time, we stayed mainly in the south. And it was just like, you know, you see so many Indians and there's definitely a connection. And you see everything religious and spiritual and cultural everywhere, which you don't see in South Africa." Raneshni returns to India repeatedly because of the sense of spiritual and personal renewal she finds there. In the India she sees, her expectations of a spiritual culture are fulfilled, and the social hierarchies that were so troubling to Shalini are invisible.[9]

Raneshni's feeling of belonging to India is strengthened through her belonging to the tech industry and her admiration for the progress India has made in the field of technology. Like those in India and Silicon Valley, Raneshni takes great pride in Indian talent as it circulates the globe, and this pride transforms the way she views her own position in South Africa. She explains, "IT and India go hand and hand. People in South Africa don't realize that the brains of IT come from India. These white guys think it comes from the Silicon Valley, but really, it comes from India, and people don't know that." Observations and comments like these cropped up throughout Raneshni's interview as well as in my subsequent meetings with her. In a dramatic contrast with Shalini's interpretation of upper-class Indians, Raneshni was impressed with how "simple" and "humble" IT professionals living in India were. Echoing the trope of avoiding materialism so common among IT professionals in India and in Silicon Valley, she saw those living in India as having overcome the materialism she sees among South African Indians, and having established a life in India that was not only wealthier, but also more moral. In these ways, Raneshni's sense of engagement in the India of today begins with her religious practice but then connects with her professional identity to expressions of national pride that closely resonate with similar articulations by professionals in India.

Finally, Raneshni articulates her Indianness through her self-consciously subordinate position in her marriage, relative to her husband. Although she earns significantly more than her husband earns and works longer hours, she is almost exclusively responsible for cooking, cleaning, and childcare in the house. Throughout her interviews, she expressed her anger and frustration with her husband's temper and insensitive expectations. But when I questioned why she did not try to change those dynamics, she explained that she was very traditional and viewed her husband as her guru, or spiritual teacher. In a double invocation of the guru principle, Raneshni explained that Swami (the spiritual head, or guru, of the Satya Sai organization) says that women must put their families first, and that she had to do her best to control her anger.

When asked what aspects of Indian culture she upholds in her own life, she responded, "Being the good wife. That means providing for your family, making sure that they're fed and taken care of and the house is clean. And the kids, you have to be teaching them whether you're working or not, that sort of thing. All the values that you learned as a kid, they have to do that too."

Raneshni's articulations of the submissive femininity she enacts in her marriage are couched in a religious and cultural language that justifies such enactments as appropriate for women, a sentiment that few other women in any of the locations I examined articulated in this way. Indeed, most Indian women in India tried to distance themselves from the kind of submissive femininity that Raneshni asserts, opting instead for a respectable femininity that sought to strike a "balance" between professional and traditional expectations. For Raneshni, however, religion, culture, and appropriately submissive femininity are almost indistinguishable from one another.

The example of Raneshni is not necessarily typical of South African Indian professional women, who articulate diverse ways of belonging to India and "keeping up" with Indian culture. Indeed, very few women I interviewed in South Africa or elsewhere justified through religion and culture the kind of power dynamic that Raneshni described in her marriage. More important for our understanding of a transnational class culture, however, is the extent to which a particular form of transnational Hinduism allows her a point of access into a discursive universe in which particular discourses of morality, respectable femininity, and Indian nationalism coalesce in a universal language of equality and righteousness. Once she has entered into this discursive universe, Raneshni can participate in the class and cultural practices of South African Indians as well as Indians living in India and elsewhere who are also occupying the same transnational Indian universe. For South African Indians who help to comprise the subaltern Indian diaspora, transnational Hinduism provides a point of contact with this universe, thus making explicit the importance of Hinduism in the consolidation of the transnational class culture of Indian professionals.

Raneshni's particular version of Hinduism, as it is practiced in the Sai organization, is similar to "thin" articulations of Hinduism described by the young and upwardly mobile in all the locations in which I conducted interviews. Cultural streamlining here occurs through the abstraction of religious principles in everyday life, and the divorce of religious identification from religious ritual that allows for little space in which to dispute a tie to Hinduism. It is much easier to reject the need for elaborate rituals that one does not understand or have time for in a busy, cosmopolitan life than to reject general moral imperatives to live a conscious life that serves others and believes in a higher power. In some sense, the perceived open-endedness of Hinduism becomes a flexible discourse of belonging to India that can conform at once to the "core" principles of family while also allowing space for individualizing, merit-based ethics to dominate everyday life. Once belonging to India and identifying as Hindu become inextricably linked, individuals participate in community cultural activities that are helping to construct an essentialized global Hinduism whether or not they consciously wish to do so. In Mumbai and Bangalore, such "rational" versions of Hinduism reflect the convergence of ideas about individuality and progress with a desire to practice a more "spiritual," "authentic" religion that bears personal, rather than simply ritual, meaning. In South Africa, the importance of this view of Hindu religiosity in comprising the culture of India's transnational class is made explicit. While this religiosity opens the door to Hindu fundamentalism, nationalism, and a host of conservative politics, more fundamentally it reflects the centrality of this sanitized version of Hinduism, free of any ties to any local context, in constituting what it means to belong to the hegemonic culture of India's transnational class.

CONCLUSION

APOLITICAL POLITICS

The extent to which Indians of all sections of the population "believe" in the IT industry and in its possibilities for individual and collective advancement is incredible. It appears that religious belief and belief in IT are the two dominant topics in newspapers and general discussion, just as there are software training centres and temples in every small town.—PETER VAN DER VEER, "VIRTUAL INDIA: INDIAN IT LABOR AND THE NATION STATE"

There is a significant difference now—consumerism, bubbling middle-class population, availability of commodities, opportunities, economic prosperity. No doubt about it . . . When I finished college twenty-five years ago, I could not even imagine an India like this.—S. MOHAN, A SUC-CESSFUL SERIAL TECH ENTREPRENEUR AND THE CURRENT VICE PRESI-DENT OF CIBER, INDIA

For India, IT is more than an industry; it is a ladder to India's future, a future that seems to have already arrived, at least in part. In this future present, temples sit alongside software train-ing centers and malls in a comfortable synergy. When we try to pinpoint who is enabling these changes, and under what circum-stances, important questions arise: Who is taking courses at the software center, going to the temple, spending money at the mall? Who is making the cultural innovations that make all of these activities compatible, even complementary? As a new mode of belonging to India is being imagined on the streets, it is also being imagined in other spheres: in homes and in offices. And, while IT professionals may proportionally comprise a relatively small slice of contemporary urban India, the India they imagine is incredibly influential: it shapes (even as it is shaped by) American corpora-tions and media outlets; it provides fodder for India's economic and development policies; and it offers a compelling ideological alternative to India's divided past by asserting the centrality of the individual and her merits.

The idea of India, like all ideas, shifts and changes constantly. The cultural innovations of India's transnational class of IT professionals have signaled one such shift. This shift is significant because it distances itself dramatically from some of the ideas most sacred to post-colonial India's political founding, which was based on a socialistic view of society, a commitment to secular, democratic ideals, and a conviction that Indians serve the nation by serving their government. While this older idea of India certainly had its flaws, inconsistencies, and contradictions, it is decidedly distinct from the idea of India that has developed in the wake of global capitalism among that class of Indians who have benefited most from it. The class of transnational professionals who dominate India's cultural and economic landscape is decidedly apolitical. Its members believe in the progress of the unfettered individual taking off on the global scene, and that Indianness is upheld in family relationships, in respectable women, in practicing a certain decontextualized version of Hinduism. However apolitical, this newly stabilized notion of Indianness —one that has streamlined myriad ways of being Indian into a short list of "core" distinctive qualities—contains an optimism that is important and contagious.

For India, the effects of this new, streamlined version of Indian culture, which transnational Indian professionals have condensed into a particular kind of appropriate difference, are many-faceted. At a time when class disparities are deepening, and when India's political system seems to foster divisiveness rather than unity, "global Indianness" provides a seemingly sunny alternative. Individualistic yet family oriented, committed to India but in an open-ended way, the notion of belonging to India in the way that IT professionals articulate it produces a "feel-good factory" not unlike the BJP's India Shining campaign of 2004. "Global Indianness," however, is likely to be more durable than the disastrous India Shining campaign. Decidedly *not* wedded to a political party, and emphasizing the fundamental goodness and superiority of Indian culture, this new, simplified version of Indianness is ultimately optimistic and seems to walk a fine line between nationalism and cosmopolitanism. Benedict Anderson characterized nationalism as a "modular" discourse promoted by culturally cosmopolitan elites, a discourse that strategically washed out difference and diversity within a culture in order to produce a new, unified difference that was ultimately politically productive (Anderson 2006). As the cultural processes I describe work in strikingly similar ways, perhaps the appropriate difference that Indian IT professionals produce through cultural streamlining could prove to be similarly productive, especially in a global cultural economy that deals in difference.

And yet, the very work of unification that cultural streamlining might perform fosters a conservative politics that fundamentally valorizes the status quo. In the convergence of glossy images of India on American magazine covers and the ponderings of professional IT women as they wonder where in the world they would live most comfortably, economic reform has been unquestioningly good for India, has brought India to the world stage, has solved poverty and destitution, and has remade the nation entirely. The global version of Indianness produced by IT workers obscures the failures of economic liberalization, which have deepened class inequalities and provided mobility only for a select few, while the "trickle-down" effects have been slower to come and harder to measure. Aside from the inequities that economic reform has perpetuated within India, global Indianness also collapses the dizzying diversity of religious and community practices within India into a singular kind of difference, just one more in a worldwide panoply of global cultures. In an unexpected throwback to the discursive effects of Orientalism, Indian cultural production becomes oriented toward something singular and nationally agreed upon, even when only a few voices have agreed, or even been consulted. Indianness becomes again a cultural commodity to be produced and reproduced, not only for a Western gaze, but also for the consumption and display of Indian cosmopolitans the world over who care to partake. These dynamics are productive of a certain kind of politics—a politics that appears interested in the collective but relies upon the ostensible self-motivation of the individual, moving away from even a superficial commitment to a more just, democratic society that is respectful of new and existing forms of difference.

When we step out of India and into the realm of social science, the cultural processes I have analyzed in this book reorient our study of cultural globalization in important ways. First, by focusing on the cultural practice of an elite class that sees itself as commonplace, I underscore the importance of class in studying the material and symbolic dimensions of cultural globalization. Although race, class, and gender have become a holy trinity of difference within the social sciences, few studies of cultural globalization engage seriously with the material and symbolic dimensions of class as a way to understand how cultural globalization works. In this case, the symbolism of middle-classness and the high status of their work lend IT professionals a cultural legitimacy that allows their cultural innovations to reflect upon the country as a whole. Class and gender work together powerfully to produce this symbolic legitimacy for the nation, making IT professional women critical navigators of cultural change, a point I will return to in more depth below.

I have also identified the work conducted in the knowledge economy in particular as a critical sphere within which class culture is produced. While a good deal of literature on globalization has examined the workplace in various ways, I have argued that the specific logics of IT workplaces are shared and thus support an ethos of individuality and merit-based advancement in a global industry that must adjudicate between carefully constructed categories of cultural difference. Indeed, the cultural innovations that IT professionals make grow out of their participation in the culture of the IT industry. In brokering cross-cultural interactions that form the economic base of the industry, the workplace fosters ideas about what Indianness is, and how to be properly Indian, in a way that is appropriate in a global workplace. Each day, hardworking, virtuous individuals with economic power carry these ideas outside the workplace, even as they reconcile the ideas of Indianness disseminated in the workplace with the complexities of the world they confront. For many of those entering the IT workforce today who come from families who already have numerous family members in IT working in India and around the world, perhaps the dissonance between the world outside IT and the world within it is even less than for others. In this sense, cultural streamlining is prompted by the culture of the knowledge economy, which subsequently produces a matching reality outside its steel and glass buildings.

India's transnational professional class, then, is a new formation that has continuity with an "old" middle class of a previous generation—made up of urban government and bank workers, long considered the symbolic referent of the Indian nation—and yet has become an elite class segment through its participation in the knowledge economy and its transnational scope. To say that class is a critical category in studying the cultural dimensions of globalization, then, means also to say that the conditions under which class and class privilege are made are constantly shifting. New approaches to studying class—that cross borders, examine symbolic power, and are tied to a workplace—sensitize us to precisely the micropolitics of globalization that can be missed with a less grandiose category of analysis. The tendency to pay attention to the small scale, while critical, should not deter us from thinking in terms of larger categories and how those larger categories are reinvented and imbued with meaning in the contexts we study.

At the heart of this project lies a very specific approach to the study of gender, one that is often overlooked in the burgeoning literature on gender and globalization. I have engaged with gender in two ways: first, by examining the convergence of class and gender in the subjectivities of symbolically powerful women, I have underscored the importance of gender in legitimating cultural projects complicit with the inequalities of globalization. Such an approach departs from social scientific approaches to gender and globalization that focus on the gendered construction of capitalist work on the one hand, and humanistic approaches that primarily engage with historical analysis or cultural critique on the other. In India, respectable femininity, as it is enacted, reinforced, and reinvented by professional women, serves as an important means through which to legitimate the fusing of "the global" into a conception of Indianness. Even in the sphere of the professional, the actions of working women underscore the progress that the nation is making and legitimate global managerial discourses about equity and merit-based advancement.

To explore gendered subjectivities, I have relied upon narratives of personal experience. Personal stories most concretely illuminate the ways in which national and global meanings work together. Narratives of experience offer valuable snapshots of abstract symbolic and material processes. The highly personal ways in which both men and women navigate social, cultural, and economic norms in their everyday lives show us *how*, in a concrete sense, the idea of a new India is created and sustained by each worker. For women, choices about how to navigate the nexus between "global" and "Indian" are heavily loaded cultural choices that play themselves out in everyday decisions. These professional women self-consciously negotiate with these different spheres, most clearly embodied in the divide between their professional and family lives. The home and family is designated as the site of Indian culture and values, while the workplace is the site of "exposure," "the global," and the "new." Cultural flows between these two spheres, however, make those distinctions more fluid than they appear at first. Still, the divide is a profoundly gendered one, and it puts women in a key position to create and negotiate identifications that meld the values of the two sites in innovative ways that are nonetheless accountable to Indian middle-class cultural norms of respectability and domestic femininity.

Yet, what I hope to underscore about gender is not restricted to the importance of feminine subjectivities in constituting a new dominant culture. I also suggest that an important part of cultural streamlining is the relegation of culture to the feminine realm of the private. In colonial times, the Indian nationalist movement located the center of culture in the domestic realm, requiring women to guard the culture of the home, while men remained free to modernize in the public realm. In yet another startling throwback, the ways in which culture becomes streamlined in India's transnational class in fact heighten the responsibilities of women and the sanctity of the private sphere in a similar manner. When Indianness is redefined in terms of its "core principles" so as to be mobile and transferable, it is primarily within the private sphere that cultural legitimacy must be sustained. In India, Silicon Valley, and even in South Africa, informants overwhelmingly articulated "good families" as the "core" of Indian culture that must remain immune to the corrupting tendencies of globalization. It is women and the practices of women that uphold these good families, and despite all of the enhanced opportunity that professional jobs bring to women, the production of a new, simplified, globalization-friendly version of Indianness means precisely that Indians must look inward to the domestic sphere to uphold that identification.

On November 26, 2008, the transnational class of Indians received a shocking wake-up call. In Mumbai, terrorists attacked the playgrounds of India's elite in a high-tech drama that played out on television screens across the country. Resulting in more than 170 deaths, the Mumbai terror attacks were quickly dubbed "India's 9/11" by the Indian media, and the interminable sixty-hour hostage situation at the elite Taj Mahal Hotel kept Indians around the world glued to the Internet's coverage of the event. Soon after, candlelight vigils cropped up around the world to memorialize those who died and call for a sense of interreligious unity and peace. This was certainly not the first time Indian cities had become targets of terrorist attacks, but this was the first time the terrorists had confronted India's elite. Several days after the attacks, in the deluge of commentary that followed, an article by Tarun J. Tejpal appeared in the political magazine *Tehalka*, a publication that has become a watchdog for the Indian public. In the article, Tejpal commented on the death of Rohinton Maloo, a strategic advisor for *Tehalka*. But this was no sentimental memoriam. Tejpal wrote,

> For me there is a deep irony in his death. He was killed by what he set very little store by. In his every meeting with us, he was bemused and baffled by *Tehelka*'s obsessive engagement with politics. He was quite sure no one of his class—our class—was interested in the subject. Politics happened elsewhere, a regrettable business carried out by unsavoury characters. Mostly, it had nothing to do with our lives. . . . In the end, politics killed Rohinton, and a few hundred other innocents. . . . I wish Rohinton had survived the lottery of death in Mumbai last week. In an instant, he would have understood what we always went on about. India's crying need is not economic tinkering or social engineering. It is a political overhaul, a political cleansing. As it once did to create a free nation, India's elite should start getting its hands dirty so they can get a clean country.

While Maloo was no IT professional, he shared with the transnational class of Indians examined in this book the common conviction of India's elite: that politics is something that was not meant for him. The reason, perhaps, that transnational Indians around the world were mobilized to candlelight vigils over the attacks on Mumbai's best hotels is precisely because it provided the wake-up call that Tejpal challenges us with.

In examining how a class of people transforms a diverse culture into something apolitical—a "difference" that feels appropriate, appealing, and non-threatening to all who encounter it—this book suggests that such a cultural process is in itself political. The disavowal of the political is something that stretches beyond the confines of India's burgeoning transnational class, which will doubtlessly continue to forge new ground in the global economic and cultural economies. Part and parcel of cultural globalization is decontextualization and depoliticization, but this procedure is ultimately artificial—a move by elites that has concrete implications for the world we live in. That this fact was brought home to Maloo and many others in such a violent way is sad, even tragic, yet it offers a lesson about the extent to which those of us who benefit from global capitalism are complicit in it.

In a deep sense, this book is a study of a culture of complicity of this kind. It maps out how it is that hard-working, moral individuals who have been actualized in the midst of the rapid social and economic changes that have lifted economic growth rates and made India a global power can, in reshaping the notions of culture they grew up with to fit their new lifestyles, support a politics that few of them bother to become aware of. It is this insight that we gain from studying middle-classness—that politics, disguised as being apolitical, make middle-class cultural innovations possible.

Introduction: On Background

1. The Bhagavad Gita, referred to here simply as the Gita and translated as "Song of God," is regarded as the authoritative "holy book" of Hinduism in popular and global parlance. This popular status belies the importance of multiple scriptures and texts within Hinduism, of which the Gita is just one. A record of a mythic conversation on the battlefield between two key Hindu characters, Arjuna and Lord Krishna, the Gita offers practical everyday advice on the importance of duty and sacrifice. Many regard the text as also outlining the fundamental principles of Hinduism.

2. All of my interviewees are identified by pseudonyms.

3. For an overview and introduction on the issues of caste and access particularly to higher education in contemporary India, see Chanana 1993.

4. In contrast to affirmative action policies in the United States, reservations policies in India operate on the basis of numerical quotas/proportions such that a particular underrepresented group receives an allotment of the available admission slots. This approach, while more radical than affirmative action in some ways, also has the effect of reinforcing the status of the underprivileged group even further. For an introduction to the arguments for the reservations system in India, especially in comparison to affirmative action policies in the United States, see Rai 2002.

5. For in-depth research on the exclusion of women from the fields of computing and IT in the United States, see Cohoon and Aspray 2006; Margolis and Fisher 2002.

6. Examples of these marriage dynamics and the ways in which these modified expectations intersect with the persistence of the gendered division of labor in the household appear in chapter 5.

7. For an extensive study on the persistence of "traditional" expectations of female engineers in India, both inside and outside the workplace, see Patel and Parmentier 2005.

8. Here, I refer to Arif Dirlik's use of the term, especially in reference to the notion of "multiple modernities." See Dirlik 2003.

9. Although the symbolic power of Indians who have joined the ranks of the world's hyper-rich, such as Narayana Murthy and Lakshmi Mittal, is indeed formidable, these capitalists make up a tiny fraction of India's transnational

professional class, and I am not primarily concerned with this minority here. Nandan Nilekani, for example, has leveraged his own symbolic power as an "ordinary middle-class" man turned industry captain to expound his vision of the future of India in his recent and much publicized book. See Nilekani 2009.

10. Workers in software, hardware, and business processing outsourcing (BPO) are often included under the same umbrella of "information technology" in official statistics about India. For purposes of this book's analysis, however, I treat the two groups as separate. Indeed, folk understandings of "IT" seldom include call center or transcription workers, and IT professionals often highlight their difference from BPO workers. For more on this distinction, see chapter 1.

11. Certainly, "globalization" is an equally contested term. Here, although I use the word "globalization" to signal the stretching of lines of production across national borders and the various cultural shifts that have accompanied it, I use the word tentatively, acknowledging various critiques of the term. My intent is to use the word "globalization" to help to describe the historical moment during which the cultural trends I observe take place (rather than as an analytical or explanatory category), and to use the word "global" as a native term that illuminates specific kinds of cultural politics.

Chapter 1: Privilege

1. The practice of women stopping work after "moving back" to India seems to be common among the growing group of returnees to India called RNRIs (returned non-resident Indians). Online blogs and articles attest to the prevalence of this phenomenon.

2. This practice is very common among Hindu women in South Africa.

3. I borrow the notion of India's middle class as being both "elite" and "everyman" from Ray and Baviskar (forthcoming).

4. Fieldwork among management both on the Indian and U.S. sides suggests that this arrangement is not so straightforward. Teams in India are very often less efficient than similar teams in the United States and often fall short when it comes to problem solving and troubleshooting. Still, the lower pay scales make outsourcing to India a financial necessity for many U.S.-based tech firms to remain competitive.

5. There is a significant range in this figure, ranging from older estimates of about one-tenth to newer estimates of one-half or less. This variation is not only the result of rising salaries but also of other kinds of costs that are not immediately visible. On average, engineers based in the United States tend to be more specialized and experienced than Indian engineers, who tend to be younger. So, an engineer in India does not exactly replace an engineer in the United States. There are additional costs for the client firm as well, including longer production cycles and longer days for employees onsite who must confer with the offshore team.

6. The "feel-good factory" borrows from the journalist P. Sainath's (2004) scathing critique of the India Shining campaign and the hype that it produced.

7. In the data from the National Association of Software and Service Companies (NASSCOM), for example, information technology is viewed as an umbrella term, and no specific distinctions are made in terms of the human resources going into software development in contrast to BPO work (see nasscom.org). Reena Patel's ethnographic work in Mumbai, however, suggests that call center firms are increasingly recruiting employees who are high school dropouts or have just recently completed high school. If this observation is part of a larger trend, then it might be that much of the panic about call center workers is also closely connected to a broader panic about youth. I return to a discussion of the symbolic hierarchies between call center workers and IT professionals in chapter 5.

8. For example, Patel's informants working in call centers reported being the subject of frequent gossip in their neighborhoods and were often stereotyped as being "not a family person" (2008, 74–75). These stereotypes were perceived as resulting from working at night. Patel calls the discourses that surround call center workers, especially women, "mobility-morality narratives," recognizing the close linkages between mobility at night and questionable morality. The quotes of IT professionals echo these views closely.

9. Similar stories of rapid mobility are present in the IT industry, but they are rare. When they occur, it is almost always men who achieve the social climb, rather than women, who are more likely to have life outcomes that are more closely aligned to their family's fortunes and wishes.

10. The significant exception to this would be the fixation of the American media in particular on female call center workers in India. See Elliot 2006.

11. Bourdieusian feminists have been particularly attentive to processes through which gender becomes symbolic capital when legitimated through middle-class status. Leslie McCall (1992) has argued that gender and class distinctions interact through embodied cultural capital, in which gender can be read as "hidden" capital—"hidden" in that it is not visible in the position that individuals occupy in social space, despite its pervasiveness, and "hidden" also in the sense that it is the most naturalized and universalized, becoming symbolic capital at once. Beverley Skeggs (2005) has also shown that once legitimated, middle-class femininity becomes, in itself, a kind of capital that women seek to embody in order to gain symbolic profit. This strategy has been well documented in Britain and in India among non-dominant groups. See also Ray 2000; Skeggs 1997.

Chapter 2: Global/Indian

1. Geert Hofstede's influential work (1980) examined the relationship between national cultures and organizational management cultures in wide-ranging comparative studies of corporate workplaces. His concept of five cultural dimensions proposes that different countries are differently oriented in their

understandings of authority, their value of the individual versus the collective, and their value for "masculine" versus "feminine" traits, among others. See also Hofstede 1980. His work has been criticized as being too homogenizing of national cultures, assuming these cultures to be uniform, distinct from one another, and relatively unchanging. See McSweeney 2002; Ailon 2008.

2. In her research, Sathaye (2007) finds an Indian IT professional who called this feeling of being "anywhere" a "space warp."

3. This interpretation is supported in Aihwa Ong's (1999) account of a "glow of fraternity" among Chinese businessmen. AnnaLee Saxenian describes the same phenomenon from an institutional and business-oriented perspective in her book, *The New Argonauts: Regional Advantage in a Global Economy* (2006).

Chapter 3: Merit

1. The question of how many people the OBC category comprises is a subject of considerable debate. The Mandal Commission found the number to be at 52 percent, although subsequent findings have put the number much lower, fueling protests that the move toward reservation rates of 50 percent is primarily politically motivated. Moreover, who qualifies as OBC varies from state to state, and the caste composition of different political parties is also a key factor in how these categories are realized in practice. See Bhalla and Jain 2006; also see Osborne 2001.

2. In an interesting contrast to perceptions of affirmative action in the United States, employees of any organization that has reservations policies in India, including the government, perceive those candidates who came into the organization because of a quota to be significantly less competent, while in the United States co-workers tend not to (at least overtly) devalue colleagues who are in the organization because of affirmative action policies. See Combs and Nadkarni 2005.

3. The success of the private sector in avoiding reservations altogether may be short-lived, however. Discussion of reservations in the private sector resurfaced in the context of legislation in 2006 to increase reservations for OBCs in government colleges and universities. Although this legislation enjoyed strong support from political parties, a small but vocal minority, including doctors and engineers, did have the effect of increasing the number of seats available to "general category" applicants as well as stalling the implementation of the legislation by a year. See Bidwai 2006.

4. This view is also deeply gendered; because men change jobs more frequently, women tend to advance because of their reliability in a firm, rather than the experience they might gain from moving between firms frequently. The few women who do constantly shift jobs find it difficult to get upper-management jobs as external applicants, so Shirin's view that moving around is merit-worthy might actually end up reinforcing a naturalized view of male IT workers being more merit-worthy than women.

5. See chapter 5 for a discussion of this important recurring folk term.
6. The Indian Institutes of Management are India's most prestigious business schools with arguably the most competitive admissions process in the world. Dhiraj's aspiration to study at IIM Bangalore indicates his ambition to acquire a qualification that would place him in an elite tier of the tech industry.
7. Despite the prevalence of this belief, interviewees suggested that there are in fact subtle concessions made for women with families. See chapters 2 and 5.
8. Here, I invoke the term "neoliberal" in its academic sense, although its popular association with unbridled global capitalism is closely related. See Harvey 2005; Rose 1999.
9. The argument that the IT industry happened by itself, and the strong evidence against such a position, has been concisely and clearly stated in Gupta 2007. For an extensive account of the importance of state and national policies in the formation of the IT industry, see Parthasarathy 2000, 2004. Three key policies were especially important. First, the STP scheme focused on building up the necessary infrastructure to allow Indian software exports to shift away from body shopping toward domestic software development, attracting better work at higher rates. With the establishment of the Software Technology Parks of India (STPI) in 1991, policies oriented toward the software industry became more autonomous from the government. Second, the National Association of Software and Service Companies (NASSCOM), established in 1988 as the national association for the promotion of IT in India, played an aggressive role in making STPI autonomous from the government and in providing a range of financial incentives for the software industry, including tax exemptions, the elimination of duties, and employee stock options. It also worked with foreign firms and encouraged local software entrepreneurs to increase exports. (See Evans 1995; Saxenian 2000.) Third, a series of sector-specific policies continued to expand the infrastructure and development of the domestic software industry. By 1998, there were twenty-five STPs in place in India.

Chapter 4: Individuals

1. A well-developed anthropological literature tended to dichotomize selves, suggesting that the bounded, self-contained individual was a uniquely Western notion, while Indian persons were substantially connected to others. For example, see Valentine 1984; Shweder 1991. In-depth studies on the ground, however, have complicated these ideas by suggesting that multiple notions of self and personhood exist in India, and that relational and autonomous notions of the self coexist and interpenetrate one another, especially when gender and the life course are taken into account. For example, see Lamb 1997; Ewing 1990.
2. Pentium processors, made by Intel, revolutionized the computer industry by their speed and efficiency. Intel has come out with new processors every few years since the 1990s, and Madhav marks his time in the industry with the

release date of each new version of the Pentium processors, which are now obsolete.

3. Mamta's views on these matters are explored in chapter 3.

Chapter 5: Family

1. I borrow the term "time bind" from Arlie Hochschild's book (2001) of the same name, which analyzes a similar phenomenon among dual-income households in the United States. In the Indian context, the time bind looks different precisely because of the myriad cultural valences associated with prioritizing the family. While the research of Hochschild and others suggest that in the United States working women are seldom able to reconcile their identities as workers with their responsibilities at home, my interviews suggest that for Indian women there exists a culturally appropriate "balance" that is acceptable in part because of the existence of cheap domestic labor that compensates for a persistent gendered division of labor.

2. See Fuller and Narasimhan 2007 for a strong supporting account of the aspirations of urban IT women.

3. For evidence of the continued discrimination that IT women face in recruiting and promotion, see Parikh and Sukhatme 2004.

4. This is a recurring theme. See Ram's comments in chapter 1, also in response to BPO workers. Some evidence suggests that call center workers are in fact younger than IT workers on average, as call centers seem to be recruiting younger and younger candidates. See Patel 2008.

5. This is the part of the sari that hangs over the shoulder, usually the most elaborately designed part. "Open" *palloos* (rather than pinned-up ones) are a more suggestive and graceful way of draping a sari in the context Meena is talking about.

6. The panics about call centers recall a more generalized panic that Indian sociologists have noted about the potential for any kind of work outside the home to destroy a woman's femininity and commitment to the family—a panic from which contemporary IT work is exempt. See Desai and Anantram 1985. Gendered moral panic over women working in new industries has also been a common theme in a gender and globalization literature. With regard to factory women, see, for example, Ong 1987; Lynch 2007.

7. This story, perhaps an urban legend, was cited as part of an editorial column entitled "Bangalore after Dark" in the *New India Press* on Sunday over eight months after this interview. This column has been posted on a Bangalore-related blog and has elicited some online discussion from Indians who are in despair over the sad moral state of India it revealed.

Chapter 6: Religion

1. There is significant scholarly debate over the extent to which Hinduism is a true "religion" and the extent to which it was "invented" by colonial and,

later, nationalist states. See, for example, a special issue of the *Journal of the American Academy of Religion* (2000; vol. 68, no. 4) for details on these debates. The constructionist view emphasizes the immense diversity of practices and beliefs encompassed by "Hinduism," while the opposite view emphasizes the long history of Hindu practices grounded in scriptural tradition. For an example of the constructionist view, see Dalmia and von Stietencron 1995. The opposite position is outlined clearly in Lorenzen 1999. The diversity of practices in the diaspora has further complicated these debates. Indeed, the cultural processes I observe in this chapter that feed into cultural streamlining seem to extend and re-create the unity of Hinduism debated in an earlier historical moment in a new global cultural economy.

2. I did not collect information about caste from my informants explicitly, as the topic is considered slightly taboo. From Upadhya and Vasavi's survey (2006) of more than five hundred IT professionals working in Bangalore, however, which concluded that 80 percent of these workers are upper caste, it seems safe to presume that the same was true of my sample as well.

3. Tejaswini Niranjana (2006) reminds us of the importance of "subaltern diasporas" in the making of the Indian nation through her examination of "Indianness" as it is negotiated in Trinidad—a destination with the same history of indentured Indian labor as South Africa. She not only explores and explains the interconnections between "Indianness" in the Caribbean and the "hegemonic construction of 'Indians'" in India, but further argues that "Indianness" in the subaltern diaspora has important implications for conceptions of Indianness "at home."

4. This contemporary role stems from the historic role of Indian women in South Africa, who, from indenture onward, have been symbolic of the permanence of Indians in Natal, as well as having been responsible for the cultural and biological reproduction of the indentured family. See Thiara 2001.

5. For example, the festival of Kavady, which is celebrated through ritual piercings of body parts and trances, is rarely seen in India today, and almost never in urban areas. Yet these practices are commonplace in Durban, especially at Tamil temples.

6. Like India, post-apartheid South Africa has made significant moves toward economic liberalization to bring globalization home. A booming economy and escalating levels of foreign investment have brought increasing numbers of high-end service sector jobs to South Africa, particularly in the areas of finance and information technology. Although the size and scope of the IT sector in South Africa is small compared to India, as the nation with the highest levels of connectivity in Africa, South Africa has significant potential to be a regional IT power. See Ord 2004.

7. Still, there was some indication from a few interviewees that among middle-class women with husbands who were well-off, in-laws and family members expected them to cut back or quit their careers. Furthermore, anecdotal

evidence from my fieldwork, especially with state and local agencies, suggests that rates of workforce participation among Indian women might be lower than for other race groups in South Africa.

8. Raneshni was one of a handful of professional women in South Africa whom I interviewed and interacted with multiple times. The analysis and overview of her story here reflects these multiple meetings and interactions, the latest of which occurred in 2008.

9. The professional women I interviewed who were a part of transnational Hindu organizations were not actively involved in the anti-apartheid struggle. It may be that involvement in the struggle dramatically changes the ways in which women express or experience Hindu identity. In previous research, however, I came across women working in other professional fields in the public sector who are involved in the Sai organization *and* are very committed to South African (rather than Indian) identity, but this seems to be more the exception than the rule.

Abraham, Itty. 1998. *The Making of the Indian Atomic Bomb: Science, Secrecy, and the Postcolonial State*. London: Zed Books.

Agrawal, Arun. 1996. Poststructuralist Approaches to Development: Some Critical Reflections. *Peace and Change* 24 (4): 464–77.

Ahluwalia, Isher Judge, Ritu Kochhar, Radhika Lal, Philip Oldenburg, and Nazneen Karmali. 2004. *India's 2004 Election: What Happened and Why*. Asia Social Issues Program. http://www.asiasource.org/asip/india_elections04.cfm, accessed June 15, 2008.

Ahmed-Ghosh, Huma. 2003. Writing the Nation on the Beauty Queen's Body: Implications for a Hindu Nation. *Meridians: Feminism, Race, Transnationalism* 4 (1): 205–27.

Ailon, Galit. 2008. Mirror, Mirror on the Wall: Culture's Consequences in a Value Test of Its Own Design. *Academy of Management Review* 33 (4): 885–904.

Amanpour, Christiane. 2003. For Love of Money. CBSNews.com. http://www.cbsnews.com/stories/2003/10/03/60minutes/main576466.shtml, accessed July 20, 2004.

Anderson, Benedict. 2006. *Imagined Communities: Reflections on the Origin and Spread of Nationalism*. London and New York: Verso.

Aneesh, A. 2006. *Virtual Migration: The Programming of Globalization*. Durham, N.C. and London: Duke University Press.

Appadurai, Arjun. 1996. *Modernity at Large: Cultural Dimensions of Globalization*. Minneapolis: University of Minnesota Press.

Arrow, Kenneth, Samuel Bowles, and Steven Duraluf. 1999. *Meritocracy and Economic Inequality*. Princeton: Princeton University Press.

Bay Area Indians for Equality. 2006. *Protest against Indian Gov't Reservation Policy at Fair Oaks Park, Sunnyvale, California*. http://bayarea4equality.googlepages.com/fairoaksevent, accessed January 2008.

Beck, Ulrich, Anthony Giddens, and Scott Lash. 1994. *Reflexive Modernization: Politics, Tradition and Aesthetics in the Modern Social Order*. Cambridge: Polity Press.

Bhalla, Surjit S., and Sunil Jain. 2006. Quota: Just How Many OBCs Are There? http://www.rediff.com///money/2006/may/08quota.htm, accessed June 10, 2008.

Bhaskaran, Suparna. 2004. Compulsory Individuality and the Trans/national Family of Nations: The Girl-Child, Bollywood Barbie, and Ms. Worldy Universe. In S. Bhaskaran, ed., *Made in India: Decolonizations, Queer Sexualities, Trans/national Projects*, 37–70. New York: Palgrave Macmillan.

Bhattacharjee, Anannya. 1999. The Habit of Ex-Nomination: Nation, Woman and the Indian Immigrant Bourgeoisie. In S. Gupta, ed., *Emerging Voices: South Asian Women Redefine Self, Family and Community*, 229–52. New Delhi: Sage Publications.

Bidwai, Praful. 2006. India: Bringing the Caste-Aways on Board. *Asia Times*. http://www.atimes.com/atimes/South_Asia/HF02Df01.html, accessed July 2008.

Bourdieu, Pierre. 1984. *Distinction: A Social Critique of the Judgement of Taste.* Cambridge: Harvard University Press.

——. 1990. Social Space and Symbolic Power. In *In Other Words*, 122–39. Stanford: Stanford University Press.

——. 1991. Social Space and the Genesis of Classes. In P. Bourdieu, ed., *Language and Symbolic Power*, 229–51. Cambridge: Harvard University Press.

——. 1995. Forms of Capital. In J. G. Richardson, ed., *Handbook of Theory and Research for the Sociology of Education*, 241–58. New York: Greenwood Press.

Burawoy, Michael, Joseph A. Blum, Sheba George, Zsuzsa Gille, Teresa Gowan, Lynne Haney, Maren Klawiter, Steve H. Lopez, Seán Ó. Riain, and Millie Thayer. 2000. *Global Ethnography: Forces, Connections, and Imaginations in a Postmodern World.* Berkeley: University of California Press.

Castells, Manuel. 1997. *The Power of Identity.* Malden, Mass.: Blackwell.

Chakravartty, Paula. 2006a. Symbolic Analysts or Indentured Servants? Indian High-Tech Migrants in America's Information Economy. *Knowledge, Technology, and Policy* 19 (3): 27–43.

——. 2006b. White-Collar Nationalisms. *Social Semiotics* 16 (1): 39–55.

Chanana, Karuna. 1993. Accessing Higher Education: The Dilemma of Schooling Women, Minorities, Scheduled Castes and Scheduled Tribes in Contemporary India. *Higher Education* 26 (1): 69–92.

Chatterjee, Partha. 1986. *Nationalist Thought and the Colonial World: A Derivative Discourse.* Minneapolis: University of Minnesota Press.

——. 1990. The Nationalist Resolution of the Women's Question. In Kumum Sangari and Sudesh Vaid, eds., *Recasting Women: Essays in Indian Colonial History*, 233–53. New Brunswick: Rutgers University Press.

Clark, Alice W. 2008. Young Women in High-Tech India: Narratives of Individuation at a Time of Rapid Demographic Change. Lecture sponsored by the Center for South Asia Studies, University of California, Berkeley, December 9.

Cohoon, J. McGrath, and William Aspray. 2006. *Women and Information Technology: Research on Underrepresentation.* Cambridge: Massachusetts Institute of Technology Press.

Collins, Patricia Hill. 1991. *Black Feminist Thought.* New York: Routledge.

Combs, Gwendolyn M., and Sucheta Nadkarni. 2005. The Tale of Two Cultures: Attitudes towards Affirmative Action in the United States and India. *Journal of World Business* 40: 158–71.

Corbridge, Stuart, and John Hariss. 2000. *Reinventing India: Liberalization, Hindu Nationalism, and Popular Democracy*. Cambridge: Polity Press.

Dalmia, Vasudha, and Heinrich von Stietencron. 1995. *Representing Hinduism: The Construction of Religious Traditions and National Identity*. New Delhi: Sage Publications.

Das, Bhagwan. 2000. Moments in a History of Reservations. *Economic and Political Weekly* (October 28): 3831–34.

Das, Gurcharan. 2000. *India Unbound: From Independence to the Global Information Age*. New Delhi: Viking.

——. 2004. India Shining (1984–2004) RIP? *Outlook India*, July 12. http://www .outlookindia.com/article.aspx?224464, accessed June 2008.

Das Gupta, Monisha. 1997. "What Is Indian about You?": A Gendered, Transnational Approach to Ethnicity. *Gender and Society* 11 (5): 572–96.

de Jonquières, Guy. 2005. "India's Knowledge Economy." *Financial Times*. http:// yaleglobal.yale.edu/content/indias-knowledge-economy, accessed May 2010.

Desai, Ashwin. 1996. *Arise Ye Coolies: Apartheid and the Indian 1960–1995*. Johannesburg: Impact Africa Pub.

——. 2002. *We Are the Poors: Community Struggles in Post-Apartheid South Africa*. New York: Monthly Review Press.

Desai, Neera, and Sarayu Anantram. 1985. Middle Class Women's Entry into the World of Work. In K. Saradamoni, ed., *Women, Work, and Society: Proceedings of the ISI Symposium*. Calcutta: Indian Statistical Institute.

Deshpande, Satish. 1993. Imagined Economies: Styles of Nation-Building in Twentieth-Century India. *Journal of Arts and Ideas* (25–26): 5–35.

——. 2003. *Contemporary India: A Sociological View*. New Delhi: Viking.

Dirlik, Arif. 2003. Global Modernity? Modernity in an Age of Global Capitalism. *European Journal of Social Theory* 6 (3): 275–92.

Dumont, Louis. 1980 [1960]. World Renunciation in Indian Religions. Appendix B of *Homo Hierarchicus*, 267–86. Chicago: University of Chicago Press.

Elliott, Michael. 2006. India Awakens. *Time* (June 18): 167.

Escobar, Arturo. 1995. *Encountering Development: The Making and Unmaking of the Third World*. Princeton: Princeton University Press.

Evans, Peter. 1995. *Embedded Autonomy: States and Industrial Transformation*. Princeton: Princeton University Press.

Ewing, Katherine. 1990. The Illusion of Wholeness: Culture, Self, and the Experience of Inconsistency. *Ethos* 18: 251–78.

Ferguson, James. 1994. *The Anti-Politics Machine: Development, Depoliticization, and Bureaucratic Power in Lesotho*. Minneapolis: University of Minnesota Press.

Fernandes, Leela. 2000a. Nationalizing the 'Global': Media Images, Cultural Politics and the Middle Class in India. *Media, Culture and Society* 22: 611–28.

——. 2000b. Restructuring the New Middle Class in Liberalizing India. *Comparative Studies of South Asia, Africa, and the Middle East* 20 (1 and 2): 88–105.

——. 2000c. Rethinking Globalization: Gender, Nation and the Middle Class in

Liberalizing India. In M. deKoven, ed., *Feminist Locations: Theory/Practice/Local/Global*, 147–67. New Brunswick: Rutgers University Press.

Fernandes, Leela, and Patrick Heller. 2006. Hegemonic Aspirations: New Middle Class Politics and India's Democracy in Comparative Perspective. *Critical Asian Studies* 38 (4): 495–522.

Frank, Andre Gunder. 1967. The Development of Underdevelopment. *Monthly Review* 18 (4): 17–31.

Freeman, Carla. 2000. *High Tech and High Heels in the Global Economy: Women, Work, and Pink Collar Identities in the Caribbean*. Durham: Duke University Press.

Friedman, Jonathan, Shalini Randeria, and Toda Institute for Global Peace and Policy Research. 2004. *Worlds on the Move: Globalization, Migration, and Cultural Security*. London: I. B. Tauris in association with the Toda Institute for Global Peace and Policy Research.

Friedman, Thomas L. 2004. The Great Indian Dream. *New York Times*, March 11, 29.

Fuller, C. J., and Haripriya Narasimhan. 2007. Information Technology Professionals and the New-Rich Middle Class in Chennai (Madras). *Modern Asian Studies* 41 (1): 121–50.

Giddens, Anthony. 1994. Living in a Post-Traditional Society. In A. G. Ulrich Beck and Scott Lash, ed., *Reflexive Modernization: Politics, Tradition and Aesthetics in the Modern Social Order*, 56–109. Stanford: Stanford University Press.

Grewal, Inderpal, and Caren Kaplan. 1994. Transnational Feminist Practices and Questions of Postmodernity. In I. Grewal and C. Kaplan, eds., *Scattered Hegemonies: Postmodernity and Transnational Feminist Practices*, 1–28. Minneapolis: University of Minnesota Press.

Gupta, Prashant. 2007. Differential Scenarios in Employment. *i4d: The First Monthly magazine on ICT4D* 5 (7): 11–12.

Hall, Edward T. 1976. *Beyond Culture*. New York: Anchor Books/Doubleday.

Hancock, Mary. 1999. *Womanhood in the Making: Domestic Ritual and Public Culture in Urban South India*. Boulder: Westview Press.

Hansen, Thomas Blom. 1999. *The Saffron Wave: Democracy and Hindu Nationalism in Modern India*. Princeton: Princeton University Press.

———. 2000. Plays, Politics, and Cultural Identity among Indians in Durban. *Journal of Southern African Studies* 26 (2): 255–69.

———. 2002. Diasporic Dispositions. *Himal* 15 (December) http://www.himalmag.com/, accessed December 2002.

———. 2005. Melancholia of Freedom: Humour and Nostalgia among Indians in South Africa. *Modern Drama* 42 (2): 297–315.

Hart, Gillian Patricia. 2002. *Disabling Globalization: Places of Power in Post-Apartheid South Africa*. Berkeley: University of California Press.

Harvey, David. 2005. *A Brief History of Neoliberalism*. Oxford and New York: Oxford University Press.

Heesterman, J. C. 1981. Householder and Wanderer. *Contributions to Indian Sociology* 15 (1–2): 251–71.

Hindu, The. 2005. "Knowledge Commission Set Up: Sam Pitroda to Head Panel That Will Give India an Edge." *The Hindu*, June 4. http://www.hindu.com/2005/06/04/Stories/2005060404541200.htm, accessed August 2010.

Hochschild, Arlie. 2001. *The Time Bind: When Work Becomes Home and Home Becomes Work.* New York: Henry Holt and Company.

Hofstede, Geert. 1980. *Culture's Consequences: International Differences in Work-Related Values.* Beverly Hills: Sage Publishers.

———. 1993. Cultural Constraints in Management Theories. *The Executive* 7 (1): 81–94.

Hooker, Clarence. 1997. Ford's Sociology Department and the Americanization Campaign and the Manufacture of Popular Culture among Assembly Line Workers c. 1910–1917. *Journal of American Culture* 20 (1): 47–53.

Hull, Glynda. 2001. Constructing Working Selves: Silicon Valley Assemblers Meet the New Work Order. *Anthropology of Work Review* 22 (1): 17–21.

Kaul, Sumeet. 2005. "More IITians Pass Up U.S. Degrees for High-Paying Jobs Here." *Hindu Business Line*, May 15. http://www.thehindubusinessline.com/2005/05/15/index.htm, accessed May 2007.

Khadria, Binod. 2001. Shifting Paradigms of Globalization: The Twenty-First Century Transition toward Generics in Skilled Migration from India. *International Migration* 39 (5): 45–72.

Khilnani, Sunil. 2004. *The Idea of India.* New Delhi: Penguin.

King, Anthony D., and State University of New York at Binghamton Department of Art and Art History. 1991. *Culture, Globalization, and the World-System: Contemporary Conditions for the Representation of Identity.* Binghamton: Department of Art and Art History, State University of New York at Binghamton.

Konana, Prabhudev, and Sridhar Balasubramanium. 2002. India as a Knowledge Economy: Aspirations versus Reality. *Frontline* 19 (2): 65–69.

Krishna, Anirudh, and Vijay Brihmadesam. 2006. What Does It Take to Become a Software Professional? *Economic and Political Weekly* 41: 3307–14.

Krishna, S., Sudeep Sahay, and Geoff Walsham. 2004. Managing Cross-Cultural Issues in Global Software Outsourcing. *Communications of the ACM* 47 (4): 62–66.

Krishnaswami, Sridhar. 2006. Now, Indian Americans Protest Quotas, June 5. http://www.rediff.com/news/2006/jun/05quota.htm, accessed June 2008.

Lakha, Salim. 1999. The State, Globalisation and Indian Middle-Class Identity. In M. Pinches, ed., *Culture and Privilege in Capitalist Asia*, xvi, 309. London and New York: Routledge.

Lal, Vinay. 2003. North American Hindus, the Sense of History, and the Politics of Internet Diasporism. In Rachel C. Lee and Sau-ling Cynthia Wong, eds., *Asian America.Net: Ethnicity, Nationalism, and Cyberspace*, 98–138. New York and London: Routledge.

———. 2004. Labour and Longing. The Diaspora: A Symposium on Indian-Americans and the Motherland (June), *http://www.india-seminar.com/2004/538 .htm*, accessed March 2007.

Lamb, Sarah. 1997. The Making and Unmaking of Persons: Notes on Aging and Gender in North India. *Ethos* 25 (3): 279–302.

Levitt, Peggy, and Sanjay Khagram. 2008. Constructing Transnational Studies. In P. Levitt and S. Khagram, eds., *The Transnational Studies Reader*. New York: Routledge.

Lorenzen, David. 1999. Who Invented Hinduism? *Comparative Studies in Society and History* 41 (4): 630–59.

Lynch, Caitrin. 2007. *Juki Girls, Good Girls: Gender and Cultural Politics in Sri Lanka's Global Garment Industry*. Ithaca: ILR Press/Cornell University Press.

MacRae, Penny. 2003. India Fetes Bride Who Said "No" to Dowry Demands. Associated Press, May 15.

Maharaj, Brij. 1996. Urban Struggles and the Transformation of the Apartheid Local State: The Case of Community and Civic Organizations in Durban. *Political Geography* 15 (1): 61–74.

Maira, Sunaina. 2000. Henna and Hip Hop: The Politics of Cultural Production and the Work of Cultural Studies. *Journal of Asian American Studies* 3 (3): 329–69.

Malik, Yogendra, and V. P. Singh. 1990. *Hindu Nationalism and Indian Politics*. Boulder, Colo.: Westview Press.

Mani, Bakirathi. 2003. Undressing the Diaspora. In Nirmal Pumar and Parvati Raghuram, eds., *South Asian Women in the Diaspora*, 117–36. Oxford: Berg.

Mankekar, Purnima. 1999. *Screening Culture, Viewing Politics: An Ethnography of Television, Womanhood, and the Nation in Postcolonial India*. Durham: Duke University Press.

Margolis, Jane, and Allan Fisher. 2002. *Unlocking the Clubhouse: Women in Computing*. Cambridge: Massachusetts Institute of Technology Press.

Mathew, Biju, and Vijay Prashad. 2000. The Protean Forms of Yankee Hindutva. *Ethnic and Racial Studies* 23 (3): 516–34.

Mazzarella, William. 2005. Middle Class. In R. Dwyer, ed., *South Asia Keywords*. http://www.soas.ac.uk/csasfiles/keywords/Mazzarella-middleclass.pdf, accessed May 2006.

McCall, Leslie. 1992. Does Gender Fit? Bourdieu, Feminism, and Conceptions of Social Order. *Theory and Society* 21: 837–67.

McClintock, Anne. 1995. *Imperial Leather: Race, Gender, and Sexuality in the Colonial Contest*. New York: Routledge.

McSweeney, Brendan. 2002. Hofstede's Model of National Cultural Differences and Their Consequences: A Triumph of Faith—a Failure of Analysis. *Human Relations* 55 (1): 89–118.

Mehta, Pratap Bhanu. 2006. To Pity the Plumage and Forget the Dying Bird. *The Telegraph* (Calcutta), http://www.telegraphindia.com/1060523/asp/opinion/story-6255404.asp. accessed May 23 2006.

Mies, Maria. 1982. *The Lace Makers of Narsapur: Indian Housewives Produce for the World Market*. London: Zed Press; distributed in the United States by Lawrence Hill.

Mitchell, Katharyne. 2002. Cultural Geographies of Transnationality. In K. Anderson, M. Domosh, and S. Pile, eds., *The Cultural Geography Handbook*, 74–87. London: Blackwell.

Mohanty, Chandra. 2003. *Feminism without Borders: Decolonizing Theory, Practicing Solidarity*. Durham: Duke University Press.

Moore, Henrietta L. 2004. Global Anxieties: Concept Metaphors and Pre-Theoretical Commitments in Anthropology. *Anthropological Theory* 4 (1): 72–88.

Myers, Rebecca. 2006. The Face of India: What It's Like to Find Yourself a *Time* Cover Model. *Time*. http://www.time.com/, accessed February 2006.

Nadeem, Shehzad. 2009. Macaulay's (Cyber) Children: The Cultural Politics of Outsourcing in India. *Cultural Sociology* 3 (1): 102–22.

Nair, Rukmini Bhaya. 1997. *Technobrat: Culture in a Cybernetic Classroom*. New Delhi: HarperCollins.

Nilekani, Nandan. 2009. *Imagining India: The Idea of a Renewed Nation*. New York: Penguin Group.

Niranjana, Tejaswini. 2006. *Mobilizing India: Women, Music, and Migration between India and Trinidad*. Durham: Duke University Press.

Nygren, Anja. 1999. Local Knowledge in the Environment-Development Discourse. *Critique of Anthropology* 19 (3): 267–88.

Ong, Aihwa. 1987. *Spirits of Resistance and Capitalist Discipline: Factory Women in Malaysia*. Albany: State University of New York Press.

———. 1999. *Flexible Citizenship: The Cultural Logics of Transnationality*. Durham: Duke University Press.

Ord, Jeremy. 2004. ICT in South Africa: Recollections of an Extraordinary Decade. In F. S. W. E. Forum, ed., *South Africa at 10: Perspectives by Political, Business and Civil Leaders*. Cape Town: Human and Rousseau.

Osborne, Ewan. 2001. Culture, Development, and Government: Reservations in India. *Economic Development and Cultural Change* 49 (3) (April): 659–85.

Oza, Rupal. 2006. *The Making of Neoliberal India: Nationalism, Gender, and the Paradoxes of Globalization*. New York: Routledge.

Padayachee, V. 1999. Struggle, Collaboration and Democracy—The "Indian Community" in South Africa, 1860–1999. *Economic and Political Weekly*, 34 (7): 393–95.

Pandey, Geeta. 2004. Dowry Woman Becomes Textbook Star. news.bbc.co.uk. http://news.bbc.co.uk/2/hi/south_asia/3696562.stm, accessed October 10 2005.

Parameswaran, Radhika. 2004. Global Queens, National Celebrities: Tales of Feminine Triumph in Post-Liberalization India. *Critical Studies in Media Communication* 21 (4): 346–70.

Parikh, P., and S. P. Sukhatme. 2004. Women Engineers in India. *Economic and Political Weekly* 39 (2): 193–201.

Parikh, Sunita. 2001. Affirmative Action, Caste, and Party Politics in Contemporary India. In J. D. Skrentny, ed., *Color Lines: Affirmative Action, Immigra-*

tion, and Civil Rights Options for America, 297–312. Chicago: University of Chicago Press.

Parthasarathy, Balaji. 2000. Globalization and Agglomeration in Newly Industrializing Countries: The State and the Information Technology Industry in Bangalore, India. Ph.D. diss., University of California, Berkeley.

——. 2004. India's Silicon Valley or Silicon Valley's India? Socially Embedding the Computer Software Industry in Bangalore. *International Journal of Urban and Regional Research* 28 (3): 664–65.

Patel, Reena. 2008. Working the Night Shift: Women's Employment in the Transnational Call Center Industry. Ph.D. diss., University of Texas, Austin.

Patel, Reena, and Mary Jane C. Parmentier. 2005. The Persistence of Traditional Gender Roles in the Information Technology Sector: A Study of Female Engineers in India. *Information Technologies and International Development* 2 (3): 29–46.

Pearson, Ruth. 1998. "Nimble Fingers" Revisited: Reflections on Women and Third World Industrialization in the Late Twentieth Century. In C. Jackson and R. Pearson, eds., *Feminist Visions of Development: Gender Analysis and Policy*, 171–89. London and New York: Routledge.

Pereira, Lindsay, Sondeep Shankar, and Dijeshwar Singh/Saab Pictures, Getty Images. 2006. A Lot of Rage, a Little Rang De. *The Reservation Issue*. http://www.rediff.com/news/2006/may/26sld1.htm, accessed June 2008.

Poster, Winifred. 2007. Who's on the Line? Indian Call Center Agents Pose as Americans for U.S.-Outsourced Firms. *Industrial Relations* 46 (2): 271–304.

Prashad, Vijay. 2005. All Smiles for Corporate America. *Frontline* 22 (14): 22.

Puri, Jyoti. 1999. *Woman, Body, Desire in Post-Colonial India*. London: Routledge.

Radhakrishnan, Smitha. 2005. "Time to Show Our True Colors": The Gendered Politics of Indianness in Post-Apartheid South Africa. *Gender and Society* 19 (2): 262–81.

Rai, Amit S. 1995. India On-line: Electronic Bulletin Boards and the Construction of a Diasporic Hindu Identity. *Diaspora* 4 (1): 31–57.

Rai, Sheela. 2002. Social and Conceptual Background to the Policy of Reservation. *Economic and Political Weekly* 37 (42): 4309–11 and 4313–18.

Rajadhyaksha, Ashish. 2003. The "Bollywoodization" of Indian Cinema: Cultural Nationalism in a Global Arena. *Inter-Asia Cultural Studies* 4 (1): 25–39.

Rajagopal, Arvind. 2001a. *Politics after Television: Religious Nationalism and the Reshaping of the Indian Public*. Cambridge and New York: Cambridge University Press.

——. 2001b. Thinking about the New Indian Middle Class: Gender, Advertising and Politics in an Age of Globalization. In R. Sunder Rajan, ed., *Signposts: Gender Issues in Post-Independence India*, 57–100. New Brunswick: Rutgers University Press.

Rajan, Rajeshwari Sunder. 1993. *Real and Imagined Women: Gender, Culture, and Postcolonialism*. London: Routledge.

Ray, Raka. 2000. Masculinity, Femininity, and Servitude: Domestic Workers in Calcutta in the Late Twentieth Century. *Feminist Studies* 26 (3): 691–720.

Ray, Raka, and Amita Baviskar. Forthcoming. Elite and Everyman: The Cultural Politics of the Indian Middle Classes. In R. Ray and A. Baviskar, eds., *Both Elite and Everyman: The Cultural Politics of the Indian Middle Classes*. New York: Routledge.

Ray, Tinku. 2007. "India IT Exodus from U.S. 'to Rise.'" *BBC News*, May 15. http://news.bbc.co.uk/2/hi/south_asia/6658527.stm, accessed May 2007.

Reich, Robert B. 1991. *The Work of Nations: Preparing Ourselves for 21st-Century Capitalism*. New York: A. A. Knopf.

Richter, Frank-Jurgen, and Parthasarathi Banerjee. 2003. *The Knowledge Economy in India*. Basingstoke: Macmillan.

Rose, Nikolas. 1999. *Powers of Freedom: Reframing Political Thought*. Cambridge: Cambridge University Press.

Roy, Subir. 2005. Infosys Builds a Realistic Dream. http://www.rediff.com, accessed July 5 2008.

Sainath, P. 2004. The Feel Good Factory. *Frontline* 21 (5): cover story.

Sarkar, Tanika. 1995. Heroic Women, Mother Goddesses: Family and Organisation in Hindutva Politics. In T. Sarkar and U. Butalia, eds., *Women and the Hindu Right: A Collection of Essays*. New Delhi: Kali for Women.

Sathaye, Sonali. 2007. The Scientific Imperative to Be Positive: Self-Reliance and Success in the Modern Workplace. In C. Upadhya and A. R. Vasavi, eds., *In an Outpost of the Global Economy: Work and Workers in India's Information Technology Industry*, 136–61. London, New York, and Delhi: Routledge.

Saxenian, AnnaLee. 2000. Bangalore: The Silicon Valley of Asia? Paper prepared for the Conference on Indian Economic Prospects: Advancing Policy Reform by the Center for Research on Economic Development and Policy Reform, Stanford, Calif., May.

——. 2005. From Brain Drain to Brain Circulation: Transnational Communities and Regional Upgrading in India and China. *Studies in Comparative International Development* 40 (2): 35–61.

——. 2006. *The New Argonauts: Regional Advantage in a Global Economy*. Cambridge: Harvard University Press.

Scott, Joan. 1988. *Gender and the Politics of History*. New York: Columbia University Press.

Sen, Geeti. 2002. *Feminine Fables: Imaging the Indian Woman in Painting, Photography, and Cinema*. Ahmedabad: Mapin Publishing.

Shiva, Vandana. 1988. *Staying Alive: Women, Ecology, and Survival in India*. New Delhi: Zed Press.

Shome, Raka. 2006. Thinking through the Diaspora: Call Centers, India, and a New Politics of Hybridity. *International Journal of Cultural Studies* 9 (1): 105–24.

Shweder, Richard A. 1991. *Thinking through Cultures: Expeditions in Cultural Psychology*. Cambridge: Harvard University Press.

Singer, Milton. 1972. *When a Great Tradition Modernizes: An Anthropological Approach to Indian Civilization*. Chicago: University of Chicago Press.

Singh, S. P., P. J. Santosh, A. Avasthi, and P. Kulhara. 1997. A Psychosocial Study of "Self-Immolation" in India. *Acta Psychiatrica Scandinavia* 97 (1): 71–75.

Sirohi, Seema. 2004. U.S. Indians Optimistic over Elections. BBC News. http://news.bbc.co.uk/2/hi/south_asia/3632085.stm, accessed June 15, 2008.

Skeggs, Beverley. 1997. *Formations of Class and Gender: Becoming Respectable*. London: Sage.

——. 2004. *Class, Self, Culture*. London and New York: Routledge.

——. 2005. Context and Background: Pierre Bourdieu's Analysis of Class, Gender and Sexuality. *The Sociological Review* 52 (2) (March): 19–33.

Sklair, Leslie. 2001. *The Transnational Capitalist Class*. Oxford and Malden, Mass.: Blackwell.

Srivastava, Manish, and Balaji Sampath. 2008. *Think Flat: Collaboration to Win in the Flat World*. Bangalore: Infosys Technology Ltd.

Suriya, M. 2003. Gender-Based Digital Divide in the IT Sector in India. Paper presented at the Forum on Women, Information, and Communication Technologies in India and China, November 5–7, University of South Australia. http://www.unisa.edu.au/hawkeinstitute/documents/suriya.doc, accessed July 2008.

Tharoor, Shashi. 2005. Imperfections in Friedman's Flat World. *The Hindu*, May 6. http://www.hinduonnet.com/thehindu/mag/2005/06/05/stories/2005060500160300.htm, accessed November 2005.

Thiara, Ravi. 2001. Imagining? Ethnic Identity and Indians in South Africa. In C. Bates, ed., *Community, Empire and Migration: South Asians in Diaspora*, 123–52. Basingstoke: Macmillan; New York: St. Martin's Press.

Tully, Mark. 2004. *India's Ruling Party May Rue Poll Slogan*. BBC News. http://news.bbc.co.uk/2/hi/south_asia/3518029.stm, accessed June 15, 2008.

Upadhya, Carol. 2007a. Employment, Exclusion, and "Merit" in the Indian IT Industry. *Economic and Political Weekly* 42: 1863–68.

——. 2007b. Management of Culture and Managing through Culture in the Indian Software Outsourcing Industry. In C. Upadhya and A. Vasavi, eds., *In an Outpost of the Global Economy: Work and Workers in India's Information Technology Industry*. New Delhi: Routledge.

Upadhya, Carol, and A. R. Vasavi. 2006. *Work, Culture, and Sociality in the Indian IT Industry: A Sociological Study*. Bangalore: National Institute of Advanced Studies at Indian Institute of Science.

Utz, Anuja, and Carl Dahlmann. 2005. *India and the Knowledge Economy: Leveraging Strengths and Opportunities*. Washington: World Bank Institute.

Valentine, E. Daniel. 1984. *Fluid Signs: Being a Person the Tamil Way*. Berkeley: University of California Press.

van der Veer, Peter. 2004. Transnational Religion; Hindu and Muslim Movements. *Journal for the Study of Religions and Ideologies* (7): 4–18.

——. 2005. Virtual India: Indian IT Labor and the Nation-State. In T. B. Hansen and F. Stepputat, eds., *Sovereign Bodies: Citizens, Migrants, and States in a Postcolonial World*, 276–90. Princeton: Princeton University Press.

Varadarajan, Siddharth. 2005. But the World's Still Round. *The Hindu*, February 8. http://www.thehindu.com/thehindu/br/2005/08/02/stories/20050 80200381500.htmaccessed November 2005.

Varma, Pavan K. 1998. *The Great Indian Middle Class*. New Delhi and New York: Viking.

Vertovec, Steve. 1997. Three Meanings of "Diaspora," Exemplified among South Asian Religions. *Diaspora* 6 (3): 277–99.

Wallerstein, Immanuel Maurice. 1974. *The Modern World-System*. New York: Academic Press.

Ward, Kathryn B., and Jean Larson Pyle. 1995. Gender, Industrialization, Transnational Corporations, and Development: An Overview of Trends and Patterns. In C. E. Bose and E. Acosta-Belen, eds., *Women in the Latin American Development Process*, 37–64. Philadelphia: Temple University Press.

Weber, Max. 1978. Status Groups and Classes. In G. Roth and C. Wittich, eds., *Economy and Society*, 302–7. Berkeley: University of California Press.

Weiss, Richard. 2005. The Global Guru: Sai Baba and the Miracle of the Modern. *New Zealand Journal of Asian Studies* 7 (2): 5–19.

World Bank. 1998. *World Development Report 1998/99: Knowledge for Development*. New York and Oxford: Oxford University Press and World Bank.

Yeoh, Brenda S. A., Katie D. Willis, and S. M. Abdul Khader Fakhri. 2003. Introduction: Transnationalism and Its Edges. *Ethnic and Racial Studies* 26 (2): 207–17.

Yuval-Davis, Nira. 1997. *Gender and Nation*. London and Thousand Oaks, Calif.: Sage Publications.

Zakaria, Fareed. 2006. India Rising. *Newsweek*, March 5. http://www.newsweek .com/2006/03/05/india-rising.html.

Page numbers in italics indicate illustrations and tables

AIIMS (All India Institute of Medical Sciences), 110
Ambition: career advancement, 97, 98, 106, 128–29, 150, 152–53, 210n4; conflict between family and personal fulfillment, 155–56; development of spiritual self through study, 175; discourse of virtue, 125–26; family priorities as limits to, 148–54; of female IT professionals, 122–25, 153–54; job changes and, 97–98, 154–55, 210n4; of male knowledge professionals, 135; personal achievement in knowledge economy, 77, 88, 95–97, 117–18, 128–29; social mobility and, 29–30
Anantram, Sarayu, 212n6
ANC (African National Congress), 181
Anderson, Benedict, 200–201
Aneesh, A., 35–36
Ant and the Grasshopper story, 111–13
Apartheid, 15, 33, 179, 181–83, 188, 190–91
Appadurai, Arjun, 19, 173
Appropriate difference: cultural streamlining and, 10, 22, 50, 73, 200–201; home-based work and, 80–82; Indianness and, 22, 50, 59; insularity of corporate workplace and, 54–55, 61–65, 116, 183–84, 210n2; IT professionals and, 35; middle-class femininity and, 50;

mind-set adaptations and, 57–59; production of Indian culture and, 35. See also Background; Indianness; the Individual; Individuality; Respectable femininity
Araoz, Zareen, 57, 65–66
Ashrams, 185, 187
Author's background, 19–20

Babri Masjid mosque destruction, 14
Background: of call center workers, 44–46, 209n8; educational, 6; familial, 121; of female bank workers, 5–6, 158, 165; global mobility and, 45; of lower middle-class families, 6; merit as overcoming limits of, 87–88; of potential brides, 7; social and cultural location of, 47; use of term, 6–7; wealth in designations of, 6, 121–24
Balance (term), 106, 147–49, 155–57, 197, 203, 212n1
Bangalore, 27–28; international airport in, 26; IT industry in, 26; middle-class background in, 7; Non-Resident Indian (NRI) relocation in, 26
Bay Area Indians for Equality, 110–11
Beauty pageants, 49
Beck, Ulrich, 118
Bhagavad Gita, 1, 207n1
Bhalla, Surjit S., 210n1
Bhattacharjee, Annaya, 15, 49

Bidwai, Praful, 89, 210n3

BJP (Bhartiya Janata party), 14, 40–42, 107, 139, 160, 200, 209n6

Bollywood, 1, 183

Bourdieu, Pierre, 16, 50, 209n11

Brahmins, 7, 119–21

Brain drain, 20, 27–28, 39

Business processing outsourcing (BPO). *See* Call center workers

Call center workers: adoption of American names and personas by, 44; age cohort of, 161, 212n4; backgrounds of, 44–46, 135, 209n8; consumption practices of, 158, 167; criticism of, 47, 158, 161–62, 167; cultural changes and, 45–46; cultural training of, 44; desirability of employment as, 43–44; economic mobility of, 47; educational levels of, 44, 209n7; English proficiency requirement for, 43–44; moral panic caused by, 46–48, 161–62, 167–68, 212nn6–7; night shift work of, 44, 167–68, 209n8; personal advancement of, 96; respectability of, 161–62, 167

Career advancement: education and, 109–10; family priorities and, 83–84, 147–54; five-year threshold, 106, 128, 150, 152–54; glass ceiling, 155; of home-based workers, 82; MBA degrees and, 95, 98, 166, 189; middle-class conventions, 80–82

Caste: background designations of, 6–7; biases toward, in IT industry, 78; Brahmins, 7, 119–21; breaking traditions of, 123–24; career choices and, 120–21; economic statue, 89; education in designations of, 8; meritocracy of IT workplace, 89–90, 91, 93–94; middle-classness and caste divisions, 8–9; OBCs (Other

Backward Classes), 89, 93, 210n3; of potential marriage partners, 123–24; reservations policies and, 9, 89, 91, 92–93, 110–11, 207n4, 210nn2–3; wealth and, 120–21

Chakravartty, Paula, 40, 59

Chatsworth (South African Indian township), 183, 185, 188

Chatterjee, Partha, 42, 49, 50, 147

Chidambaram, P., 107

Children: birth of, 31; child-care arrangements, 31, 95, 141, 152–53, 156, 193; cultural identity of, 26, 29, 32, 163; decision not to have children, 105; as factors in leaving labor force, 152; Hindu religious practices and, 176–77, 195; immorality of materialism in the diaspora, 163; sexual mores of, 169

China, 99–100

Choice: career choices of female IT professionals, 104–6, 109, 133, 145–46, 148, 153–56; decision difficulty, 31–32, 106, 151–53, 156; decision not to have children, 105; of high-tech over marriage, 129–32, 137, 145–46; ideology of merit connected to women's personal choices, 91; marriage by, 12, 123–24, 127, 153; rejection of women's place in the home, 157

Christian Indians, 184, 189, 191

Christian South African Indian women: attitudes of, toward India, 189, 191; on family life in post-apartheid South Africa, 190–91; on travel to India, 191–92

Class: background designations and, 6, 7, 29–30; business families and, 120–23; child marriages and, 169; cultural dimensions of globalization, 202–3; English proficiency and, 43–44; meritocracy of IT workplace, 89–90, 91; new middle class, 42–43, 51, 56–57, 83–85, 87–88, 92, 157–58; OBCs (Other Backward Classes), 7, 89, 93, 110–13, 210n1, 210n3; reservations policies and, 9, 89, 91, 92–93, 110–11, 207n4, 210nn2–3; stratifications of, 16–17. *See also* Individuality; Middle class; Privilege

Collins, Patricia Hill, 49

Combs, Gwendolyn M., 210n2

Communication skills, 59; with domestic workers, 77–78; education and, 74–75; English language proficiency, 5, 36, 43–44, 71; for IT professionals, 73–75; transnational experience, 75–76; uniformity of, 115–16

Congress Party, 41, 107, 139

Consumerism, 14, 28, 139, 157–62, 167

Corbridge, Stuart, 40, 89

Corporate culture, 28; of call centers, 44–46, 209n8; client relations and, 59–60, 70–71, 78–79, 167; corporate branding, 55, 67–68; dichotomies of, 90, 91; exposure to the outside world and, 97, 164–71, 203; glass ceiling, 155; global work culture, 54; homogeneity of, 56, 115–16; Indian corporate ethos in, 67–70; insularity of corporate workplace, 54–55, 61–65, 116, 183–84, 210n2; merit in, 39–40, 43, 87–90, 91, 101–3, 105, 129; outsourced data work and, 35–36, 79–80, 208n5; sense of placelessness and, 54–55, 61–64, 210n2; shaping of, 60. *See also* the Global; IT industry

Cross-cultural training: communication skills and, 71–73; difference in training methods for Indian and American workers, 57–58; empowerment in, 77; gender issues in, 85; for global work culture, 65–66; groups of mixed cultural backgrounds in, 66; individualistic selves vs. collectivist selves in, 119; simplification of Indian culture, 73; transformation of mind-set, 57–59

Cultural streamlining: appropriate difference, 10, 22, 50, 73, 200–201; of consumerism, 14, 28, 139, 157–62, 167; as corporate goal, 58; cultural globalization, 140–41, 169–72, 202; dress and, 1, 2, 4, 32, 166–67, 208n2; global work culture and, 55; Indianness and, 21–22, 50, 140–41; the individual and, 117–20, 140–41; production of appropriate difference and, 3, 5, 10; relegation of culture to feminine realm of the private and, 204; symbolically authorized middle-classness and, 51; "the global" and, 21, 54–55; transformation of mind-set, 57–59; work of unifications and, 201. *See also* Cross-cultural training; the Global; Transnational Hinduism; Transnational IT professionals

Das, Gurcharan, 40, 92

Das Gupta, Monisha, 15

Desai, Ashwin, 184, 212n6

Dirlik, Arif, 207n8

Divine Life Society, 185

Divorce, 193

Domestic help, 32, 77–78, 123, 153, 212n1

Domestic sphere. *See* Home; Respectable femininity

Dowries, 145

Economic development: call center workers and, 43; career advancement and, 98–100; critiques of, 38, 99; education and, 42–43; entrepreneurship and, 80–81, 97–100,

Economic development (*cont.*)
107; K4D (knowledge for development), 37, 38; knowledge economy, 36–40, 93–94, 117; leapfrogging, 37–38; moral lifestyles and, 109, 148–49; South African Indian women and, 188–89

Education: background and, 6, 29–30; caste differences and, 8, 109; class segregation and, 42–43; communication skills and, 74–75; continuing education and training in IT industry, 95, 98, 128–30, 150, 211n6; for the knowledge economy, 38–39; medical schools, 110; merit and, 43, 87–88, 109–10; professional IT women and, 11; public school system, 47; science education of women, 79; upward mobility and, 42–43, 128. *See also* Cross-cultural training

Empowerment: economic independence of middle-class women, 80–82; financial independence and, 80–85; flat world philosophy and, 76–85, 90; gender equity, 78–85; home-based professionals and, 80–82; through merit, 88; navigations between pressure to work vs. norm of staying home and, 80–85; pursuit of self-actualization, 98, 120, 124–25, 134, 136–37, 142, 147

English language proficiency, 5, 36, 43–44, 71

Entrepreneurship, 80–81, 97–100, 107

Escobar, Arturo, 38

Ethics, 157–67

Exposure, 97, 164–71, 203

Family, 3; appropriate sexual behavior and, 168–69; business families, 120–23; career choices and, 81, 124–26, 129–30, 147–54, 156; in categories of background, 6–8; consumption practices and, 81, 158, 160–62; defiance of dowry conventions and, 145–46; good Indian families, 11, 97, 147–48, 156–58, 160–71, 203–4; Hindu religious practice and, 14, 171, 177; independence from, 80–81, 122–24, 129–30, 132–33; individuality and ties to, 125–26; as locus of cultural streamlining, 170; morality of materialism and, 160–63; moral threat of call center workers to, 167; mothers' roles in, 26, 31, 208n1; relations of, with male knowledge workers, 137; sanctity of, 145–46; women's financial support of, 131, 148, 150, 158–59. *See also* Indianness; Marriage

Family life of professional women: appropriate difference and, 140–41, 169–72; child care arrangements and, 141, 152–53, 156, 193; cultural streamlining, 140–41, 169–72; decision difficulty of, 106, 151–53, 156; dual-income households, 212n1; economic dependence of housewives, 80–82; husbands' roles in, 31, 141, 150–54, 188–89, 196; management concessions to married female employees, 31, 95, 104–5, 154–56; materialism and, 45, 158–64, 196; preservation of Indian culture and, 21, 26, 29, 32, 147–48, 153–54, 163, 181–82, 204; prioritization of family in, 83–84, 95, 126, 147–56; quality of life in, 26–27, 81, 152; relations with parents and family, 130–34, 139; single parenting, 193; in South Africa, 189–93; time bind and, 149, 212n1; women as primary breadwinners, 153–54; work and home life balance, 83–85, 106, 147–49, 155–57, 170–71, 197, 203, 212n1

Female bank employees, 5–6, 158, 165

Female IT professionals: ambition of, 95, 97–101, 104, 125, 128–30, 138–39, 152–54; on American culture, 75–76, 140, 167; appropriate exposure of, to outside world, 97, 164–65, 170–71, 203; boundaries between Indian and global defined by, 10–11; on call center workers, 46–47, 135, 158, 161, 167; career advancement of, 90–91, 95, 98–99, 103–6, 127–30, 152–53; career choices of, 104–6, 109, 133, 148, 153–55; continuing education and training of, 95, 130, 150; dress of, 32, 138, 166–67, 208n2; economic and social mobility of, 188–89, 209n9, 209n11; economic background of, 6, 121–26, 130; educational background of, 6, 11, 128; empowerment of, 77–85, 141, 145–47; entrepreneurship and, 80–81, 99; female bank workers compared with, 5–6, 158, 165; financial independence of, 6, 81, 121–24, 129–30, 132–33; five-year threshold and, 106, 128, 150, 152–54; home-based work force and, 80–82; on homogeneity of IT culture, 115–16; individuality of, 127–33, 139–41; insularity of corporate workplace, 54–55, 61–65, 116, 183–84, 210n2; job changes and promotions of, 97, 101, 103, 105, 129, 154–55, 210n4; life priorities of, 83–84, 147–54; in management, 102–5; on merit-based advancement, 90–91, 102–5, 128–29; migration of, to the United States without husbands, 31; moral panic of, 160–63, 167–68, 196, 212n6; political views of, 139–40; as primary breadwinners, 153–54; relations of, with

managers, 104, 128–29, 154; single women as, 127–33, 153; transnational experience of, 31–32, 75–76, 122–23, 138–39; as transnational Indian professionals, 31, 138–41; on *Wired* magazine article, 1, 2, 9–10, *10. See also* Family life of professional women; Management; Respectable femininity; Silicon Valley Indian community; South African Indian professional women

Fernandes, Leela, 42, 158

Flat world thesis (Friedman), 76–77

Ford, Henry, 56

Ford Sociological Department, 56

Frank, Andre Gunder, 17

Freedom, "right" amount of, 169–70

Free market, 106, 108, 118

Friedman, Thomas, 76

Gandhi, Indira, 13

Gender: class privilege and, 50; empowerment and, 77–85; expectations of marriage, 80–84, 128–30, 148–52; feminization of BPO work, 44; gender segmentation of IT workplace, 105–6; glass ceilings in workplace, 155; job changes and, 97–98, 154–55, 210n4; in job hiring, 11; middle-class gender norms in business plans, 79; moral panic and, 161–62, 167–68, 212n6; primary breadwinner's roles and, 151–54; professionalism and gender equality, 101–5, 209n9; as symbolic capital, 16, 50–51, 209n11

Gender bias: in career advancement, 102–6, 109, 155; in education in mathematics and sciences, 11; feminization of low-end work and, 80–82; low percentages of women in upper management, 90–91, 102, 109

Gender equity: empowerment and,

Gender equity (*cont.*)
78–79, 80–85; in IT industry, 11,
77–79, 90–91, 101–6; merit and,
90–91
Gender Inclusivity Initiative, 78
Giddens, Anthony, 118
Gita, 1, 207n1
Glass ceiling, 155
the Global: corporate branding and,
55, 67–69; corporate management
and, 65, *91*; cultural streamlining
and, 21, 54–55; elite Indian IT
workers in, 35; empowerment and,
80–83; English language proficiency and, 5, 36, 43–44, 71; flat
world philosophy and, 76–85, 90;
gender equity in workplace and,
77–78; global economy as level
playing field, 76; home-based professionals and, 80–83; images of Indian women in *Wired* magazine
and, 2, 9–10, *10*; Indian culture
and, 15, 67, 69–70, 80–85; modernity and, 14, 207n8; standardized
work practices and, 70–71; symbolic language of code and, 35;
transformation of mind-set and,
57–59; use of term, 18–19, 21,
209n11; women's work in global
economy, 80–85. *See also* Cross-
cultural training
Global Education Center (Infosys), 57
Global Savvy, 65, 71
Good Indian families, 11, 97, 147–48,
156–58, 160–71, 203–4
GOPIO (Global Organization for People of Indian Origin), 183
Government employment, 9, 42, 89,
92–94, 120–21, 207n4, 210n2. *See
also* Female bank employees
Great Britain, 13, 186
Grewal, Inderpal, 49
Group Areas Act, 183
Gupta, Prashant, 211n9

Hall, Edward T., 72, 142
Hancock, Mary, 119
Hansen, Thomas Blom, 173, 180,
183–84
Hare Krsna movement, 185
Hariss, John, 40, 89
Heesterman, J. C., 175
Heller, Patrick, 42
Hindu film industry, 1, 183
Hinduism: Bhagavad Gita, 1, 207n1;
conversion from, to Christianity,
189; family and, 14, 171, 177;
origins of, 212n1; as philosophy of
individual freedom, 176; religious
instruction for children, 176–77,
195; second-generation Indian
Americans on, 177; self-inquiry in,
175; in South African Indian community, 160, 184–87, 193–97,
213n5, 214n9; temples, 186,
213n5; tensions of, with Islam, 14;
ties to India through, 174, 195–96;
transnational Hinduism, 1, 183–
87, 195–98, 214n9. *See also* South
African Indians
Hinduism Today (magazine), 186
Hindu nationalism, 13–15, 30, 40–
42, 107, 139, 160, 200, 209n6
Hinduness, 160, 171, 177–78
Hindu Sangh Parivar (Hindu family),
14
Hochschild, Arlie, 212n1
Hofstede, Geert, 58, 142, 208n1
Home: appropriate difference and,
140–41, 169–72; child care arrangements and, 141, 152–53, 156,
193; cultural streamlining and,
140–41, 169–72; decision difficulty
and, 106, 151–53, 156; dual-
income households, 212n1; economic dependence of housewives,
80–82; husbands' roles in, 31, 141,
150–54, 188–89, 196; management concessions to married fe-

male employees, 31, 95, 104–5, 154–56; materialism and, 45, 158–64, 196; preservation of Indian culture and, 21, 26, 29, 32, 147–48, 153–54, 163, 181–82, 204; prioritization of family and, 83–84, 95, 126, 147–56; quality of life, 26–27, 81, 152; relations with parents and family, 130–34, 139; single parenting, 193; in South Africa, 189–93; time bind and, 149, 212n1; women as primary breadwinners, 153–54; work and home life balance, 83–85, 106, 147–49, 155–57, 197, 203, 212n1. *See also* Respectable femininity

Housing, 26, 27, 29, 81

Husbands of professional women, 31, 80, 81, 141, 150–54, 188–89, 196

IIM (Indian Institutes of Management), 98, 211n6

IITs (Indian Institutes of Technology), 30, 39

Independence: career advancement and, 95; from family, 80–81, 122–24, 129–30, 132–33; female knowledge professionals from wealthy families, 6, 121–24; gender equality and, 80–84; migration of women to the United States without husbands, 31; of single women, 129–32, 153; work in production of, 80–85

Indian femininity. *See* Respectable femininity

Indian National Congress, 13

Indianness: apartheid and, 15; background and, 5–7, 44–47, 87–88, 121–24, 158, 165, 209n8; clothing and, 166–67; consumerism and, 14, 28, 157–62, 167; in cross-cultural training, 58, 71–73; as cultural commodity, 201; cultural stream-

lining and, 10, 16–18, 22, 50, 204; development of idea of, 12–13; in the diaspora, 15, 155–56; domestic sphere of family and, 14–15; ethnic identification in the United States, 15; family and, 140–41, 153–54; female IT professionals in South Africa and, 33; female knowledge professionals and, 145–47; globalization and, 14, 50, 54, 57, 200–201, 207n8; Hinduness and, 14, 160, 171, 177–78; and insularity of corporate workplace, 54–55, 61–65, 116, 183–84, 210n2; materialism and, 158–64, 162, 196; modernity and, 13–15, 49, 93, 207n8; mutability of, 117–18, 140–41; nostalgia for India, 26–34, 183, 191–94; prioritization of family, 83–84, 95, 126, 147–56; production of appropriate difference, 22, 45, 49, 58–59, 73, 170–71; professional IT women, 10–11; and professional women's position in marriage, 49, 196; rise of capitalism, 14–15; transformation to being global and, 57. *See also* Cross-cultural training; Family life of professional women; the Global; Hinduism; Respectable femininity; Silicon Valley Indian community; South African Indians; Transnational Hinduism

India Shining campaign, 40–42, 200, 209n6

the Individual: characterizations of self, 118–20, 122–25, 134; compartmentalization strategies and, 119; cosmopolitan sensibility and, 55; disembedded conceptions of, 118–19; empowerment of, 77–85, 90; globalization and, 55, 117–18; individualistic selves vs. collectivist selves in, 119; merit as personal responsibility, 94–95, 129; personal the Individual (*cont.*)

achievement, 118, 128–29; responsibility for risk management and, 118; Western notions of, 211n1

Individuality: class privilege and, 122–26; and conventions of marriage, 11–12, 80–85, 127, 128, 129–30; and expectations of marriage, 127–28, 147–49; family and, 119, 125–26; of female IT professionals, 122–25, 127–31; marriage by choice, 12, 123–24, 127; in masculine narratives of self, 134; rhetoric of choice, 90–91, *91*

Infosys, 56–57, *62*, 63, 76

Infoworld (fictitious firm), 78–85, *79–82*

Internet protests, 111–13

IT industry: accommodation of family needs and, 154–55; affirmative action initiatives in, 93; appropriate difference in, 58; brain drain and, 20, 27–28, 39; career moves and, 95–101, 154–55, 210n4; communication skills in, 71–75; concessions to female employees, 31, 95, 104–5, 154–56; continuing education and training in, 95, 98, 128–30, 150, 211n6; dichotomies of IT ideology, 90, *91*; employee retention in, 97, 101, 154–55, 210n4; empowerment of women in, 77–85; export policies of, 211n9; flat world philosophy and, 76–85, 90; flexibility required in, 66, 97, 101, 119; gender equity in, 11, 77–79, 90–91, 101–6; government policies in formation of, 108, 211n9; home-based workforce and, 80–82; Indian corporate ethos in, 67, 69–70; individual growth in, 77, 88, 95–97, 117–18, 122–23; mentoring in, 128–29, 137; offsite workforce and, 79–80; pursuit of

self-actualization in, 87–88, 98, 120, 122, 124–25, 134, 136–37, 142, 147. *See also* Female IT professionals; Male IT professionals; Management

IT professionals: animosity of, toward lower-class mobilization, 111–13; on BPO workers, 17, 43–45, 209n8, 209n10; career moves of, 25–26, 31–33, 95–101, 154–55, 210n4; cultural identity of, 17, 202; disavowal by, of economic motivations, 45, 121, 123, 125–26, 130, 135, 158; disregard by, for politics, 108–9, 113, 118, 205; drive of, for self-improvement, 97–101, 118–20, 122–25, 134, 136–37; entrepreneurship of, 80–81, 97–100, 107; on government policies in formation of IT industry, 108–9; ideology of merit-based advancement and, 89–91, 93–95; on international IT competition, 100–101; language of merit used by, 90; morality of, 92, 94; networking between, 33; as new middle class, 42–43, 51, 56–57, 83–85, 87–88, 92, 157–58; personal growth of, 77, 88, 95–97, 117–18, 122–23; as privileged segment of global economy, 35; production of appropriate difference, 22, 45, 58–59, 73; self articulated by, 119–20; from small towns, 29, 128, 130, 135; standardization of linguistic skills of, 71; symbolic analysts and, 35, 48; taxation of, 107–8. *See also* Communication skills; Corporate culture; Cross-cultural training; Education; Family life of professional women; Female IT professionals; Management; Merit; South African Indian professional women; *Gender headings*

Jairam, Aparna, 1, 2

K4D (knowledge for development), 37–39
Khadria, Binod, 35, 59
Knowledge economy, 36–40, 93–94. *See also* IT professionals headings
Knowledge professionals. *See* IT professionals; Male IT professionals; South African Indians; Transnational IT professionals

Lal, Vinay, 177, 183, 186
Lash, Scott, 118
Leapfrogging, 37–38

Male IT professionals: ambition of, 98, 136–37; career advancement and, 97–100; continuing education and training and, 95, 98, 150, 211n6; decisions of, to move to the United States, 19–21; disavowal of, of economic motivations, 45, 135; entrepreneurship of, 97–100; expectations of, of wives' priorities, 151, 154; on gender equality, 102; individuality and, 136–37; interaction of, with colleagues abroad, 98; interests of, in spirituality and philosophy, 175–76; management skills of, 136–38; as primary breadwinners, 151; on wives' domestic roles, 136–37, 150–52; working abroad, 98
Malik, Yogendra, 89
Management: absence of women in upper management, 90–91, 102–3, 109; concessions by, to female employees, 31, 95, 104–5, 154–56; female IT professionals in, 90–91, 109, 137, 155–56; female managers' relationships with female employees, 104–5; the Global and, 65, 91; mentoring by, 104–5, 128–29,

137; paternalism in, 136–38; relations of, with female professionals, 90–91, 109, 137, 155–56
Mandal Commission Report, 89, 110, 210n1
Mani, Bakirathi, 15
Mankekar, Purnima, 50, 89
Marriage: ability to be a good son and, 137–38; arranged marriages, 11–12, 127, 132, 145–46; bride's background check, 7; cancellation of, 145–47; child marriages, 169; by choice, 5, 11–12, 123–24, 126–27, 139, 153; choice of high-tech education over, 146; divorce and, 193; dowries and, 145–46; of female IT professionals, 123, 126–30, 139, 141, 148–53; Hindu-Christian, 190; husbands as primary breadwinners, 151–52; in-laws' control of, 80, 156; love marriages, 12, 127; of male knowledge professionals, 137–38; migration to the United States and, 31, 125; personal wealth and, 123; social class and, 169; submissive femininity in, 196–97; virtuous individuality and, 134; women's empowerment, 80–81, 145–47
Materialism, 45, 158–64, 196
MBA degrees, 95, 98, 166, 189
Mbeki, Thabo, 182
McCall, Leslie, 209n11
Medical students, 110
Mehta, Pratap Bhanu, 93
Merit: affirmative action policies and, 89, 93–94; caste-based exclusions and, 89–90; education and, 43, 87–88, 109–10; female IT professionals on advancement based on, 90–91, 103–5, 128–29; gender equity and, 90–91; government jobs compared and merit-based advancement, 89–91, 93–94; individual achievement and, 93, 128–31; as

Merit (*cont.*)
  personal responsibility, 94–95,
  129; personal transformation by
  way of, 87–88; reservations policies, 9, 89, *91*, 92–93, 110–11,
  207n4, 210nn2–3; as signifier for
  upward mobility, 43; tensions with
  social justice, 111–14
Meritocracy, 87, 90, 93–94, 99, 101,
  106–10
Middle class: American automobile industry and, 56; Brahmins as, 120;
  as consumers, 56; designations of,
  6–8, 34, 49–50; dowries and, 145;
  formation of American middle
  class, 56; gender as symbolic capital, 209n11; government employment and, 9, 42, 89, 92–94, 120–
  21, 207n4, 210n2; government
  workers as old middle class, 42,
  202; in imagining the Indian nation, 16, 41–42; IT professionals as
  new middle class, 8, 42–43, 51, 56–
  57, 83–85, 87–88, 92, 157–58;
  opinions of, on BPO jobs, 43–44;
  out-migration from India, 19–20;
  reservations policies and, 9, 89, *91*,
  92–93, 110–11, 207n4, 210nn2–3;
  reservations policies protests and,
  89; segregation of, 42; women in,
  49, 51, 79, 80–82, 188
"Mind the Gaps," 76
Modernity, 13–15, 49, 93, 207n8
Mohan, S., 199
Mohanty, Chandra, 38, 48
Morality: of call center workers, 44,
  46–48, 161–62, 167–68, 212nn6–
  7; economic opportunity and moral
  lifestyles, 109, 147–48; of materialism, 45, 158–64, 160–63, 196; new
  middle class and language of morality, 92, 94; sexual morality, 167–69,
  212nn6–7; transnational Hinduism, 197

Murthy, Narayana, 56–57
Muslims, 14, 97, 184

Nadeem, Shehzad, 48
Nadkarni, Sucheta, 210n2
Nair, Ruhimi Bhaya, 39
NASSCOM (National Association of
  Software and Service Companies),
  78, 209n7, 211n9
National Knowledge Commission, 37, 93
Nehru, Jawaharlal, 13, 42, 59
the New India: awareness of, 31–32,
  179–80, 184; feminine imagery in
  portrayals of, *3*, *4*; Indianness and
  the new Indian woman, 49; India
  Shining campaign, 40–42, 200,
  209n6; portrayals of, *3*, *4*; repre-
  sented by professional class, 41;
  Wired magazine, 1, 2, 9–10, *10*
New middle class, 42–43, 51, 56–57,
  83–85, 87–88, 92, 157–58
New Zealand, 36
Non-Resident Indian (NRI), 22, 24–
  28, 30–32

OBCs (Other Backward Classes), 7, 89,
  93, 110–13, 210n1, 210n3
One-third world/two-thirds world
  framework, 38, 48
Ong, Aihwa, 16, 17, 210n3, 212n6
Ord, Jeremy, 213n6
Osborne, Ewan, 210n1
Outsourced data work, 35–36, 79–80,
  208n5

Padayachee, V., 180
Parthasarathy, Balaji, 211n9
Patel, Reena, 43, 209nn7–8
Phoenix (South African Indian town-
  ship), 183
Pink, Daniel H., 1
Prashad, Vijay, 76
Prashanti Nilayam (Sai organization
  ashram), 185, 195–96

Private sphere: consumption practices in, 158, 160–62; cultural standards in, 9; exposure to the outside world and, 97, 164–71, 203; femininity in, 50, 204; good Indian families and, 11, 97, 147–48, 158, 160–71, 203–4; husbands as primary bread-winners and, 151–52; middle-class Bengali women in, 49; reservations policies and, 9, 89, *91*, 92–93, 110–11, 207n4, 210nn2–3; state government tensions with, 93–94; work and home life balance, 83–85, 106, 147–49, 155–57, 170–71, 197, 203, 212n1. *See also* Family life of professional women; Government employment; IT industry; Respectable femininity

Privilege: construction of cultural meaning and, 18; and motivations for independence, 122–25; privileged One-Third world, 48; repatriation as, 32; reservations policies and, 9, 89, 92–93, 110–11, 207n4, 210nn2–3; travel to India and, 33, 34. *See also* Caste; Class; Education

Promiscuity, 161–62, 167

Puri, Jyoti, 49

Radhakrishnan, Smitha, 15

Rai, Amit, 186

Rajadhyaksha, Ashish, 183

Rajagopal, Arvind, 42, 158, 173

Rajan, Rajeshwari Sunder, 49

Ray, Tinku, 27, 209n11

Reflexive modernization (Beck), 117

Reich, Robert, 35

Religious pilgrimages, 185, 187

Repatriation to India: ambivalence toward, 31–32; consideration of, 31–32, 156; of IT professionals, 25–26, 30–32; quality of life as reason for, 26–27; transnational Indian professionals, 27, 29

Reservations policies, 9, 89, *91*, 92–93, 110–11, 207n4, 210nn2–3

Respectable femininity: and avoidance of materialism, 158; and balance of work and home, 106, 147–49, 155–57, 170–71, 197, 203, 212n1; and exposure to outside world, 97, 164–65, 170–71, 203; feminine domesticity, 156–57; Indianness and, 170–71; insularity of corporate workplace, 54–55, 61–65, 183–84, 210n2; Nisha movement and, 145–47; submissive femininity and, 196–97; as symbolic capital, 16, 50–51; transnational Hinduism and, 197

Retirement from work force, 99, 125, 175

RNRIs (returned non-resident Indians), 26–27, 29, 208n1

Romanticization of India, 29, 32, 140

Rose, Nikolas, 118

Roy, Arundhati, 111–12

Roy, Subir, 57

Sahay, Sudeep, 59

Sai Baba, Sri Satya, 185–86

Sai organization, 185–87, 195–98, 214n9

Salaries, 26, 44, 64, 80–82, 208n5

Sampath, Balaji, 76

Santosh, P. J., 89

Sarkar, Tanika, 49

Satya Sai organization, 195–97

Saxenian, AnnaLee, 27, 210n3, 211n9

Schafer, LuEllen, 53–54, 65, 71

Scope of research, 17–18

Sen, Geeti, 49

Sexual morality, 167–69, 212nn6–7

Sharma, Nisha, 145–47

Shiva, Vandana, 38

Shopping malls, 27, 132

Silicon Valley Indian community, 47, 58; anti-reservations protests and, 110–11; Bay Area Indians for

Silicon Valley Indian (*cont.*)
Equality, 110–11; cross-cultural
training, 65; on good family as core
of Indian culture, 204; growth of IT
sector in, 30–31; Hindu religious-
ity, 160, 176; interior office environments, 61; materialism and
erosion of family values and, 163–
64; merit and, 88; office architec-
ture in, 63; repatriation of, to India,
26–27, 31–32, 156; transnational
Hinduism, 187; work-home balance
in, 31–32, 155–56
Silicon Valley Indian women: on materialism and erosion of family
values, 163–64; on work-home balance, 31–32, 155–56
Singer, Milton, 119
Singh, Arjun, 112
Singh, Manmohan, Prime Minister,
37, 41
Singh, S. P., 89
Singh, V. P., 89
Sirohi, Seema, 40
Skeggs, Beverley, 118, 209n11
Sklair, Leslie, 17
Software sector in India, 78, 108,
211n9
South Africa: apartheid in, 15, 33,
179, 181–83, 188, 190–91; economic liberalization in, 213n6; Indianness in, 15; IT sector in, 188,
213n6; as rainbow nation (Mandela), 179, 182, 184
South African Indian community:
Hindus in, 160, 184–87, 193–97,
213n5, 214n9
South African Indian professional
women: attitudes toward India,
189, 191; culture of transnational
Indian professionals and, 180–81;
economic and social mobility of,
188–89; economic privilege of, 188;
expectation of, of working outside

the home, 188, 213n7; experiences
of, with India, 193–94; identification of, with Indian culture, 33; Indian identification of, 192–93;
involvement of, in anti-apartheid
struggle, 192–94, 214n9; nostalgia
of, for India, 33–34, 190; political
activism of, 192–94; in roles of traditional wives, 190; social mobility
of, 194–95; South African identity
of, 189–90, 214n9; on travel to India, 191–93, 195–96; on unique aspects of being Indian, 192–93
South African Indians, 18; accultura-
tion of, 183–84; apartheid and, 15,
33, 179, 181–83, 188, 190–91;
awareness of, of the new India,
179–80; connectedness of, to Indian homeland, 33–34, 179–80,
182–83; economic mobility of, 33–
34, 183–84; on end of apartheid,
181–82; family ties of, in India,
191; Indian culture embraced by,
180; interconnection of India as
homeland, 181; minority identity
of, 179–80; multigenerational re-
moval from India, 33–34, 179; residential communities of, 183;
segregated neighborhoods of, 183;
travel to India by, 33–34, 183,
191–93, 195–96
South African Indian women: attitudes toward India, 189, 191; class
histories of, 188; identification of,
with Hinduism, 184, 195–96,
214n9; identification of, with the
new India, 184; images of, 182; impact of apartheid policies on, 188;
on lifestyle of IT professionals in
India, 196; preservation of classical
Indian arts by, 181–82; in public
life, 182; religious affiliation of,
185–86; ties of, to India, 195–96;
ties of, to India through profes-

sional identity, 196; workforce participation of, 188, 213n7
South Indian Brahmin women, 119
Spirituality, 34, 175–77, 184–85, 187
Srivastava, Manish, 76
Stock exchange workers, 104
STPI (Software Technology Parks of India), 211n9
Suriya, M., 90
Symbolic capital, 16, 50–51

Taj Mahal Hotel terrorist attack, 204–5
Tamil people, 179–80, 213n5
Taxation policies, 107–8, 139
Tejpal, Tarun, 205
Temples, Hindu, 186–87
Tharoor, Shashi, 76
Time bind, 149, 212n1
Traditionalism, 3; compartmentalization strategies, 119; women's family roles, 80–85, 190, 195–97; work and home life balance, 83–85, 106, 147–49, 155–57, 170–71, 190, 195–97, 203, 212n1
Transnational, 16–19
Transnational Hinduism: film industry, 1, 183; Indian diasporic communities' influence on rise of religious nationalism in India, 186; Indian identity and, 184–85; religious goals of, 187; respectable femininity and, 197; Sai organization and, 185–87, 195–98, 214n9; Satya Sai organization and, 195–97; in South African Indian community, 160, 184–87, 193–97, 213n5, 214n9; transnational religious exchanges, 185–87
Transnational IT professionals, 39, 194; boundaries of national and international development and, 39; construction of Indianness by, 10, 16–18, 200, 204; cultural innova-

tions and, 200; disregard of, for politics, 108–9, 113, 118, 205; Indian identity of, 32–33; individual merit and, 39–40, 200; one-third world/two-thirds world framework and, 48; repatriation of, to India, 26–27, 31–32, 156. *See also* Cultural streamlining; the Global; Indianness; Silicon Valley Indian community; *South African Indian headings*
Travel to India, 33–34, 36, 183, 185, 187, 191–94

United Kingdom, 13, 186
United States: female IT workers in, 122–23, 141; Indian diasporic communities' influence on rise of religious nationalism in India and, 186; Indianness in, 15; migration of professionals to, 5; offshore outsourcing model and, 35–36; sexual freedom in, 168–69
Upadhya, Carol, 15, 58–59, 94

van der Veer, Peter, 50, 173, 186, 199
VHP (Vishwa Hindu Parishad), 183, 186
von Stietencron, Heinreich, 212n1

Wallerstein, Immanuel, 17
Walsham, Geoff, 59
Weber, Max, 16
Weiss, Richard, 185
Whitefield (town outside Bangalore), 34, 60–61
White National Party, 181
Wired magazine, 1, 2, 9–10, 10
World Bank, 36–38
The World is Flat (Friedman), 76

Young, Michael, 87

Smitha Radhakrishnan is an assistant professor of
sociology at Wellesley College.

Library of Congress Cataloging-in-Publication Data
Radhakrishnan, Smitha, 1978–
Appropriately Indian : gender and culture in a new
transnational class / Smitha Radhakrishnan.
p. cm.
Includes bibliographical references and index.
ISBN 978-0-8223-4843-6 (cloth : alk. paper)
ISBN 978-0-8223-4870-2 (pbk. : alk. paper)
1. Information technology—Economic aspects—
India. 2. Information technology—Social aspects—
India. 3. Globalization—Social aspects—India.
I. Title.
HC440.I55R334 2011
305.5'530954—dc22   2010031782